ADVANCE PRAISE

"*Cover My Dreams in Ink* is Jessie Dunleavy's accounting of—and reckoning with—the life and death of her son Paul, who in 2017 fell victim to the opioid crisis. Partly by using poetry he wrote in his lifetime, Dunleavy searches for answers, fully presenting his life and their relationship, warts and all. It's a powerful technique, and *Cover My Dreams in Ink* is a worthy elegy for a young man who never got the chance to fully become himself."

> —Ben Westhoff, award-winning investigative journalist, author of *Fentanyl, Inc., How Rogue Chemists Are Creating the Deadliest Wave of the Opioid Epidemic*

"Paul was a warm, creative, and loving individual who defied labels. He had many challenges, diagnoses, medications, and, tragically, self-medications. But he also had friends and loved ones, one of whom—his mother, Jessie Dunleavy—has given us this remarkable, searing memoir. Through it, she lets us love Paul, too, and opens our minds and hearts to the struggles of all who cope with disability, alienation, and addiction."

> —Roger Parloff, award-winning journalist, regular contributor to *Yahoo Finance* and *Newsweek*, former editor-at-large for *Fortune*, and former editor-in-chief of *Opioid Watch*

"*Cover My Dreams in Ink* is a book with a vital purpose. Jessie Dunleavy's bravely told story of her son, Paul, relates how he, like so many others, was repeatedly let down by the educational, mental health and addiction treatment systems meant to protect him. It illustrates how stigma and misinformation around drug use greatly exacerbate drug-related harms. And it powerfully shows how his suffering and tragic death fueled her own journey into advocating for the harm reduction interventions, drug policy reforms and attitudinal changes that we desperately need."

—Will Godfrey, human rights journalist, editor-in-chief of *Filter*, a contributor to *The Nation, Salon, Pacific Standard*, former editor-in-chief of *TheFix*, and founding editor-in-chief of *The Influence* and *Substance.com*

"Jessie Dunleavy's memoir is a riveting reminder of the ultimate toll of the addiction crisis. An honest and relatable tale that hits home for far too many families. *Cover My Dreams In Ink* is a must read for any person wondering what it's like to walk a lifetime in the shoes of a loved one suffering."

—Ryan Hampton, national advocate and bestselling author of *American Fix: Inside the Opioid Addiction Crisis--and How to End It*

"A gut-wrenching and poignant memoir, *Cover My Dreams in Ink*, illuminates the multiple forces that, in concert, ultimately doomed Paul's fight to live, and leaves the reader with a deepened understanding of the tragic reality that Paul's death, like so many, was preventable, exposing the ways in which the war on drugs and an antiquated treatment ethos are killing people. Paul's story instills a passion to stand up for the vulnerable and to rail against the multiple barriers to needed reform."

—Benjamin A. Levenson, Founder, Origins Behavioral Healthcare, substance use disorder treatment expert, international advocate for humanitarian drug policy

"Jessie Dunleavy has written a beautiful memoir about her son Paul who died from a drug overdose at the age of 34. The book is a searing account of the dysfunctional and negligent US drug treatment system that failed her family. The tragedy of Paul's death made the author into a fierce supporter of harm reduction, an advocate for medication-assisted recovery and an activist against the War on Drugs. The other bonus of *Cover My Dreams in Ink* is Paul's poetry—each poem offers a glimpse into his humanity, into a life of loneliness and pain but also one of joy and connection."

—Helen Redmond, LCSW, expert in substance use, multimedia journalist, senior editor for *Filter Magazine*, sought after speaker in the US and abroad, adjunct faculty Silver School of Social Work, New York University

Cover
My Dreams
in Ink

Cover
My Dreams
in Ink

A Son's Unbearable Solitude,
A Mother's Unending Quest

a memoir
with selected poems
by Paul

JESSIE DUNLEAVY

Apprentice
House Press
Loyola University Maryland

Library of Congress Cataloging-in-Publication Data has been applied for.

First Edition

Hardcover ISBN: 978-1-62720-259-6
Paperback ISBN: 978-1-62720-260-2
Ebook ISBN: 978-1-62720-261-9

Printed in the United States of America

Acquisitions & Editing: Kelly Lyons
Design: Apprentice House Press
Promotion plan: Grace Marino
Cover painting by Taliah Lempert / bicyclepaintings.com
Photo of Paul on back cover: Joe Heimbach
Photo of Jessie on back cover: Ana Fallon
Family wedding-day photo: Phil Sapienza

Published by Apprentice House Press

Apprentice House Press
Loyola University Maryland
4501 N. Charles Street
Baltimore, MD 21210
410.617.5265
www.ApprenticeHouse.com
info@ApprenticeHouse.com

For Keely

CONTENTS

AUTHOR'S NOTE

I HAVE ALWAYS been told that I have a good memory, and I guess I do. I know some studies suggest that the brain transforms stressful or traumatic experiences into more lasting memories, which could account for some of my clarity on the events detailed in these pages. But I remember the good times too, and we had plenty of them.

I could not, however, have completed this project without the journals that I kept over the years. Funny, because I am not a born journaler. It's just that, in caring for Paul, I had to write things down. And not because the act of writing was therapeutic for me, but because I was trying to make sense of it all, keeping track, understanding my role. In addition to my notes, I drew from Paul's school and medical records and, of course, his journals.

The fact is, I throw nothing away. I don't clear out my emails or voicemail messages as I should, and I shudder to even think about all that's stowed in my attic. It occurs to me that there could be a correlation between hoarding and a good memory, with both representing a tendency to hang on, no matter what, when maybe what you need is to declutter—to sort out what's worth keeping and dump the rest.

Writing this memoir was healing in ways that I didn't anticipate at the outset, a time when—in spite of my overwhelming drive to take it on—I was uncertain of where it would go. More than a few friends have suggested it was my way of continuing the fight for Paul. Maybe it was. In the beginning, I was dedicated to the process—absorbed in gathering the information and pulling it together. As it unfolded, there were times when I felt as though it was leading me, instead of the other way around—a reality I couldn't easily explain other than to say it took on a life of its own.

I came to see that recalling painful events catapults you back in time, forcing you to live them again and to suffer just as you did. But, then, getting these experiences down on paper—putting them out there—in many ways frees you from the burden of what you may have kept hidden from others, and even worked hard to do. And whether it was stoicism or secrecy that motivated stuffing it down, keeping it to yourself, it's freeing to let it out. A weight, lifted.

In the end, seemingly disparate segments of the past converged to expose connections otherwise unknown to me. What I hope readers take away, more than a knowledge of the struggles or the heartaches we may have faced, is the discovery of a deeper truth, one that doesn't dwell in the past but informs the future. In other words, the value lies not in what I brought to it, but in what it brought to me and hopefully to others.

This memoir draws on my personal knowledge and depicts actual events that took place in my life. All people are real, but some names and settings have been changed to protect privacy.

I should mention that I chose not to correct Paul's spelling, a decision I wrestled with, and one that I may feel differently about tomorrow. After all, the best of writers have editors. But I decided that Paul's idiosyncrasies were integral to knowing him. There were certain conventions or societal norms that he just didn't get. A square peg in a round hole. An exception to the rule. Regardless of how his distinctiveness may have been characterized, I didn't want to smooth over any of it.

PROLOGUE

MY SON PAUL was different, and that is not just my opinion. Some described him as "unique," but, regardless, the sentiment was the same and would be corroborated by every professional we encountered. His condition defied a label.

These differences not only presented learning challenges but also masked the ways in which Paul was gifted. Capable of higher-level reasoning than he was able to verbalize due to a language impairment, and equally trapped by a hand tremor that hindered adequate use of a pencil, Paul was underestimated both in and out of school. Not knowing anything different in his early school years, he toed the line, was liked by others, and was characterized as sensitive and kind. For the most part, he was shy and withdrawn, overly dependent on the teacher.

Placed in special education classes where often he was unchallenged, though sometimes lost, Paul increasingly suffered the frustrations of being misunderstood and, in many ways, his basic needs were unmet.

Marginalized and often mistreated, Paul harbored deep-seated feelings of inadequacy and over time developed a sense of hopelessness. The absence of affirmation and recognition, to say nothing of praise, dovetailed with failed systems—school, health care, legal—to create the perfect storm.

*

ANNAPOLIS, WHERE I grew up and raised my children, is a small city as state capitals go. Intertwined by narrow, colonial-era streets leading down to the harbor and the Chesapeake Bay, it was designed for horse-drawn carts, not today's automobiles and bicyclists, who pretty much ride at their own risk. But Paul loved navigating these streets on his bike. As he raced across the bridge connecting the two parts of town—making deliveries for a local sandwich shop—he felt exhilarated by a sense of purpose and an independence he had rarely experienced.

Going into his apartment the day after he died shattered my state of disbelief, or shock, or whatever mindset I'd inadvertently adopted to protect myself. But seeing his bike propped up against the mantel in his bedroom, just as he'd left it after his last shift only two nights before, was as close to unbearable as any moment I've known.

I had been to his place so many times, once even without him during his recent hospitalization, and always found it comforting. For me, the apartment represented all the progress Paul had made; for him, it was a source of genuine pride, one he acknowledged with uncharacteristic candor.

With grief squarely upon me, I swung into caretaker mode, checking his mail, gathering some papers on his desk, and scanning the rooms for lights left on or a window left open.

Back home a few minutes later, I again slid into the shelter provided by a combination of denial, the distractions of people looking after me, and the pace of preparations for a memorial service. In moving Paul's papers to a corner of the room for safekeeping, I noticed a receipt from the pawn shop. It was for his laptop. So that's how he got the money. The money I had refused to give him I would now eagerly spend to buy back his computer.

Paul had turned to writing as a means of self-expression when he was young, filling countless pages with mostly illegible run-together words, often left crumpled in the trash. I had dozens of journals from his teenage years and remember his writing in them with a flashlight under his covers at night. Though his handwriting was nearly impossible to read—an effort further challenged by his spelling—I was able to decipher enough to be impressed, even surprised, and typed a few of his poems. Back then, I told him he should show his work to a teacher, but he had already decided there was no use. School was a place where he was underestimated, and the teachers thought he was slow and therefore didn't ask much of him. After so many schools, and as many dashed hopes, he couldn't afford to expect anything more.

And now here I was, all these years later, opening his laptop. My hands shook as I disabled the face recognition, typed in his password, and began to explore parts of his world not fully shared. Saved in files Paul titled "On Blog" and "Journals" are writings that span a decade, extending well beyond his teenage years. Everything I read, whether new to me or not, exemplified the vast discrepancy between Paul's ability to think and his ability to articulate his thoughts.

This experience plunged me into a wild and merciless sea of emotions. I found myself starring down the barrel of a reality altogether too brutal for my capacity to take on. The finality of it all: The gifts Paul can never reveal; the inner life that most who knew him wouldn't recognize and can never come to know; and the tragic forces that conspired to take his life, to take him from the world, and from me. I was also struck by the ways in which his writings tell his story.

*

AT FIRST, I just wanted to publish my son's poetry. I wanted to honor him and show off his work—something he never did.

As I thought about it, I realized presenting Paul's poetry apart from his life would be difficult for me—not to suggest I took the easy way out in writing this book. But knowing his life story as I do, I could see it provides a deeper understanding of his writings; I came to see the reverse is just as true—his writings illuminate a life otherwise obscured from others and even, in some cases, from me.

To intertwine the two, I open each chapter with several lines from one of his poems, which is then printed in its entirety—with its title and format as Paul created—in the back of the book. Also, I have interspersed a few of his writings in the body of the text where I thought it helped in telling his story. *Cover My Dreams in Ink*, a line taken from one of Paul's poems—*Pleading With Gravity*—jumped out as a fitting title. Even though the words are Paul's, the sentiment, now recast, is mine too.

As close as I was to my son, I am aware of a presumptuousness in telling the story of another, even in the form of a memoir that is clearly from my perspective. In some ways, a mother knows her child better than others do, even better than the child knows himself. But only to a point. And I have to say he knew me too and could have told his own narrative about that.

Paul's story didn't end well but, God willing, it can triumph in its capacity to shine a light on all that he kept hidden. And for others suffering as he did, I hope it can lend some insights, promoting hope over despair.

Chapter 1

PURE GOLD

Hope was painted yellow,
lighting a path and guiding us when we thought we were blind.
Compassion was painted blue,
the color of the sky, because once it's within us, it goes on forever.
Last but not least is love, which was painted gold,
because there is no value greater than its gifts.

IT WAS OCTOBER 1982. The nurse dialed the number and handed me the receiver, attached by a long cord to the phone on the wall in the mostly barren recovery room.

"Mommie! I had a boy!" I exclaimed.

"You did not," my mother replied, expressionless.

She was a gracious and genuinely sweet person whom we all called "Mommie"—which she emphatically spelled with an "ie" and not a "y"—but she could be so deadpan.

"I did! Really! I'm lying here in the recovery room; I'm LOOKING at him!"

"I know you are pulling my leg because you haven't been in the hospital long enough to have had the baby," she said with the utmost confidence.

I don't remember exactly how our brief conversation ended, but I can tell you this: I made no headway. I do remember thinking to myself that my mother was right—I hadn't been there "long enough" if you calculated averages, even if you cut a wide swath in doing so.

Paul was born within twenty minutes of my hospital arrival, surprising everyone, including my husband, Don, who barely made it in time for the delivery, and my doctor, who told me an hour earlier I had plenty of time. But I knew too that my mother found the "boy" part of my news as far-fetched as the twenty-minute labor and delivery. You see, I came from a family of three girls and, at the time of Paul's birth, I had a daughter and my older sister, Jennie, was the mother of three little girls. Paul broke the mold.

When I was pregnant with our daughter Keely back in 1979, an era when the baby's gender was unknown until birth, Don and I decided that if we had a son we would name him after my father. We also agreed we'd call him "Paulie," my father's nickname as a young child. On the day of Paul's birth, I realized further merit: The name certainly wouldn't hurt as my mother adjusted to this obvious curveball.

Weighing eight pounds even, Paulie was precious—fair skin and reddish hair—and healthy, as verified by looking at him, hearing his cry, and learning of his Apgar test scores. Furthermore, we now had the perfect family—a girl and a boy, spaced three years apart, just as Dr. Spock had championed.

*

BORN A FEW blocks from home at Anne Arundel Medical Center, Paul came into this world as a fifth generation Annapolitan and a member of an exceptionally close extended family. In fact, my sisters and my mother were my best friends.

My own childhood had been idyllic, and my family was a huge part of my identity, as well as a source of pride. The household of my youth included my mother and father—whose enduring romance was an inspiration to all—my two sisters, my mother's father, and my father's brother, all characters who, to put it mildly, kept life interesting. Love was unconditional. Mutual support was a given. And we shared countless good times.

My father's family had moved to Annapolis when he was in the fourth grade, meaning he wasn't—and never would be—an Annapolitan. This was enshrined in my mother's book of gospel. Even though he attended St. Mary's, where he also was a member of the parish and an altar boy, graduated from Annapolis High School and St. John's College, and ultimately became a civilian English professor at the United States Naval Academy, Mommie said, "You and your 'people' have to be born in Annapolis for you to qualify for the distinction." This was not debatable.

Mommie was born and grew up in the heart of Annapolis' historic district. She was proud of the small town where her father was a prominent figure. The Alderman of Ward One for twenty-six years and the Fire Chief of Annapolis for nearly thirty, he was a respected voice within the city government.

As newlyweds my parents moved to Washington, D.C., where my father taught at George Washington University. After a year of living there, my mother missed her parents so much that she and my father moved back to Annapolis and into her parents' home, where they remained, caring for her parents, for the rest of their lives. My father then commuted to GWU until my older sister was born, at which time he sought a position in Annapolis. While he was a superb teacher and undoubtedly found his niche within the world of English literature, his family life drove his place of employment, not the other way around.

My father left the house to meet his classes and promptly returned home to study and correct papers. Of my childhood friends, about half had working mothers. Mine did not work outside the home and in fact was the consummate homemaker. I recall being asked if my mother was home when my school day was over. "My mother *and* my father are home when I leave for school and when I return!" I said.

For both my parents, family was everything. My father was particularly close to his mother and sought her company frequently, prompted by enjoyment rather than obligation. He also was close to his siblings, deriving much pleasure from time spent with his two brothers. One of his brothers never had children and in many ways functioned as another parent to us, living and vacationing with our family when we kids were little and subsequently assuming parental roles for many years after our father's untimely death.

While my parents were fun lovers, open minded, and encouraged acceptance of people who were different from us, flexible thinking did not apply when it came to their expectations for our education. In truth, I'd say they were downright rigid. The bar was set high. And being good kids, we fell in line, racking up advanced degrees and maintaining a strong work ethic along with a commitment to devote ourselves to a noble cause.

*

AMONG MY TWO sisters and me, we had eight children within a ten-year period. In addition to Jennie's three and my two, my younger sister, Erin, had three children. "The cousins," as we called them, grew up within blocks of one another. Family gatherings for every holiday and birthday, local events, as well as Friday pizza nights, brought the whole clan together with great frequency, most often in one of our homes. Bound by blood, proximity, and friendship, "the cousins" also shared the same middle name—Dunleavy. As young girls, my sisters and I had decided on this strategy to keep our name alive.

Our mother remarried when Keely was five and Paul was two. She was lucky. Not only had she and my stepfather grown up together, but also there were intersections in their adult lives, stemming for the most part from his career as a civilian French professor at the Naval Academy. I was nothing but happy for my mother, but I didn't even stop to think about how much this man would enrich *my* life. I think

I can safely speak for my sisters in saying they felt the same. And beyond our gaining a stepfather, our children gained a grandfather who loved them as his own and, along with our mother, was a central figure in their formative years. For Keely and Paul, he was the only grandfather they ever knew.

Just a few months after my mother and stepfather married, Don and I separated. In the end, it was my idea that we do so, but I didn't feel there were other options available to me. While I had gone into the marriage as madly in love as I'd ever been before, and quite frankly since, the disappointments for me were overwhelming. I'm sure some of the blame lies with me; maybe I expected too much. It's hard to say. But I could see that family life wasn't an important priority for Don, and I found myself increasingly alone with the children, often for breakfast, lunch, *and* dinner.

I had stopped working when Keely was born, and Don had started his own architectural business, the demands of which I understood and supported. The fact is, I was enamored of his work and shared his excitement for each new project landed. And I knew from the start that a big part of my investment called for a sacrifice that included long hours of tending to the homefront. But as I suffered the loneliness, and gradually figured out that it wasn't always work that kept Don away in the evenings, I took a stand.

Some moments in life are forever etched in memory. For me, this is one: I was driving Keely and a couple of her pre-kindergarten classmates to school. As we rounded the corner from Church Circle onto Duke of Gloucester Street, Keely said, "I haven't seen my Daddy in days and days and days." Another child in the car innocently responded, "I see him all the time. Last night he took me bike riding!" This was my first clue that Don wasn't always honest with me, a realization that hit me hard. How I kept the car from running up on the sidewalk, I still do not know.

Even though I didn't jump to any specific conclusions, my plight was worrisome enough that I briefly became somewhat of a sleuth. During my stint as a covert operative, I do remember steaming open the American Express bill—a skill they don't teach in school and something that isn't as easy as it looks.

As I struggled with the task, Paulie toddled through the kitchen to the playroom and announced to Keely: "Mommie's cooking mail." Startled by his having noticed, I swung into cover-up mode, speaking sternly so as to derail any further communication, "No, Mommie is paying bills—that's all."

During the first year of the separation, we didn't see much of Don. At the time, I figured the children's lives weren't as disrupted as mine, given that our routines stayed pretty much the same. I was the primary caretaker, and we remained in the family home. One day, several months after Don had moved, he walked up to our front door.

Paul saw him first and came running into the kitchen to alert me, exclaiming, "Uncle Daddy is at the door!" I had to smile to myself as I considered his point of view—to little Paulie all men were called "uncle-something" and he knew this guy's name was Daddy. Made sense!

As Paul tried to follow the mailman down the street or chose to hang out with the dryer repairman for the duration of his time in our basement, I realized his hungering for male attention. My sensitive and good-hearted stepfather didn't miss a beat in taking Paul under his wing. In fact, the bond formed between Paul and his grandfather was a blessing for which I remain thankful.

*

THE GRANDPARENTS LIVED in the Wardour neighborhood, just a few blocks from my home and those of my sisters. One of the amenities of their old and quirky house was a huge screened-in porch where the entire family, and then some, could gather for a meal or just sit and talk. And talk we did. If there wasn't a new matter at hand, we would happily rehash what we had talked about the day before. In either case, our topics ranged from local politics to world events, and from our problems and triumphs to those of our friends and neighbors.

Screened in on four sides and surrounded by massive old trees, the porch provided camaraderie, a respite from the heat, and a view of a good-sized yard with a pool where our children played for countless hours as summer days became summer nights. We gathered at "Grandmommie and Granddaddy's" for occasions throughout the year but always looked forward to the warmer weather when life could be lived outdoors, usually kicked off by an elaborate Easter egg hunt for our children and their friends. Fortunately for all of us, we had twenty years of this sanctuary with our parents, years that ushered our children into young adulthood.

In addition to his recognition of Paul's emotional needs, Dad—as I came to call him—often stepped in to meet the practical needs, an increasing challenge over the years due to Paul's medical appointments and the uniqueness of his school situation, not to mention my being a single parent with a demanding job.

For Paul, spending time at his grandparents' home was routine. If Granddaddy was cutting the grass, you can bet Paul would be out there too. I can picture Paulie now, pushing his plastic lawnmower about ten feet behind his grandfather.

The longest section of my parents' fenced-in backyard was bordered by a deep ravine, once the right-of-way for the old Baltimore and Annapolis Railroad. To empty the lawnmower bag, my stepfather would lift it over the fence and, with arms extended, hold it open to allow the grass clippings to go down the steep vine-covered embankment.

One day, as my stepfather was performing this ritual, the weight of the grass shifted, causing him to lose his grip. The bag and its contents tumbled about halfway down the ravine before getting snagged on an old tree root. Because the bag was out of reach, the drop nearly straight down, and the stability of the terrain unpredictable at best, there was no way my stepfather could have retrieved it. Therefore, against my mother's pleas to the contrary, he decided to tie a rope around his little buddy Paul's waist, loop it over the fence, lower Paul down until he could reach the bag, and then hoist Paul back up and over the fence. The operation was a success. Even though I wasn't there, I have a clear image of this event in my head thanks to my mother. After losing the debate over the safety and wisdom of this maneuver, what did she do? She ran inside and got the camera!

Absent the benefit of mainstream schools or even consistency in schools, Paul didn't have a lot of friends, a fact that was compounded by his lack of social confidence. Because our family was close, his cousins and their friends were his primary social contacts, providing much-needed consistency as well as a safe haven.

Chapter 2

"I'M TIRED OF LETTERS"

Off in the sunset, resting on the cue of night,
There lies a horizon, sinking in neon light.
While nature below rustles in its chilling gust,
Trees dance to its music, all throughout dusk.
Then as we sleep, by enormous shaded skies,
The western world awakens with day light at its side.

AFTER PAUL HAD spent just a handful of days in pre-kindergarten, he climbed into the car one afternoon and announced, "I'm tired of letters." *Great,* I thought, *they're just the foundation for literacy.* But we had time—lots of it.

Even though Paul's teacher the prior year had expressed concern about his ability to engage, or to take his turn when prompted, I was more amused and endeared by him than I was worried. I could see some of his differences. Of course I could. But he was beautiful, he was remarkably sweet-natured, and he was happy. And I am an optimist.

His biggest impediment by far was inattentiveness. Even at home, where individual attention was more the norm than in a classroom, there were many times when he didn't realize he was being addressed, and even a gentle touch on his arm or the side of his face had no effect whatsoever. He simply went somewhere else. I used to joke that you could stick a pin in his arm and he wouldn't know it. I never tested this theory, but I still think it's the truth. When he came back from wherever he'd been, he would carry on age-appropriate conversations with me or Keely or other members of our family, always as if he didn't know he'd gone away for a little while.

I recalled that I had not been the most focused child either. The fact is, I was the child whose stage debut was to have been at the Annapolis Recreation Center in a kindergarten class performance of *H.M.S. Pinafore*. In spite of what must have been weeks if not months of rehearsals, I missed my cue and failed to go out on the stage for my part. Backstage, sitting Indian style—as we said back then—and wearing what seemed to me to be a ball gown, I was mesmerized by a bug on the wall. The next thing I knew, it was too late. While I don't recall being upset, I do remember fleeting thoughts of my parents out there in the audience but concluded they wouldn't have noticed. I was wrong.

And Paul's father didn't hear half of what was said to him. But Don was brilliantly successful, and my guess is that I had excelled beyond what my elementary school teachers or my parents might have predicted. After all, I had gone on to earn a master's degree, graduating with honors.

As a three-year-old, Paul was screened by Child Find, a service provided by Anne Arundel County for preschool children to determine if a disability interferes with learning and, if so, whether special education services may be recommended. Their findings were inconclusive, a fact that, frankly, allowed me at the time to continue to rationalize that Paul's differences didn't warrant undue concern. *Just as I thought*, I said to myself. *Nothing to get worked up about.*

But by the time Paul turned four and his pattern of drifting away had continued, I took him to a psychologist, Anthony Wolff. If nothing else, I knew Paul would benefit from one-on-one attention. And I needed to check my own thinking, or at least have a sounding board. I had to admit Paul was a mystery, and I knew I shouldn't bank on his outgrowing the distractibility that was impeding his learning.

Dr. Wolff quickly won Paul over. In fact, Paul loved going there. They played games, inside and out of the office. The results of a formal assessment, were summarized in writing:

Paul is an affectionate, endearing child who wants to please the adults in his environment. However, his behavior can best be characterized as globally immature. We have dealt with certain psychosocial issues, such as the relative lack of involvement of his father, which are significant but in my opinion not the main issues with respect to his cognitive development or academic performance.

Despite his episodic but quite noticeable symptoms of ADD, I have been conservative and hesitant to apply that diagnostic label to Paul on the theory that he may be on an atypical developmental course. However, Paul's failure to benefit optimally from his pre-k class prompted me to recommend finally that a trial of medication be instituted.

It is not my impression that Paul suffers from a serious emotional disorder per se although he certainly is at risk for developing a secondary emotional problem if his primary problems, in the cognitive and academic domain, are not improved.

As I now read that final sentence, all these years later, it feels like the first time. I was a devoted mother to Paul. I have no doubt about that. And I have a pretty good, if not very good, memory. But I didn't absorb the meaning of those words as maybe I should have. I was concerned about kindergarten and, beyond that, first grade. I absolutely didn't think long-term. Instead, I was slugging it out one day at a time. And, ever the optimist, I didn't realize the full extent of this child's vulnerability.

DESPITE MY INITIAL skepticism, we started down the medication route for Paul. As a school administrator, I had first-hand knowledge of children whose lives were saved by strategies that included medication. I witnessed kids whose disorganization compromised their potential and for whom a small dose of Ritalin (the most frequently prescribed medication for ADD or ADHD at the time) was a miracle. Success was noted literally overnight. Paul was not one of those kids.

Ritalin for Paul made a marginal difference in enhancing his concentration but, unfortunately, the slight and uneven boost in his productivity did not outweigh the side effects: weight loss, fidgeting, and nervousness that exacerbated his tremor, compounding his difficulty with fine motor skills. Dexedrine was tried next and, working with his pediatrician and psychologist, we experimented with the dosage before determining, some months later, that the Ritalin was more beneficial and that Paul would acclimate to the side effects.

I was fortunate to be able to stay home with my children in their early years (until Keely was seven and Paul four) and to jump back into the professional world in a way that blended with my parenting. Until Keely was born—the year I turned thirty—I had been an academic librarian at the University of Maryland, College Park, a place where I enjoyed accolades for my work and made lifelong friends.

When Keely started school as a three-year-old, I volunteered in the library at her school, a pre-kindergarten through twelfth grade independent school in Annapolis. Within a couple of years, I was on the payroll. And by the time Keely started second grade, and Paul was entering the four-year-old program, I was the librarian—a full-time position. The following year, I joined the school's administration, working twelve months and assuming increasing responsibilities over what would end up being a thirty-year career.

The school's campus included fifteen buildings and was located on an old estate that had been a gentleman's farm from the late 1880s to 1940 or so. Beyond being a home-away-from-home for the three of us, the school was a place where good people joined forces, where intellectual zest and creative thinking filled the air, and where the commitment to individuality and to new ideas was exciting. Along with opportunities for tremendous professional growth, I gained a greater exposure to my children's teachers and a greater respect for their work.

I remember going into Paul's classroom one day at lunchtime, just as he was given his mid-day dose of medication. The little boy seated next to him said, "Why did you take that pill?"

Even though I was across the room, Paul called out to me, "Hey, Mommie—why do I take pills?"

I explained he took them to help him pay attention and concentrate.

A worried look crossed Paul's face as he responded to me. "I hate to tell you this," he said, "but when I take that pill, it goes down; so I don't think it's helping my brain."

I didn't think it was helping his brain either.

The summer before Paul's kindergarten year, when he was five-and-a-half, I turned to a local organization that provided diagnostic evaluations and tutoring support. After a series of sessions with Paul, including a battery of tests, they sent me a written report that included:

Test scores must be accepted cautiously as they are considered a minimal estimation of Paul's true abilities. The pervasive pattern is one of attentional limitations. Until the correct dosage of medication is met, further definition of Paul's learning style is tentative. He appears to be a creative thinker who has difficulty with sequential delineation, poor control over his pencil, and a lack of confidence for academic tasks. The result of this constellation of patterns is that Paul may try to manipulate or avoid task completion altogether as a means of disguising his undeveloped skills.

After receiving the report, I hired a tutor to work with Paul.

The common thread in Paul's many assessments, beyond just the poor scores, was the challenge of determining his ability level, due for the most part to his distractibility, but also to his unique approach to testing. It was understood that Paul's scores reflected his performance rather than his ability. One of the teachers recounted the following exchange:

Teacher: "Susie had five hair ribbons and she lost three of them. How many did she have left?"

Paul: "Did she find them?"

Teacher: "No. She lost them . . . If she had five to start with and lost three, how many did she still have?"

Paul: "Did someone help her?"

Teacher: "Yes, of course . . . But my question is: How many did she have? Start with the number five and take away three."

Paul: "Was she sad?"

As the teacher explained to me, "None of Paul's responses were unintelligent but, in scoring the test, no points were given."

In a different setting, Paul was asked to name things "to ride." In the allotted time, he had just one response: "A house." At the end of the testing, Paul was asked to explain his logic.

"My mom told me they can dig them out, put them on a truck, and move them," he said. "*How* do they do that?"

When I heard this, I knew. Just a few days before, I had told Paul about a couple of houses in Annapolis that had been moved when I was young. Paul was intrigued and, even though I did my best to answer his follow-up questions, he continued to ruminate on it. Since Paul's ability to adjust his response to suit a particular setting was an area of weakness, he came up with what was on his mind.

Again, no points. But as the diagnostician told me, "Clearly there is verbal reasoning ability evidenced in several of Paul's responses, but their uniqueness did not meet the test criteria and are not reflected in his scores."

The tutoring bolstered Paul's academic progress, with his learning to read in kindergarten as a noteworthy example. While this gave his teachers and me some insight into his brightness, unfortunately, the windows of time when he was able to focus, and therefore learn, were unpredictable. His teachers communicated their ongoing concerns about his skill development and his well-being, with written reports that provided a fuller picture:

> Paul is a particularly sensitive child, always kind to his teachers and his classmates. He does not have negative interactions but is instead too withdrawn. His delayed response time impedes normal peer relationships. He often engages in perseverative behaviors, which consist of being overly focused upon a particular detail. On days when he is alert, his ability to comprehend new material is startling. But his good days are sporadic. Most of the time he is unable to work independently or in a group.

During an appointment Paul had with his pediatrician, I explained the school's and my concerns. I will never forget sitting in that little exam room that evening as the doctor broke it to me that he could no longer treat Paul, explaining that his own areas of expertise didn't align with Paul's apparent needs. This was a huge setback for me and, as I heard his words, I began to cry. The doctor, also Keely's pediatrician, took the time to hear me out.

I was worried; worried the medication wasn't right; worried Paul's future at the current school was tentative and our options limited; then suddenly, without forewarning, I was worried about finding a pediatrician—a critical part of the team needed to minimize all that I was worried about. I felt a great deal of pressure to move forward and my role as the "go-between" with the two doctors, as well as each doctor and the school, was stressful enough.

Here I was sitting in the largest and most respected pediatric office in town, from which I now felt blackballed, and was about to leave without so much as a referral. And if this group of doctors couldn't treat Paul, who could? Fully aware that I had no say in the matter, I made my way to the front desk, where I learned my balance due was twice that of a regular appointment. When I questioned it, I was told the charge was for an "extended visit" because we had been in the exam room with the doctor beyond the standard number of minutes.

I was tempted to ask, "You charge for crying?" But I was too fragile to take issue. I simply paid the bill and left.

Driving home, I was thankful that Paul was buckled into his car seat and unable to see me because I cried again. This was the start of my somewhat routine "crying in the car" period, which I was usually pretty good about limiting to times I was alone. No matter how hard things got, I didn't want the children to know.

*

TAKING ADVANTAGE OF a professional development opportunity, two colleagues and I went to Loyola University in Baltimore for a talk on learning and the brain given by Martha Bridge Denckla, a professor of neurology at Johns Hopkins University and Director of Developmental Cognitive Neurology at the Kennedy Krieger Institute. It didn't surprise me that the auditorium was packed. Dr. Denckla was internationally renowned for her expertise.

After this incredibly enlightening experience, I fantasized about a professional of Dr. Denckla's caliber working with Paul, then a first grader. Despite the odds, I picked up the phone. Getting through to a member of her staff, I was able to share our story and initiate a process that started with paperwork for Paul's teachers, doctors, and me to complete and submit.

Emily Legum—Paul's first grade reading teacher and a gifted learning specialist—spearheaded the school's response, writing a five-page summary of Paul's strengths and weaknesses and attaching the results of her extensive diagnostic testing as well as Paul's written reports. In conclusion, she wrote:

> All Paul's teachers feel a strong personal concern for him and his academic advancement. His mother has always worked with his teachers in a most positive way and is a loving and supportive parent. We believe Paul is very bright but his inability to attend impedes his success. Despite extensive remediation strategies and individualized instruction with learning specialists, his skill development is impaired, and his learning behaviors are a puzzle to us.

It wasn't long before we had an appointment.

As Paul and I arrived at the Kennedy Krieger Institute, I was full of mixed emotions. I was thankful for what I saw as an auspicious opportunity, but at the same time I was saddened to be there, to have to take my little boy to this place, respected as it was. When I spotted their logo featuring a child in a wheelchair, it just about did me in, and I fought hard to choke back my tears—a reaction I now see as somewhat idiotic and even shameful, but nonetheless the memory is crystal clear.

To my utter surprise, a week or so later, Dr. Denckla called me at home. She told me she had put a sticky note on the lamp by her bed to remind her of Paul. I don't recall all of what was said in that conversation, but I remember this particular exchange as though it were yesterday.

"I have never seen anyone quite like Paul," Dr. Denckla said. "I can't believe I'm telling this to a mother."

And I said, "I can't believe *I* am the mother."

This revered doctor—internationally known research scientist in behavioral and cognitive neurology whose groundbreaking work I'd first read about years before and who must have been in her mid-fifties at the time—had never seen anyone like Paul?

I was not offended—every mother thinks her child is one-of-a-kind—but I was, I don't know, numb. On the other hand, I was grateful for her interest and genuinely touched by her call. She told me about some highlights of her findings, such as Paul's visual perception being in the ninety-ninth percentile, a significant strength that he couldn't readily reveal due to his poor fine motor skills. She also told me her written evaluation was forthcoming and said she'd like to follow up with us periodically, which, over the years, she did.

The evaluation arrived some days later and included:

Important findings of my evaluation on 11/22/89 were that indeed extremely poor concentration was characteristic of Paul and that it is very difficult to maintain his attention, even while on medication. Although he is a child who has a strength in visual perception and visually guided reasoning, he was below the 3rd percentile on the visual retention tests that depend upon visual attention. He had problems on virtually every one of the tests that require careful looking or listening and controlled responding.

Neurodevelopmentally, it will come as no surprise that he does have confirmatory "neighborhood" signs in areas of motor control with failures for his age in all areas including gait and balance, with poor control of foot and finger movements, plus hypotonia.

Barkley Home Rating Scale [used to assess ADHD] was not out of normal range for Paul's age.

The medication issue will be an ongoing difficulty, I am sure. However, with some "tinkering" I believe it can be gotten under control. If there is no success with the reduction of Ritalin and with the possible transfer back to Dexedrine, I would have the psychopharmacology clinic referrals with highly specialized persons known through my affiliations with the Kennedy Institute and Johns Hopkins in Baltimore.

School seems to be an issue for which no perfection can be obtained. There is no perfect school or even excellent school to which I can point. If there were a school that was oriented toward the serious attentionally impaired youngster such as Paul, I would recommend it! Absent that possibility, one is again "tinkering" to come up with a solution that is the best we can do.

In January of Paul's first-grade year, following Dr. Denckla's advice and in conjunction with his teachers and his new pediatrician, Raymond Srsic, we began the process of reducing the Ritalin, ultimately ruling it out altogether. After trying Dexedrine at various dosages without success, I called the Psychopharmacology Clinic at Johns Hopkins Hospital, where we were able to get an appointment with the director, a Dr. Reiss. I had no illusions at this juncture of a quick fix, but I hoped this level of expertise could provide the help Paul desperately needed.

With few exceptions, Paul was still unable to focus well enough to be successful in either large or small groupings. Even though Paul continued to be characterized as cooperative and kind, he was unsure of his place within a group of classmates. In fact, when the children played games, he preferred to sit alone and mostly depended on the teacher for reassurance.

Paul's writing was weak and labor intensive. I remember a call from his first-grade teacher, telling me he had written his very first sentence in his journal that day.

"What did he write?" I asked.

"I wish it was summer," she said.

*

THANKFULLY, PAUL WASN'T a self-centered child, and the absence of ego-boosting experiences never caused him to resist going to school. Paul loved his teachers and had developed a close friendship with Scott, a fellow first grader. At home, Paul functioned happily, playing with Keely, his cousins, and a couple of close neighborhood friends.

The only time I saw Paul upset at school was on the day of the first-grade play. Just minutes before it was to start, Paul was told his participation wasn't needed. Everyone in the class was in the play, and he'd worn the designated outfit to school that day. This news came as a surprise and a blow to him. I learned of this situation just minutes before Paul did and was asked to get him from the wings of the stage, take him back to his classroom, and wait with him until the others returned.

As I intercepted Paul, I could see he was confounded. He ran ahead of me as we crossed the campus, and when we entered his empty classroom, he grabbed a plastic basket full of crayons and threw it to the floor. He sobbed and, in so many words, asked me why he was singled out. I held him and tried to soothe him, but I had no answer.

I was careful not to feed his anger, but I was upset too. After his crying subsided, we picked up the crayons and I read a book to him. He never mentioned this incident again.

By March, first grade for Paul had deteriorated entirely due to the instability brought on by switching the various medications (nortriptyline, clonidine, desipramine, imipramine), with each drug generating different effects and the transitioning itself adding to the instability. On one medication, Paul became overly agitated; on another, he couldn't stay awake. I remember going into our bathroom at home early one morning, thinking I was the only one up, and finding Paul passed out cold on our bathroom floor.

Paul needed routine EKG and blood tests, all of which he stoically tolerated, but he could no longer go to school, and it was obvious he was not remotely prepared for second grade for the upcoming year. Because Paul was already an old first grader, a repeat was out of the question.

I was anxious. I wanted this experimental phase behind us and, frankly, grew impatient with it. At the outset of this trial period, I hoped that by some miracle Paul would get the right treatment, be able to take advantage of his brightness, catch up academically, and end this roller coaster ride. But I knew this was a long shot, and my realism was starting to temper my optimism. My focus was on his fate for the upcoming school year, and I didn't yet see even a glimmer of light at the end of the tunnel.

May 27, 1990
Dear Dr. Reiss,

My son, Paul, is under your care, through his pediatrician, for determining the best possible medication for his attentional impairment.

As we began to experiment with various medications this spring, Paul initially suffered withdrawal from the stimulants to the point where he was rolling on the floor in his classroom, making high pitched noises, and displaying other disruptive behaviors. Once on a full dose of nortriptyline for the requisite period of time, Paul did present as the happy, well-adjusted child that I had known him to be most of his life. However, his ability to learn (even in a 1:1 setting) was nonexistent.

Hence we began the clonidine and all of the negative behaviors that accompany any change for this child were evidenced. Whereas I realize it is not possible to avoid the ramifications of weaning from one medication and beginning another, I have never been told what to anticipate, what to tolerate, and when to express concern. Also, I have not been told what length of time is necessary to begin to evaluate any positive effects of these two medications.

As of today, Paul is on .2 mg of clonidine. Other than the morning nap he needs as a result, he is able to enjoy riding his bike and playing in the afternoon. He cannot, however, do any academic work and is no longer able to attend school. I learned through the pediatrician yesterday that we will proceed in two more increments to .3 mg of clonidine. At that time, I suspect we will rule out the clonidine. I can only guess, however, as to what will be decided and when, and why, and to what end. And each day without success is long and painful. I know this entire process requires patience, yet without a full understanding of the process itself, patience is difficult. Moreover, I am not convinced my patience to date has served my son.

The bleakness of our current situation contributes to my frustration. I know we are fortunate to have your involvement, yet I feel too removed to feel confident that Paul's best interest is being served. In short, I am frustrated by the questions I cannot ask, and the input I cannot give.

Please give me the benefit of your advice.

Thank you,
Jessie Dunleavy

I received a reply from Dr. Reiss, encouraging me to persist as long as I felt the "deleterious effects of the medication trials do not outweigh the potential advantages to be gained" and clarifying that he was serving as a consultant to Dr. Srsic, with whom I should share my insights and concerns.

Finally, a medication we tried late that spring, desipramine, seemed to help Paul and he was able to return to school, although there were just a few days left in the year. The teachers reported Paul was more aware of his environment, more outgoing and communicative with his peers, and more focused on completing his work. One day, Paul's teacher was so excited by his performance that she called me during the school day. Unable to reach me, she asked my administrative assistant to give me this message: "Paul is having the best day ever!"

None of these positives suggested that Paul was functioning well enough to be able to make up for lost time, particularly in short order. Still, I was heartened and extremely relieved that it looked as though we had landed on the right medication.

Within a few days of this respite, I got a call from Dr. Srsic, who told me he had just received the June 1990 issue of *The Medical Letter*, a bi-weekly journal providing evaluations of pharmaceutical drugs for physicians. Its lead article—*Sudden Death in Children Treated with Tricyclic Drugs*—concerned him greatly and, as a result, he was unwilling to continue to prescribe desipramine. I couldn't believe it! I was heartsick. From there, we tried an alternative that supposedly provided similar benefits. This may have been true for some children, but it wasn't for Paul.

Earlier in the spring, I had started to consider school alternatives for Paul. There weren't many choices, but I learned a lot about special education resources within a thirty-mile radius of our home. I fell in love with one school I visited in Washington, D.C., but decided our neighborhood public school would be the better option. Confident that Paul would qualify for special education services, I could see the merit in joining forces with the team of available experts. Even though I was heartbroken that Paul had to leave the school where Keely and I were rooted, I gradually had learned to let go of an all-too-elusive ideal and accept the reality. But I never let go of hoping for the best for Paul and believing it was out there somewhere.

Paul was tested by a county school psychologist whose results were very much like those we had accumulated to date. She clearly liked Paul—a fact that soothed my wobbly heart.

In her summary, she wrote:

Paul's greatest area of deficit is in the distractibility arena, with scores falling significantly subaverage. The strengths Paul brings to learning include his curiosity, his humor, persistence, diligence, and a generally high frustration tolerance.

After the bumpy ride that was spring for this child, I chose to delay telling him about changing schools, waiting until August to do so. I knew he would fret about the unknowns, and I figured at least I could shorten the duration of unease and let him settle into summer and regain his footing in this world. Furthermore, by August, I too would've had time to catch my breath, time to collect my thoughts and introduce the new school—Annapolis Elementary, otherwise known as Green Street—with enthusiasm.

As the time drew near, I rehearsed what I thought was the best way to explain the situation. Then August came, and I told him.

Paul had only one response: "What is Scott going to do without me?"

Chapter 3

RUNNING TOWARD MORNING'S DOORWAY

Miracles are sometimes stretched few and far between hardships.
And though battles may rage in our communities
and though our hearts keen sense of injustice may be felt;
when miracles surface, they will carry us back to refuge.

DESPITE MY MOSTLY optimistic outlook, juggling life's demands as a parent, a homeowner, and a professional presented challenges. Sometimes I felt buoyed by my ability to manage, and manage well. Sometimes I was lonely; other times I felt discouraged by competing needs that pretty much ruled out my ability to live up to my own standards, at work or at home.

When the children were still pretty little, I signed up for an exercise class that met one time a week in the early evening, something I saw as a luxury but good for my overall health, even though I'd have to figure out childcare each week as the day approached. To enable my getaway one winter evening, I took Keely and Paulie to my neighbor's house.

By the time I returned home, snow had accumulated, and I decided to steal a few extra minutes to run inside, grab the broom, and clear our front steps and walk before having the children underfoot. Later, when the three of us were settled back in the house and I was getting dinner together, a gust of bitterly cold air whipped in from the playroom, prompting me to yell to the kids, "What is wrong with you? Close that window! It's winter, for God's sake!!"

Keely, the appointed spokesperson for the twosome, came into the kitchen and said, "We didn't open the window, Mommie."

I walked in there. The window was wide open. I closed it before noticing the shards of glass at the top of the basement steps. Checking for additional signs that would help calibrate my reaction, I went upstairs and discovered my ransacked bedroom and eventually my missing jewelry. The police came and investigated, telling me the thief had entered by breaking the basement window. They surmised he was caught off guard when I returned home, and, rather than exiting via the front door, he jumped out the playroom window located at the back of the house and beneath which they could see his footprints in the snow. I knew then that I had startled him when I ran in for the broom and was thankful I hadn't come in to stay, with the children in tow.

The whole thing unnerved me. I soothed the kids, fed them, and began to clean up the mess and anticipate the repairs, the insurance claims. I would not have considered myself a jewelry person, and was far from dripping in anything, but when adding up every piece of jewelry accumulated in your whole life, it's more than you'd think. I learned that without a separate rider for jewelry on my homeowner policy, the coverage would be a mere fraction of the total value of what I'd lost.

My insurance agent then suggested I reconsider and take out a jewelry rider on the policy. While I could have cried, I actually laughed. "Run this by me one more time," I said to him. "Despite my years of premium payments, you can't pay *me* the money to cover my loss but, instead, I can pay *you* additional money to cover that which I no longer have and cannot replace. Is that what I heard?"

I was sad mostly for sentimental reasons. Among the things I lost were a gold charm bracelet my parents had given me for my sixteenth birthday with accumulated charms representing many a milestone. Also gone were gold earrings my father had given my mother, gold cufflinks she had given him, my engagement ring, the diamond bands Don had given me when each of the children was born, and a watch I loved. Sometimes I still wish I had those things, but they were just things.

Don had remarried as soon as our divorce was finalized, just as Paul was entering pre-kindergarten and Keely second grade. While he didn't tell me or the children directly, I had heard about the engagement and the pending wedding. From the start, his relationship with Lucy ushered in a more regular visitation schedule, which I welcomed—just as I did the fact that Lucy was a likable and family-oriented person. One has no say in who will become a step-parent to their children; let's just say I was grateful. Some years later, Don and Lucy would have their own child, a daughter named Annie.

Even though life was full of challenge, I wasn't interested in pursuing a relationship during my first couple of years as a single parent. Without giving the matter much thought, I instinctively focused on the children. In any case, they were my highest priority and their world had been disrupted enough. And frankly, even in my younger carefree days, I valued breathing room between romantic relationships.

It stands to reason that another influence on my thinking was rooted in the heartaches of a failed marriage. But regardless of the forces at play, about which I am not entirely sure anyway, we were a pretty happy threesome—Keely, Paulie, and I—and even took to calling ourselves "three peas in a pod," a reference to our bond that cropped up now and again in many a light-hearted moment for the duration of our years together.

Eventually, however, I agreed to unleash one particular friend, Linda, whose extroverted personality suited her matchmaker aspirations. Since this was the 1980s, there was no such thing as Match. com, but Linda's reconnaissance on my behalf would stand up to any comparisons. Linda was a born social butterfly who was pretty, and she knew it. And while she was a faithful wife and a devoted mother, she loved to flirt and was in her element in scouting out men. Linda recruited several candidates, each of whom met her rigorous criteria: nice looking, social, and successful. Over time, she introduced me to a lawyer, an airline pilot, and a judge. As a result, I dabbled in the dating world and admit I did have some fun, even though I often felt it was more trouble than it was worth, mainly because I shielded the children from my activities.

One date stands out. Mike, the attorney, invited me to go out on his boat with another couple. We agreed to meet at the dock at the end of my street and from there motor over to Mill Creek for dinner at Jimmy Cantler's Riverside Inn, a wildly popular waterfront crab house, an Annapolis icon. I had not met Mike or his friends but was instantly at ease and enjoyed the cruise and the dinner.

Navigating the waterway in and out of Whitehall Bay—linking Mill Creek to Annapolis' Severn River—is tricky, something I knew well. The Bay is deep and narrow, with shoals on either side, requiring careful attention to channel markers and charts. We made it in without any problem, as had always been my experience, but got stuck on the way out, a situation that was made worse by the motor getting hopelessly tangled with crab pots, abundant in this particular area.

Keely and Paul's babysitter that evening, Andrea, was a young teenager who lived in the house directly behind ours, and I had told her I would be home by 11:00. I think we ran aground about 10:30. Efforts to free the boat, followed by attempts to flag down another boater, failed and eventually my three companions—none of whom had children at home—went below to sleep. I sat there all night, helpless, with no possible way to communicate. My degree of misery was such that I contemplated swimming, but I decided a temporarily missing mother was better than a dead one. Still, my suffering grew along with the seemingly endless night.

As the sun finally peeked over the horizon, I was able to wave down a passing boater who agreed to take me to the City Dock, less than a mile from home. I will never forget walking into my house, disheveled and in my rumpled dress, where I found Keely and Paulie at the kitchen table eating cereal. Seated with them was Andrea's father, who had relieved his daughter at some point and stayed the night at my house, no doubt waiting . . . wondering . . . I was so sorry! How I looked, how the situation seemed, I can only imagine. The same goes for what poor Keely and Paulie thought upon realizing my absence as they got up that morning, seeing my made bed without me in it. And Mr. Seabrook's presence! I had some explaining to do.

I used to think of that as the worst night of my life, often recalling it as Andrea—who in the blink of an eye grew up to become a successful journalist—hosted favorite programs on NPR, and even now as I continue, some thirty years hence, to catch up with her parents over the back fence.

Throughout my time as a single parent with young children, I was lucky to have bonded with several neighborhood teenagers, one of whom—Molly Wanamaker—became family to us. Molly was eleven when she first knocked on our door, and she helped me in countless ways until she left for college—and even then was a presence during school breaks and throughout the summer months, whether or not I was going out. We baked cookies together, carried out the work of Santa Claus, and battened down in preparation for a hurricane barreling up the Atlantic. Molly would spend the night sometimes, and even vacationed with us and my extended family over multiple summers.

The best thing I had going for me was the camaraderie and the backing of my family, with their unconditional love for the children providing emotional support as well as "another pair of hands" when needed. I took much comfort in the fact that Keely and Paulie hadn't lost fifty percent of their daily adult network, as would be the case for many children of divorce. In essence, their world continued to include a grandmother, a grandfather, two aunts, and two uncles, all of whom they saw at least weekly and who played meaningful roles in these critical years. In time, I came to see that I was rationalizing the reality of divorce and that—in spite of these very real advantages—recurring sorrows are part and parcel of a fragmented family. Nevertheless, we had plenty of love; there was no doubt about that.

At some point in here I started to date Jerry, a college professor I met through my work. It was a relationship that I was not quick to divulge to the children and one I initially didn't take very seriously. It was fun; that was all. And I loved teasing Linda, telling her I met him all by myself. But things evolved and we grew closer, with a bond that was enhanced by a common passion for education. Eventually, Jerry asked me to marry him.

As Paul's second-grade year and Keely's fifth unfolded, I began to consider Jerry's proposal. He was more confident than I of the merits of this idea, and I pretty much dragged my feet for the better part of that year. However, in weighing all the pros and cons, ultimately, I was persuaded by several factors. One, Jerry was a born teacher and, despite being childless, he would be a "natural" in a caretaker role. Two, he was highly energetic—having completed his doctorate while teaching full time was just the tip of the iceberg in terms of his productivity—and eager to take on the duties of parenthood. This was explicit as he continually made his case. "Come on!" he'd say. "Tell me—who else has the energy to help you raise your children?"

Also in the plus column was Jerry's sense of humor and what I saw as his unwavering devotion to me. After all, he was in his thirties and had never married. And maybe, just maybe, six years of going it alone was enough for me.

*

THIS DECISION-MAKING PERIOD coincided with Paul's year at Annapolis Elementary School. At that time, we had settled on a somewhat satisfactory medication regime and I was thankful for the consistency. I had no complaints with the school per se. Paul's classroom teacher was kind and supportive, as was the special education teacher, who devoted a couple of hours a day to working with him. Even so, as I dropped Paul off on my way to work each morning, I watched him walk up the front steps of the school, hang his head, and wave to me by extending his arm behind his lower back and wiggling his fingers. I don't think I rounded the corner from Green Street onto Compromise Street one time that year without tears in my eyes.

While Paul toed the line with little complaint, school was a place where he stayed to himself and, for the most part, was unaware of his surroundings. His teachers reported, for example, that he remained seated at his desk as the other children lined up to go to the cafeteria for lunch. When prompted to join them, he often needed to be reminded to take his lunch box.

Having entered the world of special education within the county system, I would become all too familiar with ARD committee meetings, otherwise known as Admission, Review, and Dismissal—the official name of the committee responsible for making educational decisions for a student. Parents are members of the committee, as are designated educators who bring their expertise to the meetings where together an Individualized Education Program, often referred to as the IEP, is written and the child's placement is determined. The placement is denoted by a particular "Level," indicating how much of a child's school day is spent in a special education setting, with federal laws defining Levels I through V. The higher the level, the more special education services are required.

In an ARD committee meeting in early May, it was evident that, by all measurable standards, Paul's year had not been successful, and he would need increased services for third-grade. The upshot of the meeting was the county's recommendation to change Paul's designated placement of Level III (providing thirteen hours of special education support per week) to Level IV (twenty hours), meaning Paul would have to attend Central Elementary School in Edgewater, Maryland—the only public school in the area equipped to provide Level IV services.

After thinking about this decision for a couple of weeks, I realized I was more puzzled than resolved, and I decided to ask for another review:

May 28, 1991
Anne Arundel County
Department of Special Education

To whom it may concern:

I am writing to request a formal hearing to review the proposed educational placement for my son, Paul—currently a second grader receiving Level III special education services at Annapolis Elementary, a place where he has been well cared for, yet his educational needs have not been met in general or in special education classes. Because Paul has not been successful, Level IV services are recommended for the coming year.

After further consideration, I must question how twenty hours of services is preferable to thirteen hours, when Paul's time in the special education setting this year did not meet his needs. In other words, I do not understand how this proposed change—essentially the continuation and extension of the same methods that didn't enable success—provides hope for improvement for Paul (educationally, emotionally, or socially). In fact, I fear further setbacks as he continues, in a different setting with a different peer group, in a system that cannot cope with his differences.

Please notify me regarding the appropriate next step for an appeal process.

Sincerely,
Jessie Dunleavy

Finding the right school environment for Paul was a conundrum that kept me awake at night, but my pending marriage, initially requiring a little more adjustment on Keely's part than Paul's, was a good thing. I looked forward to becoming a family unit and having a partner, a shoulder to lean on, particularly in considering the challenges I faced with Paul, an old house, and a job with increasing demands. Jerry and I were married at the end of the academic year, and he subsequently moved into my home—the only home the children had ever known.

Our strengths included respect for each other's career and work ethic, good friends with whom we socialized frequently, and the support of my family members who embraced my husband from the outset. But, catching me off guard, significant challenges surfaced early on. Jerry had what I then would have described as temper tantrums.

The frequency of these often frightening outbursts ranged from a couple of times a month to multiple times in a given day. During a typical episode, Jerry would simultaneously shout—launching unfounded and often vicious verbal attacks—and stomp from room to room and up and down the stairs from one floor of the house to another repeating himself over and over. In sum, he lost control and, along with it, the ability to reason.

This behavior was shocking and incomprehensible to me, and initially I was handicapped, thrown off balance by confusion. I know I adopted a protective mode—protecting myself by making a conscious effort to maintain my composure and not let him upset me while also protecting the children to the extent I could, often making light of any verbal attacks they could overhear.

For a long time, I thought my reasonable approach would win out. Basically, I was good at influencing others. Additionally, I was eight years Jerry's senior and had faced more challenges than he. I was confident in my ability to communicate and to establish standards. At times I thought maybe my efforts were helpful, extending the periods of smooth sailing.

Part of my quandary was figuring out what provoked Jerry's anger—a piece of the puzzle I could rarely grasp. But even when I could, I didn't get why his reaction was out of proportion, more dramatic than the circumstance warranted with accusations and personal attacks that knew no limits. And because this correlation with reality was shaky at best, there often was no way out of the labyrinth he created.

Making matters worse, it wasn't long before these bouts of hostility turned on Paul, whose reactions, depending on the specific situation and his own degree of fragility at the moment, included crying, words of self-defense, and occasionally even assuming a more "adult" role, accepting the assigned blame just to minimize the drama. Nothing worked. Nothing but time.

Generally, somewhere between one and three days after an outburst, Jerry adopted a conciliatory manner, "making things right" with acts of kindness. While I was sincerely grateful for his gestures, he rarely acknowledged his destructive behavior. Nor did he retract the insults that bore no resemblance to the truth. I walked a tightrope—trying to keep the peace, minimize the toll taken on the children, and defend Paul when I could do so without fanning the flames.

One evening, a year into our marriage, Jerry became infuriated because Paul was having trouble completing his homework. I think it's fair to say every parent in the country, or maybe the world, has experienced similar frustration and may well even overreact as a result. I know I have. But this scenario triggered an episode of outrage on Jerry's part, and among the hurtful things he repeatedly yelled at Paul were:

"It's no wonder you can't read and write like other children your age!"

"You will continue to be weak. I guess you think it's okay to be weak!"

"Go cry to your mother. She likes you to be weak!"

No resolution was reached and no words of respect or regard were spoken. When Paul was ready for bed that evening, I quietly went into his room to say goodnight and, if nothing else, give him a hug. He asked me if it was true that he couldn't read and write like other children his age, and I did my best to point out his strengths and to explain the array of differences among various learners, in terms of ability and pace. I also said there were many whose skills may have advanced beyond his, but there were others less capable than he, telling him too that the poor reader may be the fastest runner, or that the child with disabilities may become an engineer, a famous artist, or a world leader.

I usually tried to provide comfort without directly countering one of my husband's declarations, something I saw as necessary in keeping his reactions in check lest he accuse me of undermining "his authority."

However, as I left Paul's room that particular night, I do remember saying, "By the way, Paul, you are not weak. And you know you aren't."

"Goodnight, Mom. I love you."

*

AS SUMMER AND our family's annual two-week trip to the beach approached, Jerry said to me, "I am not going to do anything with, or for, Paul while we are on vacation, unless you want me to be volatile with him. Actually, it's your choice; so just let me know what you decide."

He repeated this for days, always emphasizing that I was in the driver's seat—it was my choice. Elevating himself to the benevolent position, he reiterated that he would simply go along with my decision. One hardly needs to be a psychologist, or even a tad insightful for that matter, to see that I had no choice. The fact is, this twisted maneuver was nothing but a threat, a strategy to keep me on edge.

In spite of the fabricated land mine I was trying to navigate, we had fun on our family vacations, and I found that the network of adults—whether friends or family—served to keep Jerry's unreasonable behavior in check. As a matter of fact, the beach trips were good for us, reminding me that we could laugh and be light-hearted.

This particular year, the eight cousins—ranging in age from two to thirteen—could go out unsupervised after dinner in the little oceanfront village where we stayed. One night they were out on foot, except for two-year-old Molly who they put in her stroller with Caitlin, the oldest cousin, at the helm. It was getting dark, and as they approached the path to the beach, they were frightened by a man on the walkway who reportedly was wearing a long black hooded cape— with the hood up, concealing his face. They were spooked and took off running for home! As they burst in the door, breathless, with all of them talking at once, we had to laugh at the vision of them running for their lives, all the while pushing the stroller over some pretty rugged terrain. Little Molly's hair was slicked back as if she'd been in a wind tunnel! We took some pride in the fact that they didn't abandon the stroller, given their state of high alert. For the rest of our vacation, they swung into investigator mode, fixated on discovering the real "cape man," who obviously lurked among us, and deciding whether or not he was a threat to the safety of this otherwise tranquil community. While I don't think they solved the mystery, theories abounded, and "cape man" was a legend for years to come.

A passage from Paul's laptop files:

Of all the places in the world I could want to be, the beach house was the place. It was a place where dreaming stopped and where real living began. All of the memories of the beach in Delaware make me wishful to be a child again, carefree and down at that same beach chasing the crashing waves back into the ocean. If only life could be so simple, I would be a millionaire.

Back at home, another incident between Jerry and Paul took place that same summer. On this particular day, Paul's crime was leaving our neighbor's garden hose running. Our street is lined with old houses that are just about as close together as detached houses can be, so much so that in looking down the street, you see the eaves of the roofs overhanging one another. Our easement, a little more generous than some, provided a narrow side patio used in common with our neighbor Mandy, a circumstance we enjoyed, and one that over the years led to a deep friendship between Mandy and me as well as among her three children—Josh, Danny, and Lara—and my two, all close in age. Not only were the children back and forth between our two houses, but Mandy and I shared garden tools, the lawnmower, detergent, anything and everything.

As Paul came inside, I heard Jerry ask if he had left the hose running. Although in another room, I braced myself.

"Yes," Paul said.

This prompted an outburst that started with, "That was the wrong thing to do."

"I didn't mean to," Paul interjected.

The drama took its course anyway, as the statement of wrongdoing was repeated with the classic irrational fervor and rapidly escalating personal attacks.

Paul then said, "I won't do it again."

Grabbing Paul, picking him up and putting him in a chair while squeezing his frail arms (in front of his cousin with whom he'd been playing), Jerry screamed, "Don't you *ever* talk to me that way! You will not treat me like that! I am trying to tell you something! You were wrong! You were wrong!"

Paul started to cry, and Jerry continued to yell: "You never said you were sorry! You don't care about Mandy!"

Crying harder, Paul said, "Yes, I do."

Now in full-blown rage, Jerry screamed, "No, you don't! No! You do not! You do not care about Mandy! That wouldn't be your style, would it? You didn't even say you were sorry!" All of this, with the emphasis on Paul's supposed character flaws rather than his forgetfulness, was repeated more times than I care to report, or even want to remember.

As a school administrator, I advised many a parent over the years, frequently emphasizing the importance of respect (we cannot expect to receive that which we don't give); modeling the behavior we want our children to assume; consequences for poor choices that are fair and understandable to a child, bearing in mind that discipline is a component of love. And probably the most important: Don't put yourself on the child's level. They have to know you are in charge and when you lose your cool, you lose your effectiveness. None of us is perfect, and children press our buttons. We are human and we make mistakes.

But Jerry broke all the rules, and my desire to share my perspective was often thwarted by fear.

For me, being in a therapist's office had become almost as routine as going to the grocery store, but at this juncture I couldn't convince my husband of the merits. So his explosive tactics continued despite my efforts and the warnings voiced by a couple of Paul's teachers and mental health providers. Mundane occurrences, such as a misplaced remote control or the way laundry was folded, could prompt a no-win interrogation followed by a blow-up and literally days of hostility.

In some ways I became immune to the yelling, but he employed other subtle forms of manipulation, strategies to belittle me or trivialize what mattered to me. One school morning when Paul was a little older, we were having breakfast when Paul announced he needed to take a set of dress clothes to school for that day's mock job interview.

Mildly impatient with him, I uttered one of those classic parental refrains, "Paul, you need to tell me these things the night before."

Perceiving this as my reluctance to help him, Paul said, "Please, Mom, I won't pass my competency if I don't have the clothes."

Naturally I got them together. Then, while Paul was at the front door watching for the bus, it dawned on me I had forgotten to pack his lunch. Knowing I was cutting it close, I dashed into the kitchen to pull something together. Jerry entered the kitchen, stood there for several minutes watching me as I flew around, making the lunch.

I said, "Do you think I'll make it in time?"

He said, "No . . . because the bus already came and Paul left."

I didn't say anything more.

*

BY AND LARGE, with some exceptions, Keely was spared the personal attacks. Maybe this was because she was as close to a perfect kid as you could get but, more likely, I think she was spared because she was a girl. While I knew she paid a dear price for his antics at home, I appreciated the void he was able to fill in her life even though, through no fault of hers, it contributed to the trap I was in.

Later on, I came to understand that my husband's behavior had nothing to do with me. The fact is, he wanted to dominate and control me and thus created an oppressive environment with verbal abuse as his greatest weapon. I learned too that the pain of verbal abuse is as great as physical abuse, but in some ways more insidious because it's hidden and the perpetrator routinely denies it. And while he inflicted unnecessary pain, he did not destroy my sense of self. Maybe it's because I didn't crumble that he picked on the most vulnerable among us, as bullies do, knowing too that Paul was my Achilles Heel.

While I have avoided revealing the most egregious incidents, these challenges were part of the reality of our journey and significant in Paul's development. The fact is, my shame in having made this choice, and then tolerating the circumstances, trumps any remote temptation to cast aspersions on an individual who is long gone from our lives. Unable to change the past, and fully acknowledging my own failing, I can only hope to help others who may find themselves in a similar trap and for whom my insight may have some value. So often, when in the midst of difficult times, we can't see the way out.

When a therapist asked me why I stayed, I gave it a lot of thought. Naturally, it was complicated. One thing I realized—beyond my trying to make it work, hoping it would get better, not wanting to give up—was the degree of turmoil in my life that depleted the sort of reserves needed to take on disruption. Also, the children did benefit from my husband's good qualities. He taught Keely to ride a bike and to love opera and taught Paul to ski, something they did together every year.

Paul's few friends, outside the network provided by our family and friends, lived far and wide, and Jerry thought nothing of giving up a Saturday to drive to Leonardtown and back, for example, so that Paul could have a playdate. While they loved their biological father, his presence in their lives fluctuated, and they clamored for what children need most—time. And as they lapped up the attention their stepfather did offer, they learned to turn a blind eye to his hurtful behavior. And lastly, I would have been embarrassed within the community we shared, even though I'm now ashamed to admit that "appearances" could have kept me from doing what I knew in my heart was right for me.

The fact is, during these years, my children did not have a predictable home life or an environment in which adult wisdom and dignity were the norm, making me all the more grateful for the grandparents and aunts and uncles whose stability was reliable.

I alone brought this into our world. It is among my greatest regrets.

Chapter 4

FIGHTING FOR OUR RIGHTS

Lame but expected to carry
Simple but demandingly complex
Creative but left without canvas
Anxious but made to sit
Different but pressured to conform

I SAT ANXIOUSLY in the ARD committee meeting as Paul's placement was debated. It was July. And all these county officials were seated around the table because of my objection, after the fact, to the outcome of the spring meeting. When a decision was finally reached, I was relieved. Paul's placement changed from Level IV to Level V— full-time special education services.

It was just after this meeting, and by happenstance, that I became aware of a letter, written in June to the county coordinator for special education and signed by nine professionals who worked with Paul during his year at Annapolis Elementary, including his teachers, the school principal, and the school psychologist:

Unique is an adjective that has been used frequently to describe Paul. . . . Every effort has been made to help Paul gain the necessary learning behaviors for school success. Paul is a delightful child but we have failed to find strategies that would enable us to meet his needs. In our collective educational experience, Paul is unique. His needs cannot be met in a traditional public school setting. We believe his needs exceed our school system and we look to you to help us find the appropriate educational placement.

I was deeply moved by this expression of concern for Paul and by the collaborative effort to highlight the extent of his needs. In fact, their advocacy was powerful, and I could see that, maybe, it wasn't just my persuasive gifts that had inspired this recent placement decision. Regardless, I was on to the next hurdle: Level V services were not provided within any public school in the state.

As mandated by the Rehabilitation Act of 1973 and the Individuals with Disabilities Act of 1975, all children with disabilities in the United States have the right to a free and appropriate education. So we needed to seek a non-public school that could meet Paul's needs, one that was approved by the Maryland State Department of Education. *Wow*, I thought, *we have less than six weeks before Paul's third-grade year is to begin.*

By August, despite the joint efforts of the county officials and myself—casting our net in a thirty-some-mile radius—a viable, or even marginally acceptable, school had not been found. I was left only one alternative—a new school located about twenty miles north of Annapolis with a curriculum designed to serve students with learning differences. But despite the professional credentials of the staff, the small class size, and the remedial program, the school did not have MSDE approval. This meant that the steep tuition, as well as transportation and all other costs, fell to the parent. I was relieved to have found a school, and even hopeful about its being a good place for Paul, but I was worried about sustaining the financial commitment into the future.

In a repeat performance of just one year earlier, I told Paul in August that he'd be starting a new school, The Meadow School. On the morning of the first day of school, I put Paul's clothes out on his bed as I usually did to help him get himself ready.

He promptly came into my room, with the clothing in his hand, and said to me, "These are the clothes I am NOT wearing to the school I am NOT going to."

I don't remember my reply but do know that Paul's resistance must have been fleeting, as we arrived on time to his new school, where Paul was immediately welcomed with open arms.

The director of Meadow School suggested I hire an attorney to pursue funding in accordance with my rights as a parent of a handicapped child. She said the tuition at Meadow was comparable to what the county would have paid for any of the non-public alternatives they had sought for Paul. She also said if his case was approved for funding, it could pave the way for other students in her school who may have, or may obtain, Level V eligibility. She gave me the name of a specific attorney—the principal of a special education law firm in Washington, D.C., who she said was widely recognized for his legal prowess and his successes in securing appropriate placements for students with disabilities.

I met with the attorney, Michael Eig, and retained his services. While his legal fees would be at my expense, Mr. Eig had confidence in the merits of our case and explained the possibility of his fees being covered, along with the tuition, if we prevailed. Come what may, I decided to take the risk.

After failing to come to a resolution working within the county school system, Mr. Eig submitted a formal request for a due process hearing at the state level. The hearing—to take place in Lutherville, Maryland, in front of a judge and three impartial hearing officers— was scheduled, and more than a dozen individuals were summoned to provide testimony.

I had a lot riding on the outcome of this case, and when the day of the hearing arrived, I was anxious. Paul had no knowledge of any facet of this legal process and went off to school that morning as he did any other day, except for the excitement of taking cupcakes for all his classmates. It was his ninth birthday.

The hearing itself, for me, was brutal. I don't know if the fact that it was Paul's birthday heightened my sensitivity. But I do know that it was hard to sit there and listen to the multiple "experts"—none of whom had ever met Paul, much less worked with him—deliver what I remember as hours of testimony riddled with inaccuracies and designed to make the case to deny funding for his current school. I wanted to set the record straight when incorrect or misleading information was presented, but I wasn't given the opportunity. I looked to my attorney, whom I had come to admire and whose reputation I knew was well deserved, but I don't remember feeling satisfied that critical facts were clarified. My only saving grace was that my sister Erin had accompanied me and corroborated my sense of it all.

During my year of working with Mr. Eig, his teenage son was killed in a freak accident. Sometime after this tragedy, I was on the elevator going up to his law office and somehow knew that the woman next to me was his wife. I remember how she looked—grief stricken—but I couldn't relate to how she must have felt. Yet standing next to her that day is engraved in my memory. At the time, I knew my problems paled in comparison to hers and my heart broke for her and her husband. I have no idea whether this tragedy had an impact on his performance on Paul's and my behalf during that pivotal hearing. But if it did, I can more than understand.

It would be days before we received the hearing review board's twelve-page decision. It was not in our favor. This was a blow to me, intensified by reading the findings—chock-full of information that just wasn't true. For example, it stated that I had two other school offers before enrolling Paul at Meadow School. I did not. I had *no* other offers.

Mr. Eig offered to continue to represent us on a contingency basis and I decided to go forward. In December, he filed a formal complaint, appealing the decision to federal court. Already daunting, this prospect grew more formidable when I received the official paperwork declaring: PAUL, a minor by his parent and next friend, JESSIE DUNLEAVY, Plaintiffs, v. WILLIAM DONALD SCHAEFER, et al, Defendants. *Geez*, I thought to myself, *Paul and Jessie, toe-to-toe with the governor.*

Fortunately, this drama never played out because some months down the road the county made a settlement offer—a funded placement at the current school in exchange for dismissal of our pending federal suit. I accepted and the case was closed.

Paul had a pretty good run throughout his third- and fourth-grade years. I knew the school wasn't the perfect match for him, as did the director when he was admitted, but I knew too—as Dr. Denckla had said—that perfection in a school for Paul was not to be found. Nevertheless, I was grateful that his teachers loved him, and he them; that he made some academic gains; and that he was popular among his peers. In addition to reading and mathematics, Paul had classes in social studies, science, art, and music and also received much-needed speech therapy and occupational therapy. Paul's medication—imipramine and Dexedrine—had stayed the same since concluding the trial phase of his first-grade year. However, his attention deficit continued to be a significant challenge and I knew his academic potential was far from realized.

*

BY THE END of fourth grade, I noticed Paul becoming increasingly fragile, more readily prone to tears. I knew the discrepancy between his ability and his performance must have been a source of frustration, and I figured he might have been more aware of his differences as he matured. These concerns prompted me to take him to

Jonathan Watkins, a child psychologist in Annapolis with whom Paul began weekly therapy sessions.

With no signs of improvement in Paul's spells of unresponsiveness, I also had him tested for seizures. A sleep-deprived EEG was performed with results that came back normal, without any evidence of seizure activity. This would be the first of several such tests, but the results were always the same.

Dr. Watkins and I agreed that it was time to re-evaluate Paul's medication, and he suggested local psychiatrist, Norman Roberts, to help manage it. Dr. Roberts referred us to a neurologist—Thomas Hyde, in Chevy Chase, Maryland—for an assessment. After Dr. Hyde worked with Paul and provided a written report, Dr. Roberts decided that we would discontinue the Dexedrine, which we did right away, and increase the dosage of the imipramine, which would have to be incremental since it required monitoring with blood and EKG tests. Medication changes were always difficult for Paul, and for me, and this one was no exception. I can't overstate the challenge of managing Paul that summer, a situation I knew called more for patience than for discipline.

Before we had reached the better side of this tough transition, the school year began, and it didn't surprise me that Paul's behavior was adversely affected, with the first two weeks of school being the worst. For the first time, he talked back to his teachers, questioned certain routines, and one time even threw his books to the floor. He never took his frustrations out on another student. The fact is, Paul remained popular with his peers but nonetheless was a challenge for some of his teachers.

Several weeks into the school year, as Paul had begun to settle in and benefit from the medication change, Dr. Watkins visited the school to observe classes. He reported back, telling me he felt Paul's current level of "acting out" represented a positive step in his development and said Paul was by no means a clinically challenging child. Paul was questioning things that didn't make sense to him and standing up for himself in a more aggressive manner—a heartening change from the withdrawn child he had been. Dr. Watkins also noted that the teachers would benefit from advice on classroom management, telling me he saw them as relatively unsophisticated in this arena, something I felt was understandable for a new school with a new team.

Paul's first report card was issued in November, by which time the medication transition was behind him and his behavior had resumed an even keel. His homeroom and reading teacher wrote:

> Paul is a wonderful child who is in the process of redefining who he is. Last year, I saw this withdrawn, quiet student who was not always available for learning. This year, I see a child hungry to learn new things. He asks questions, expresses opinions, and shares his feelings. While these expressions may not always be presented in the most socially correct manner, he is taking risks and learning his ideas and thoughts have value.

Later that fall, the school began a behavior modification plan for all students in Paul's age group that would put him at a disadvantage. Before it was implemented, Paul's homeroom teacher called me to express her concern. After explaining that the plan came about because some of the children were hurting each other's feelings, she said, "Since Paul's behavior has improved, and, considering he was never guilty of being hurtful to his peers, I'm worried that if Paul feels the plan is unfair, it could spark a setback for him." I appreciated her thoughtful communication but don't remember feeling worried.

When Paul came home and talked about the new system, I didn't detect any apprehension on his part either. The children were to carry a chart to each class, and those who met the standards for behavior would get a star; those who did not would get a check. Three checks in any given day for a child would require a conference with the parents.

Several days later, the director called me to say I needed to come in for a conference the following morning because Paul had received three checks that day. I said I would be there and was sorry to hear he was having trouble. I told her about the homeroom teacher's concerns and said that I too hoped this new strategy didn't represent a setback for Paul, mainly because he'd been doing so well and was not a part of the troublesome behavior that precipitated the need for this system.

The director's response was confusing. "Paul was the sole reason for the implementation," she told me. "I don't know where the homeroom teacher is coming from."

I rescheduled my work obligations for the next morning and went to the conference, eager to meet with the teacher and the director to learn about Paul's behavior and the ways I could support him and the school. To my surprise, Paul was a part of the conference, meaning I was unable to clear up my confusion. At the end, I said I had a question that I would prefer discussing without Paul. The director said she needed to walk Paul back to class but would return. I waited with the teacher, but she never made it back.

It wasn't long before I was called to come in again for a conference. Paul had received three checks that day in one forty-five-minute class, something I didn't think was possible based on the premise that a student was to receive either a star or a check for each class. Even so, I went in, but the director did not attend the meeting. In truth, I never had any further communication from her about anything.

Because Dr. Watkins believed that the methodology behind the behavior management system was indeed working against Paul—just as the homeroom teacher had surmised—he called the school and scheduled a meeting with the director and the teachers. His appointment was canceled by the school twice, and his third attempt was answered by the school's newly hired psychologist, who would be the point of contact from there on out.

I didn't get why the school kept Dr. Watkins at arm's length. But eventually, he was able to work with the school's psychologist, which turned out to be productive. Together they devised a new system for behavior management, which took effect in March. Shortly thereafter, Paul's teacher reported: "Paul is responding well to the system devised by Dr. Watkins. In fact, he has earned the maximum number of points in ninety percent of his weekly classes."

In spite of the mysteriousness surrounding some aspects of the home-school communication, things were going well for Paul, and I was grateful. But in the spring, at what I thought would be a routine ARD committee meeting with county officials and the school's new psychologist representing the director, I was told Paul could not return to Meadow School for his sixth-grade year. I was shocked. With my heart pounding, I struggled to maintain my composure.

"Why?" I asked, incredulously.

After a minute of deafening silence, I looked directly at the school's psychologist, "Is this decision based on Paul's academic standing or his behavior?"

This man, whom I barely knew, slammed his fist on the table and said, "Both!" That would be the only explanation I would ever receive. On top of the fact that I didn't understand, I was alarmed by the lack of professionalism, not to mention compassion. Trumping this poor showing, though, was the implication for Paul's fate. I desperately wanted consistency for him, and I knew all too well that our options were dismal. But one thing was certain: I was powerless. And my confusion took a back seat to my worry.

Even though I was upset about the school's decision, which was not documented in the report cards or elsewhere, I did not broach the subject with Paul's teachers. I decided that when the time came for the year-end parent-teacher conferences, I would listen more than talk. I felt it was imperative to maintain the bond I had established as a parent at the school. For one thing, Paul loved these people and, for another, I didn't know when we might need them again. Furthermore, I did have others with whom I could commiserate about this unexpected turn of events and the treatment that I saw as appalling.

In the conference with Paul's two primary teachers, I was pleased with their feedback. Mirroring the written reports, they raved about Paul's sensitivity, his sense of humor, and his academic progress. I was told his teachers were sad to see him go and did not agree with the administrative decision. They said Paul was far from the biggest academic or behavioral challenge facing the school and reiterated how well he had weathered the storm of the medication change that had plagued him at the start of the year. They also lauded Dr. Watkins' advice to the school in general.

One of the teachers told me it was a challenge for the school to adjust to being accountable to the county for the few funded children enrolled there. She mentioned too that the county paid for a classroom aide the school said Paul needed, who wasn't used for Paul. I did not know whether any of this was a factor in Paul's dismissal, but I wondered. In fact, as one is prone to do in a communication vacuum, I wondered many things. Maybe I had been a pawn from the outset, a test case to pursue funding without the school having to conform to the full-blown MSDE approval process. I will never know. But this was another undeserved blow in Paul's journey, one with tentacles reaching into the future.

*

LUCKILY, I FELT a kinship with the special educators in the county, and I sensed the feeling was mutual. We may not have always seen eye to eye, but we were always respectful. One county professional and I went together to Baltimore to visit a school, which we then agreed to rule out for Paul. The school was impressive but served students with head injuries, multiple physical handicaps, and emotional disturbances. Paul had come into his own with his peers at Meadow School, and we didn't want to see him lose that. We also noted the skill level of the students in Paul's age group was beneath his. Every professional we worked with, including Dr. Denckla, agreed.

I worried about the detriment of a program that would teach to Paul's weakness. Because his test scores were poor and he was often hard to reach, he was easily underestimated. However, he was capable of critical thinking and needed intellectual stimulation lest he wither away in the pitfalls of low expectations, which frightened me more than anything.

The county submitted applications for Paul to a couple of other schools located in the Baltimore-Washington vicinity where, once again, we were disadvantaged by the late application. Further working against us this time around was the perplexing dismissal from Meadow School.

I couldn't help but get my hopes up when The Lab School—my first choice—invited Paul to spend a day. A few weeks after Paul's visit, I was able to speak with an admission officer who said a space for Paul was unlikely but gave me feedback about his visit. "In many ways, Paul looked familiar," she said. "He was receptive to the instruction and was dutiful and polite, but his processing seemed to be an area of difficulty. He was not inattentive by choice and certainly not rude, but he couldn't always focus."

She also said Paul was cautious in his interactions, and she noted his tremor, asking me if he was a nervous child. I said he was not, but in a new setting he was shy. She told me they might end up with a space before school started but then said she was concerned about why Paul had not been invited back to Meadow School.

I knew it. I was painfully aware of the fine line I walked. If I was candid, pointing to the school's absence of professionalism in providing me needed information, I risked being perceived as a problem parent. At the same time, I was desperate to keep Paul from being unfairly judged. I suggested she contact Paul's teachers directly, as well as Dr. Watkins, for additional information.

Aware that I had skirted the issue, I wrote a follow-up letter to the admission office, which may well have been overkill on my part, but I didn't want to leave any stone unturned. The thing is, I had fallen in love with the school and wanted it so badly for Paul that I could taste it.

June 17, 1994
Dear Admission Office,

Thank you for the information you provided regarding Paul's application. Although this process is stressful for me, and I do worry it is tiresome for you, I am dedicated to providing all the information I can.

Despite my many unanswered questions surrounding the current school's re-placement decision, which is not documented in the report card or elsewhere, I have a good relationship with Paul's teachers who all stand ready to provide information in support of his application. I am attaching his year-end reports.

I sensed during our conversation that one of your concerns had to do with his interaction with others. I understand your reasoning based on his visit, but he works well in a group and is sought out by his peers. Paul is taking Karate classes, which was his idea, with mainstream children and is doing well. Also, he is registered for overnight summer camp—a week camping in Shenandoah—again with mainstream children ages 10 to 13 who he doesn't yet know; this too was his idea.

At the end of the year, the dispatcher at Associated Cab Co., who provided Paul's ride to and from school each day, called to tell me Paul is the nicest child they have ever transported. Recently, Paul found a twenty dollar bill in a public parking lot, which, without my knowledge, he took to a homeless shelter in our neighborhood. In fact, Paul is amazingly well-adjusted considering his differences, the ego insults he has endured, and his untapped potential.

Because I agonize over whether you will accept him, I forgot to mention that, if you do, he will bring much to your school.

While my contacts at the county are optimistic about the space situation, I am obviously anxious.

Thank you again for your time.

Warm regards,
Jessie Dunleavy

A space never materialized.

I took Paul to a well-known educational consultant, Ethna Hopper, located in Washington, D.C., for an assessment and for her advice. Paul's long-time summer tutor since kindergarten sent a letter to Ms. Hopper in advance of our visit, providing an overview of Paul's progress and distinguishing the deficits she believed were due to Paul's handicaps from those she saw as programmatic. In conclusion, she wrote:

My history with Paul is perhaps unique in terms of its duration. As with any successful teacher-student relationship, roles frequently reverse. Paul has taught me a great deal about diligence, flexibility, selflessness, and humor, all often in the face of great strain. He is undeniably a gifted, talented child who seeks the appropriate instructional format for reaching his high potential.

In addition to the schools where we had already applied, Ms. Hopper suggested a school for bright children in need of an individualized program in Charlottesville, Virginia, where Paul would have to board—a concept I just couldn't imagine but one I probably should've considered. She agreed that Paul didn't need a clinical setting and said Paul's dismissal from Meadow School probably poisoned his pending applications. Lastly, she urged me to ask the county to strike from his record the statement that he required a classroom aide, considering he didn't have one.

*

IN AUGUST WE left for our annual two-week beach vacation with my extended family. I was determined to have a good time but was unsettled by not knowing where Paul would go to school. With several balls in the air, and the need for me to ride herd on the process, I took my notes and the needed phone numbers along to the beach. Our cottage didn't have a telephone and, with cell phones off in the future, I used a pay phone across the street. After days of multiple calls and lengthy discussions—keeping me on the pay phone or standing by it awaiting a call—I finally moved a Rubbermaid chair across the street, parking it next to the phone for the duration of our stay. At least then I could sit as I watched my family members head over the dunes to the ocean. I think they would vouch for the fact I spent half my vacation tethered to that pay phone.

In spite of my focus and determination, we returned home without a solution. By the end of the month, with only a couple of remote possibilities still in play, the county put another option on the table—six hours per week of what they termed "home and hospital teaching."

The first day of school came fast. Foreseeing the lack of resolution, I had taken a couple of days of leave from work. After getting Keely off to school, Paul and I went to the Baltimore Zoo for the day. We had fun, and I was able to leave my troubles behind. After we saw all the animals, and I mean every last one, and had lunch, we went to the gift shop where I told Paul he could select a small stuffed animal based on his favorite of the day. A lover of all living creatures, Paul couldn't decide between the giraffe and the prairie dog.

"The giraffes were the most interesting," he said, "but the prairie dogs were the most cute!"

He asked me to decide. We got both.

The next day, we went to Ikea and got Paul a desk and chair and supplies for setting up a homeschooling work area, which we did in a sunny nook in a back room of our house. Over his desk, we hung a bulletin board and a small framed print, selected for its fitting message, "*Dreams are Travels for the Soul.*"

Thankfully, my parents took over after day two, but I was determined that this gap would be short lived. Taking the county up on the six hours of instruction per week, I got to work on figuring out how to cover the other twenty-some hours and, by October, I had devised a full schedule that would suffice while we continued to seek school alternatives. As an educator myself, I was fortunate to have connections. Supplementing the county teacher, who came to our house three times a week for two-hour sessions, I hired three other teachers: One was a colleague of mine, one had taught Paul in his most recent school, and the other was a special education tutor I knew of through my work.

There were lots of logistics that needed my attention, both practical and programmatic, but I was energized by what I had come to see as an opportunity for Paul. After all, he often needed one-on-one attention to learn and, even though he had made academic progress in recent years, he fell far behind the averages for his age and, more important, he fell far behind what he was capable of achieving. Maybe, with the focus and attention of this team of talented teachers, Paul would realize more of his academic potential and fare better in the admission process at one of the schools that could accommodate his unique strengths and weaknesses. In all, I found this far superior to parking him in a catch-all school that would eventually stifle his desire to learn.

After a routine ARD committee meeting in November, during which I updated the team about Paul's progress, the director of special education for the county gave me the name of an attorney who she said may be helpful in seeking county funding for my plan. I was grateful for the tip, which I acted on the same day, but was surprised—and touched—that a person in her position was arming me with what I needed to challenge the system she represented. I didn't know where we would land but, that aside, I was reminded of human goodness and the merits of teamwork.

The attorney, Wayne Steedman, was located in Towson, Maryland, and couldn't have been more different from my former special education attorney. There was no high-rise office building and no slick facade. In fact, there was no firm. Formerly a social worker serving special education students, Mr. Steedman had seen too many children whose needs had slipped through the inevitable cracks of the bureaucracy and decided a law degree would further empower his advocacy for these deserving kids.

Mr. Steedman found Paul's case compelling, and I retained him to represent us. As I peruse my files, I'm reminded of the many back and forth letters, including declarations from the county attorney, that were initially upsetting to me. But, without going to court, we came to a resolution by late winter. While the school year was more than half over, I was pleased with the outcome and grateful to have encountered another good person along the way.

At the end of each day that year, Paul was dropped off at my office, located in an old three-story house that had been converted to office spaces, where he quietly entertained himself from 3:30 to 5:30. He had a box of things he played with, mostly paper clips, string, and sundry office supplies he had accumulated, which he kept in the eaves on the third floor.

In the grocery store one winter day, Paul picked up a pack of valentines and put them in our cart. "Paul," I said, "you can have the valentines, but who are you going to give them to?"

"All my friends in your office," he replied, as if it should be obvious—"Rene, Charlene, Irfan, and Uncle Goldblatt"—a name, to the amusement of all, that Paul had somehow adopted for my boss.

The teacher Paul spent the most time with that year was Gretchen Nyland, a veteran art teacher whose dedication to providing multidisciplinary experiences for Paul was matched by her endless creativity. In one of their many projects, Paul made a pinch pot mouse out of clay, which they glazed and fired. Paul loved the experience and wanted to make more. One thing led to another, and Paul ended up producing dozens of these little guys. Subsequently, Gretchen convinced Annapolis Pottery—a well-known shop in downtown Annapolis—to sell Paul's mice. These tiny creatures were placed on the counter near the cash register with a little sign that said, "$2 each." Several of my friends and family members bought one, except for my mother, who I think bought five! The day I came home with my purchase, Paul looked at it, then looked at me, and said, "You bought the mean one."

Annapolis Pottery gave Paul the option of selling all his mice to the shop or stopping in at regular intervals to collect his portion of the proceeds. He chose the latter, and Gretchen helped him open a bank account, where they made frequent deposits and kept track of his money.

Sarah Hyde, Paul's primary academic teacher for the year and a highly respected and experienced special educator, wrote a brief summary as the year came to an end:

> Paul is intellectually curious, expressive, well-behaved, charming, exceptionally empathetic, and fun. His strengths include his visual perception, his memory, his sense of humor, and his ability to get along with others. His weaknesses are his fine motor skills, his written language, and his math concepts with his primary weakness being his inconsistent attention span.
>
> Paul probably learned more during this particular year than any other of his life. Some of his learning was rote—he memorized his multiplication tables, for example—but also his curiosity about the world and his interest in history, politics, music, and art soared. In general, he had a lot of self-doubt regarding his differences and had noticed that every time he left a school, the other children stayed. But he felt good about himself during this year, and I think we both had turned lemons into lemonade.

Chapter 5

CRAVING CONNECTION

Then there's my heart that craves
Mostly connection
And a good deal of rest
In between conversations
So that I can be recharged
And ready to talk again.
My life… It means everything
That I get the chance to connect
I don't know how else to put this into words
I'd give you a hug but my hands,
They're behind my back.

I WAS WORRIED. Paul was making progress, but he needed a peer group. He continued to be sweet and good-natured, but he needed a place to belong. It was 1995. Paul would be entering seventh grade, and his pending adolescence ramped up my sense of urgency. I was determined to get him in a school where he would thrive—and stay! A school that would recognize his strengths and engage him. A school that knew how to accommodate his unique challenges.

I feared his being underestimated as much as I did his being overwhelmed. Or worse yet, overlooked.

Of all the schools I came to know, The Lab School continued to be my favorite. Designed for children with language-based learning disabilities, it stood out as a place that could inspire and support Paul.

When I visited there, I saw creative teaching that didn't short-change intellectual development and a broad curriculum intertwined with the arts. Without question, it was a place that wanted kids to blossom more than it wanted to keep them in line. And, at the risk of sounding corny, it spoke to me; I just knew it would make a big difference for Paul. It was my dream.

The school was located in Northwest Washington, D.C., a good hour from our house, which, as Paul got older, seemed more reasonable. When we'd applied there before, it was late in the season, and spaces for new students were hard to come by. During Paul's year of homeschooling, his application for seventh grade was submitted on time to Lab and a couple of other approved schools.

To give Paul a fighting chance, attention to his medical needs in light of his deficits was a top priority. Even though it was tempting to leave well-enough alone, I wasn't prepared to settle. I knew we needed to keep pursuing the right therapy, one prong of which was medication management.

During Paul's year of homeschooling, we had experimented by substituting the combination of Prozac and Dexedrine in place of the imipramine, something more doctors were finding a good option at the time for hard-to-medicate attentional issues. Even though imipramine had proved to be most effective in helping Paul pay attention, it was prescribed with caution due to its risk of cardiac arrhythmia—irregular heartbeat. Routine EKG tests monitored this risk for Paul but, if the combination of medications could provide the same benefit, the absence of risk would make it preferable. If not, we would double back. Even without a school setting that year, it became clear to me that the imipramine was more beneficial for Paul and I was in favor of resuming it.

I wished Paul could have been easily characterized and summarized, condensed on paper with standardized testing results and conventional school records. But this would never be. Test scores were all over the road, and most often reflected glaring weaknesses. As we'd known for years, test results for Paul revealed his performance on the test, not his ability. Paul had significant deficits, without question, but test scores in isolation simply didn't align in a way that provided a road map for his programmatic needs. It was anecdotal information from firsthand experiences with Paul—tapping into his thought process and the ways he interpreted meaning—that provided an understanding of his depth, his sensitivity, and his interest in learning.

I always thought Paul's intuition and his emotional intelligence were strengths. Every teacher Paul ever worked with had emphasized his remarkable capacity for empathy and compassion. When Paul was barely six years old, he asked me, "Do you like going to work?"

My answer, "Yes, I do," apparently didn't satisfy him.

"But how do you feel when you get there? Do you feel happy? I mean, when you walk in the door, how do you feel?"

Around this same age, we went to New York City for several days during a school break. Just after we hopped in the back of a cab, Paul looked at the driver, then turned to me. In a decibel I would've reserved for announcing an imminent safety threat, Paul asked, "Is he happy?"

Trying to soothe his concerns without involving the cab driver in our conversation, I quietly replied, "Yes, I imagine he's happy."

As Paul continued to look at me, I knew my credibility was tanking—by no means a first.

He then matter-of-factly said, "He doesn't *look* happy."

A day or so later, we headed out for sightseeing and dinner. As we waited to cross 57th Street, we saw two homeless men sitting on a sidewalk grate. Bearing in mind the fact Paul was still worried about the cab driver, one can imagine the number of questions this sighting inspired. When Paul wasn't hungry for his dinner that evening, I didn't think too much about it until he asked for a doggie bag. Then I knew what was coming. As we headed back to the hotel, he asked that we retrace our steps. No words were spoken, but Paul delivered his dinner to the two men.

We went to Disney World when Paul was twelve and Keely fifteen. Paul loved everything about the experience and at the end bought a picture book he actually slept with for weeks. As we were driving home from the airport, and Paul was looking through the book for the thousandth time, he asked me, "Was that trip expensive?"

I frankly don't remember my explanation, but I do remember saying, "Why do you ask?"

Paul replied, "I just want to make sure I can do the same thing for my children."

I could write pages about Calvin and Hobbes—his beloved gerbils—and Ruff-Ruff—a stuffed dog Paul loved like a human and made things for—a house, clothing, and, I'm not kidding, a baby book. Don't you know when I cleaned out Paul's apartment, I found Ruff-Ruff at the bottom of a trunk Paul had moved from place to place over the years, wrapped in a baby blanket Paul also had saved for sentimental reasons.

Just a couple of years ago, Paul told me he had seen the movie *Twelve Years a Slave*. In recounting part of the story, he started to weep, which I could tell caught him off guard. Even so, he continued telling me about it through his tears. "All she wanted was soap, Mom. She was beaten because she used a little piece of soap. I don't think you should see it. It's just too sad."

In addition to Paul's genuine concern for others, he was insightful. Because his social cueing was an area of weakness, he was often isolated in a group situation. But he would later report to me what he took in about others. He spotted the disingenuous with remarkable accuracy as he did those who were truly kind.

He just read people. And he amused me with his reports. Recently, he asked me, "You know that friend of yours who walks her dog in the neighborhood?" I answered, "Elizabeth? Donna?" He said, "I think, Elizabeth . . . Well, anyway, she worries about me."

"That doesn't surprise me either way, both are sweet people and my friends, so it stands to reason." I said. "But how do you know?" I asked. "She just does." I, of course, knew my friends were concerned for his well-being and somehow Paul knew it too.

I learned to rely on Paul's intuitive gifts. I also came to know that the disabled are often more keenly aware of authentic kindness for the simple reason that one can indeed judge the character of a person by how he treats those who can do nothing for him. When Paul said someone was kind, I knew every single time that he was right. He was well wired to assess the difference between *acting nice* and *being kind.*

*

PAUL WAS ALSO a creative thinker and benefitted from teachers who recognized this and stimulated him to think more deeply. A recent reminder came to me in a sympathy letter from Paul's homeschool teacher, Gretchen Nyland:

May 2017
Dear Jessie,

I cannot hope to "alleviate, assuage, take away, appease, soothe, allay, mitigate, ease, lessen, soften" your grief. This was our method—Paulie's and mine—to think of all the ways we could express one thought and then end up in the dictionary amazed at how many more ways there were.

He shared with me a good year of his young life. One that I've always cherished. Perhaps because it was one on one—and our attention was always with each other for those hours each day.

I can't imagine your grief for losing Paulie. I can only hope it will subside, abate, lower ("Not as many good words here," Paulie would have informed you.)

It is probably hard to smile right now, but it will come back as you remember the goodness of his life, for he was a good, gentle person—gone too soon.

I'm sad, but smiling in thinking about him.

Much love,
Gretchen

In thinking about the school situation, I knew we were fortunate to have Paul's homeschool teachers as references. They all loved him, and knew him well, which I figured would help us live down the regrettable circumstances that had tainted his applications the year before.

When Paul was accepted to the summer session at The Lab School, I was thrilled! It was a very good sign, I thought. They would have time to get to know him, and there was no doubt they would love him. Everyone did. The summer session ran from late June through mid-August, and Paul's medication changeover began in early June. Knowing that the transition period would be hard for Paul, I was eager to get it behind us and was focused on realizing its benefits in time for his Lab School classes.

To reach the optimal dosage of 100 mg of imipramine per day, the plan was to start with 50 mg and, after obtaining EKG results and consulting with Dr. Roberts, to increase the dosage by 10 mg—with this pattern repeating every four days. I had this sequence mapped out on a calendar and felt confident about the time frame. If I was efficient in getting the EKG tests, we would be in good shape.

What I didn't anticipate was the lag time between submitting the lab test results and Dr. Roberts returning my calls and sanctioning the increased dosage. As we stalled in the changeover process, I could see that Paul wasn't functioning as well as he did on a full dosage of either medication regimen, and I deeply regretted making this change during this critical time.

Apparently, my voicemail messages—pleading our case—fell on deaf ears. And the excruciating delay in response from the doctor at every possible turn landed us in the last quarter of the summer program before the medication changeover was complete, at which time, as we had expected, Paul began to function at his best. This was heartening, for sure, but was it too late for him to demonstrate his strengths in a setting where he had little time remaining? And where he had not been himself for the first four or five weeks of a six-week program? Needless to say, I was incredibly frustrated, which I lamented to Dr. Watkins more than once during those painful days as I felt my hopes being thwarted yet again.

In spite of the challenges beyond Paul's control, he enjoyed the summer program, and his feedback to me about his experiences was encouraging. He spoke each day about his friends—Matt, Seth, Kia—and the course work, the field trips, and the projects. He never complained about the ride, left the house cheerfully each day, and began to refer to Lab as "my school."

In late August, the school notified me that there was not an available space for Paul. I knew the summer program had been a test case for their admission decision and I was beside myself.

Since Paul had come into his own in the home stretch, and I was interested in the school's perspective and, frankly, still hanging on to a thread of hope, I called the summer program's lead teacher. I told her about the medication transition. She said she did see Paul becoming more interactive and alert in the final days, as had a couple of other teachers. She suggested I write a letter to the school explaining the details of Paul's transition, which I did in short order—even jumping at the chance, while knowing in my heart that it was a lost cause and that they were probably sick of me and my letters. Dr. Watkins called the same teacher who told him Paul was never a challenge behaviorally, that he'd endeared the teachers and, if his attentional issues could be better remediated, he would fit within the parameters of the program.

As my hopes steadily plummeted, I began to try to accept the fact that Paul would have to attend Harbour School, a Level V school just outside of Annapolis serving children with multiple handicaps, which I had visited a couple of times and did not feel was right for Paul. My heart was broken, but I had to resign myself to the reality.

I called the county and was astounded to learn they had somehow assumed Paul was enrolled at Lab School for the coming year and, because of this, had passed up a space for Paul at Harbour School, which I foolishly had thought of as a perpetual backup. Nothing more could be done, I was told, until the next ARD meeting, set for mid-September.

Yet again, the first day of school was upon us, and Paul had no place to go.

I was in for another big surprise when, on that first day, a school bus arrived at our house to take Paul to Lab School, representing a detail the county overlooked and one of a string of snafus on the horizon. Was I ever tempted to put him on that bus!

I was upset with the county for the balls dropped. Making matters worse, I was the only one to show up for the scheduled ARD meeting, which then had to be rescheduled for later in the month.

Because Paul was staying home alone while I went to work, even a small delay was painful. When we finally had our ARD meeting, I was offered ten hours per week of homeschooling. I petitioned for more hours, and was prepared to go to battle on that front, when I learned of a space for Paul at Harbour School, where he enrolled as of November.

As far as Paul knew, I was delighted with the placement and, as always, I formed good relationships with the teachers. Paul complained about the school, but I told him to look for the good. He did make a new friend, another Scott, a boy whose love for playing the guitar matched Paul's and led to them forming a band with another boy in Scott's neighborhood in Laurel, Maryland. While Paul liked saying he was in a band, practices were limited by the distance between the boys, and they didn't exactly have any gigs lined up. But I do remember them performing once at school and another time in a line-up of other bands, an opportunity kindly arranged by Paul's guitar teacher. Despite Paul's challenges, he was innately musical, and these experiences for him warmed my heart.

Often I was asked if Paul's disability had a specific label. Was it merely Attention Deficit Disorder? Or, maybe, Attention Deficit Hyperactivity Disorder? But the fact is, Paul never fit a precise description of any one diagnosis. I remembered Dr. Denckla had said, "ADD with other neurological involvement." Considering Paul was not hyperactive, maybe ADD was most fitting. But I knew it was more than that.

Dr. Hyde, the neurologist Paul had seen when he was eleven, said Paul had elements of Pervasive Development Disorder and that his episodes of unresponsiveness likely represented an abnormality related to an underlying disorder of the central nervous system. Years later, I would come to think Paul was on the autism spectrum, as Pervasive Development Disorder suggests. No matter what, I knew it wasn't the label, but the treatment, that mattered.

Paul needed a psychiatrist and continuing with Dr. Roberts was out of the question. He cost Paul a placement at Lab School—a loss that I couldn't forgive. Dr. Watkins did not disagree and, knowing the vital role a psychiatrist would play in Paul's well-being along with the absence of a viable alternative in Annapolis, he referred us to Alan Zametkin, a psychiatrist in Kensington, Maryland.

Dr. Zametkin evaluated Paul when he was twelve, just before he started Harbour School. While noting that Paul didn't always hear what was said and his response rate was slow, Dr. Zametkin was optimistic on several fronts. "Paul was an extremely cooperative young man whose self-esteem at this point is excellent," he wrote, "and the parenting skills are very good as well."

Recognizing Paul's need for ongoing psychotherapy and oversight of medication, as well as support for me in the management of Paul's care, Dr. Zametkin referred us to Ellyn Stark, a psychiatrist whose office was a little closer to us in Hyattsville, Maryland. While the weekly visits to Hyattsville were inconvenient and Paul complained profusely about the forty-five-minute ride, Dr. Stark's insights and investment in Paul made her a perfect choice, and I welcomed the relief from the back-and-forth scenario with a therapist and a psychiatrist whom we saw separately.

Paul would stay at Harbour School from mid-year seventh grade through tenth grade. While he valued the relationship he formed with his kind guidance counselor, Claire Tartasky, and for the most part had caring teachers, he longed for what he called "real classes." I countered his requests to explore options, pointing out the good things about his school and telling him there was life outside of it.

Over and over, he said, "I want to take science, and history, and music, and read novels." Paul also longed for more social opportunities.

When he was a seventh grader, we went to Connecticut for a wedding. With the reception featuring live music, Keely wasted no time in getting her brother out on the dance floor. I was a little surprised that he readily joined her, but astonished that he danced with abandon. He even danced with me! The next morning—the minute he lifted his head from the pillow in our shared hotel room—he said,

"Wasn't that so much fun?" My heart soared, but little did I know that he would never again have the same opportunity.

To supplement school, Paul had weekly guitar lessons with Mike—a dynamic and caring teacher with whom Paul formed a lasting bond—and we maximized summer opportunities to enrich his experiences. Also, Paul was reading for pleasure on his own. His favorite book at that time was *Love Story* by Erich Segal, a then twenty-five-year-old book he found in a box in our attic. He loved it so much that he re-read it several times and was thrilled when I told him there was a sequel, which I was pretty sure was also in the attic. He knew about the movie but didn't have as much interest in it. Even so, just two years ago, I emailed Paul an article on the reunion of Ali MacGraw and Ryan O'Neal at Harvard. His reply to me, at the age of thirty-three? "Awww."

*

PAUL'S COUSIN CAITLIN died the summer after his seventh-grade year, an unimaginable loss that shook our world. The oldest of "the cousins" and Jennie's firstborn, Caitlin had been diagnosed with Hodgkin's Disease a year or so before. After the initial round of treatment, including chemotherapy and radiation, her prognosis had been quite good. But the disease returned the following year, meaning a bone marrow transplant was warranted. This arduous procedure ended with good results, and optimism returned until complications arose and the follow-up treatment failed. Tragically, Caitlin died the summer before she was to have begun her freshman year at Bryn Mawr College.

Coping with the heartache and the sheer absence of such a young and vital personality brought forth challenging days for us all, particularly for Caitlin's mother and father and two sisters, followed by Keely, who was closest in age and a friend and classmate as well as a cousin. One never plans for how to begin to cope, much less behave during such times, but the family was thrown together like never before. In my memory, we traveled in a pack, or in subsets of the pack, licking our own wounds but striving every day to nourish Jennie and her immediate family.

As Paul stuck with his cousins more than ever, he fortunately had Dr. Stark with whom he could share his personal feelings and his overall consternation. I remember he talked with her about not knowing how to help and, in particular, expressed concern about Keely, as he had never seen her so sad. Keely's cheerfulness had been unwavering in Paul's life and he didn't know what he could do for her. He joined his cousins in singing a song at Caitlin's memorial service and, later that fall, in planting a tree in her honor.

But otherwise, he felt helpless.

The following summer, Paul attended Brendan Sailing Camp for learning disabled youth, where he encountered a couple of old friends from his former school. Among his new acquaintances that summer was Sara, who ended up being the star sailor of the whole group, winning top accolades on the last day of camp. Paul's prize was for asking the most questions!

On that final day, families were invited to take a sail with their child, enabling each camper to show off the skills he or she had acquired. Paul took Keely and me out on the water—just the three of us in the small sailboat he was maneuvering. He was pleased with himself. Because I'm a good swimmer, as is Keely, I could at least muster up enough control to act relaxed about it. All those little boats, each manned by a novice kid, going every which way out there . . . I can see Keely now, looking at me with eyes as big as quarters.

Sailing camp was good for Paul, and he returned the following summer, the summer Sara would become his first girlfriend—a relationship that evolved over many years, and grew into a deep friendship that lasted the rest of Paul's life.

While Paul was under the care of Dr. Stark, we once again switched back to the combination of Prozac and Dexedrine, a decision made due to ongoing concerns about the risks of imipramine. This was okay with me since Paul's school didn't challenge him enough for me to scrutinize the difference.

When all else fails, lower your standards.

But, when I learned that Dr. Stark was leaving the area, I couldn't breathe. *Please, no*, I thought to myself as I reckoned with the scope of this loss. I wanted continuity for Paul, and the important role Dr. Stark had played in his life for nearly two years was going to leave us with big shoes to fill. Another setback and another unwelcome change.

Knowing there was not an alternative in Annapolis, I decided to stay with the same practice, inheriting another psychiatrist, Dr. Felt, who over time I came to see as mostly disinterested. Seeking more support, we started to see a psychologist in the same office, continuing with Dr. Felt whom we needed for medication management. The psychologist, Dr. Crain, was superb and genuinely invested in our well-being from the start.

Paul's ninth- and tenth-grade years in school were difficult. He didn't like school, mostly for the reason that he objected to the track he was in, but also he felt the school didn't listen to his concerns. He enjoyed his two academic classes, but otherwise he was scheduled in the career center for a transition-to-work plan, which he felt was uninteresting and too manual, especially in consideration of his poor motor skills. He had few social contacts and was increasingly suffering bouts of anxiety along with feelings of inadequacy. School wasn't his only problem, as I would learn down the road, but it was a huge part of his life and he just didn't like it.

I was worried about Paul, but the constancy of the state of worry can have a numbing effect. He would lie in his bed at night and write. His handwriting was mostly illegible, but what I could decipher was full of themes of angst and heartache. Things weren't right and I had adopted a one-day-at-a-time "accept the things you cannot change" way of life, which maybe serves a purpose, but only to a point. His anxiety, a new addition to his diagnosis, was hard for him to manage as it was for me, and it spilled over into every facet of his life.

When Paul was fifteen, I took him for his third evaluation with Martha Denckla, who remained interested in him and whose insights I found extraordinarily meaningful. She said Paul continued to demonstrate superior abilities in visual-spatial reasoning, but sadly his fine motor skills remained very poor—in the second percentile—a weakness that, in light of his age, was unlikely to improve.

"In other words," Dr. Denckla explained, "Paul is gifted in terms of what comes into his brain, but he cannot use his motor output to show what all his excellent visual perception has to offer."

Then another remarkable strength emerged: Paul achieved a superior score on concept formation, a test highly respected as an indication of intellectual reasoning, putting him cognitively at the level of the third or fourth year of college. I knew he was smart, but I was encouraged by his test performance, and not in the interest of high test scores but by virtue of his demonstrated capability through a traditional measurement system, something that could prove advantageous for him. Yet this revelation represented another dramatic skew, unique to Paul.

"Paul is still language impaired," Dr. Denckla told me, "and has difficulty formulating sentences, retrieving words, and putting together adequate verbal expression of what is on his mind."

Summarizing these findings, Dr. Denckla wrote:

When one meets a person like Paul, one remembers 'use your words' as the didactic approach to handling anger and frustration, but one sees that with his language impairment, Paul is still not up to handling that task. . . .

I cannot overemphasize how much Paul's output skills, both what comes out of his mouth and what comes out of his fingers, are really holding him back and that much of his higher capacity is frustratingly locked-in. We must understand what this frustration means for Paul and work diligently to offer him opportunities to make detours around his expressive language impairment and fine motor difficulties.

She also explained that when Paul's strengths are unrecognized, and he is lumped in with those who are less capable, his frustrations exacerbate his deficits. "There are unusual aspects to Paul (he has never fit neatly into one diagnostic category), and his school activities should be carefully scrutinized and further individualized to make use of Paul's considerable abilities," Dr. Denckla said.

I understood what she was saying. Paul was gifted in terms of his ideas, but in conversation he wasn't fast enough to organize and retrieve the information needed to make meaningful connections. But I didn't understand what to do. Paul's school didn't seem to recognize his strengths, much less know how to tap into them given his weaknesses. I did share her findings with the school but didn't detect any motivation to consider change.

Keely left for college as Paul started tenth grade. Since she was in upstate New York, we wouldn't see her until Thanksgiving, and this was a big adjustment for Paul. Their relationship, like that of most siblings, had gone through different stages over the years, but they were always loving and kind to each other. When young, they had played together endlessly. With three years age difference, they instinctively met somewhere in the middle, creating elaborate fantasy worlds with their stuffed animals, their trolls, their dress-ups, and the countless games that they devised inside and outside our house.

Keely had been pretty much oblivious to her brother's differences when they were little. He may have tuned out in school, and certainly did at home, but he was just Paulie, who mostly never shut up when the two of them were playing. He was an irritant on occasion, no doubt—particularly the day he hit her over the head with a bicycle pump.

Four-year-old Keely had been innocently sitting in her Tyke-Hyke chair watching her coveted *Sesame Street* with her back turned to her thirteen-month-old brother and the rest of their playroom. Paul picked up the pump and, as he attempted to lift it, its weight threw him off balance. In trying to recover, he stumbled forward, then went down. As he did, the trajectory of the pump's arch ended squarely on the top of Keely's head, which proceeded to spurt blood, as even a superficial head injury can do. Because I saw it happen, I knew it was an accident, but from poor Keely's point of view, she'd been attacked . . . for no reason! While it wasn't funny at the time (well, for me, it was a little funny), the three of us laughed about it for years—as we did about so many things.

Just after our arrival at the beach for our family vacation when Keely was six years old and Paul was three, I was trying to unpack the car and get settled. Because Keely and Paulie were overly excited and getting in my way, I suggested they ride around the block—she on her two-wheeler with training wheels and he on his Snoopy scooter—something they frequently did together at home.

It was days later when Paul said, "When I was on the highway on my Snoopy scooter, it was hard to go as fast as I can on a sidewalk." Startled, I said, "*What* are you talking about? *On the highway?*" Paul replied, "You told Keely and me to ride around the block." I then realized. The neighborhood had only one road that paralleled the ocean with two others running perpendicular and providing entrance to the private community; therefore, a literal interpretation of "around the block" would have to wrap in the highway. I was both horrified and amused but mostly grateful that my mother would never know.

The year Paul was in first grade and Keely in fourth, the three of us were having dinner a few days after Christmas. "I need to think of what to take to school on Monday," Paul said, "because it's my turn to tell my class about something of mine that I bring in. It has to be interesting, but it can't be a toy."

Keely instantly decided what it should be. "Take that beautiful pop-up book on the cavemen that you got for Christmas."

"Keely!" Paul said. "I can't do that! No way! There are *naked people* in that book! The kids will laugh at me!"

His sister, the young sophisticate, replied in her haughtiest voice: "I am in the fourth grade, Paul, and we are studying the human body in science; there is nothing funny about the human body."

Her superior tone made me wonder if Paul would feel diminished, but he surprised me. "Yeah, well," he said, with a confidence matching his sister's, "I am in the first grade, and the human body is funny."

Another memorable story was from the year Keely was in seventh grade and Paul in fourth. We'd gone to the beach for a few days in mid-winter and stayed in a hotel with an indoor pool and sauna. Paul was so excited! But when we went to the pool area, Keely wore jeans and her new Birkenstocks rather than a bathing suit and chose to sit on a lounge chair and write in her diary.

Paul, in the pool within two seconds of our arrival, kept saying, "Come on, Keely, get in!"

She finally acknowledged him, looking up only momentarily. "No," she said. "I need to finish my diary entry."

Dumbfounded, Paul stared at her for a minute, then turned to me and said, "I liked her better before she was cute."

I could go on, explaining the time we lost Paul at Vista Point, an overlook near Sausalito, California, because he—even though we had arrived in a rental car—got on a tourist bus thinking we would do the same. This, of course, was funny only in hindsight, but we got our mileage out of it; just as we did in recalling the time we discovered that, for years, Paul had thought his favorite gourmet cupcakes were actually made by our auto mechanic whose shop was located near the bakery. Gives new meaning to greasing the pan . . .

The three of us shared so much and, in all, the two of them shared even more than I know. Paul was going to miss her terribly.

Fortunately, he was able to see his friend Sara most Sundays during his tenth-grade year. Sara's parents were protective and therefore cautious regarding her relationship with a boy. But Sara pushed hard—with what I'd call a singular focus—to see Paul.

I think her parents recognized that Paul was a sweet boy and decided that the best way to accommodate Sara was to take Paul to church with them, after which he could join them for their church and family activities. As a result, I drove him to Sara's house in Gambrills, Maryland, on Sunday mornings, most often returning to pick him up in the early evening.

I appreciated their friendship, especially since Paul was often lonely and, in many ways, increasingly lost. He was mostly afraid of Sara's mother—not a bad thing!—and came to see her gentle father as a father figure of sorts. Most important, Sara was a good girl and as true a friend as I've ever known.

*

THE SUMMER AFTER tenth grade, Paul and Sara went to a Young Life camp in Saranac, New York, where Paul, despite his growing anxiety, was able to participate in fun and challenging activities in a beautiful lake setting. This experience emboldened Paul's stance that he would be better off in a more mainstream school.

I was perplexed by Paul's schooling but recoiled at the thought of another futile, and heartbreaking, school search. Keeping my head above water without a mooring or a direction, I was stuck between the risks of disturbing the status quo and the perils of accepting mediocrity. Was I being complacent? I didn't know.

I was well aware that our school choices were limited at best, but at the same time I realized I couldn't continue to use that as an alibi for doing nothing. Paul remained a Level V special education student, ruling out any public school. Level V non-public options basically fell in two categories: those that mirrored his current school, and those that had a greater academic focus and where, by and large, he had been denied admission in the past. I was hindered by a cyclical thought pattern and I knew I needed help.

I turned to Dr. Crain, who had read Dr. Denckla's report, and we agreed she would do two formal assessments of Paul—cognitive and psychological—each critical to making informed decisions. I scheduled Paul for the multiple sessions required.

Dr. Crain's five-page cognitive report included a summary recommendation that was not a surprise to me. "Given Paul's overall level of functioning from an intellectual point of view, he needs to be presented with academic material that is more challenging."

The psychological evaluation, utilizing seven standardized tools to measure emotional and behavioral functioning, culminated in a ten-page report that explained the test analysis and made recommendations. Highlighting the degree of Paul's suffering, the findings shook me from any residual numbness.

The report's summary included the following:

Paul was polite and cooperative yet anxious. At times his anxiety seemed overwhelming and he needed support to stay on task. Paul asserted that he has had emotional challenges and is depressed with his current school situation. He feels he gets along well with family members but elaborated it is easier for him to relate to women, specifically, he feels close to his mother and sister.

Projective testing revealed that Paul is predominately action oriented in his thinking and is more reactive than reflective in decision making. It is difficult for him to differentiate salient from tangential cues in a given situation. As a consequence he may become overwhelmed by the seeming complexity of a situation and it may be challenging for him to develop more simplified solutions when needed. There is evidence that he maintains a state of hyper-alertness, a reaction to some concerns that he needs to be defensive and protective in a world in which he must be on guard in order to assure his well-being.

In a situation of elevated stress, Paul's emotions can cloud his judgment and contribute to more illogical problem solving behaviors with increased likelihood that he will become distorted in his thinking with actions that may be quite outlandish. Due to current high stress levels, Paul has little capacity to gain longstanding control over his impulsivity and emotional disruption. However, he does seem to manifest underlying potential resources for more controlled behaviors but access to these is currently compromised by inner emotional turmoil.

Paul harbors a tremendous amount of feelings that he is not expressing to others. Therefore, the depth of his emotional turmoil may not be overtly apparent. Paul seems both simultaneously angry and concerned about being victimized himself as many of his responses involved aggressive themes and issues related to harm and potential annihilation. He is very confused by his feelings and is at increased risk when provoked to act in a way that may not protect his own safety.

Paul views himself less favorably when compared to others. He perceives of himself as damaged and inadequate. He is also preoccupied with issues of bodily concern, as his ideas of being damaged seem related to both physical and mental status.

Paul is intensely more negative about himself than seems warranted. While this can be a common finding in adolescents with long-term learning issues, the level of Paul's discomfort with himself and self-negativity seem out of proportion to his abilities and to his positive qualities, and may be related to his suspiciousness. He is mistrusting of the intentions of others and feels vulnerable in a world he views as more threatening. He is guarded and preoccupied with issues of autonomy and personal space.

Paul needs to be in therapy to assist him in modulating behavioral reactions and to decrease his aggressive pre-occupation. He needs to continue with his psychiatrist for medication management and further determination as to the roots of some compromising factors. His innate and underlying psychological resources need to be capitalized on to increase his access to emotional controls.

Even though it would be years before I would come to understand all of this report, its gravity did help resolve my ambivalence about exploring options for Paul's schooling. And I hoped the results would sound an alarm for Dr. Felt, inspiring a greater investment in Paul's needs.

We submitted an application to Chelsea School, a school for bright students with learning disabilities located in Silver Spring, Maryland, where Paul had been denied years earlier. Paul was invited for an interview, and he was accepted. I don't know which one of us was more excited! Paul would be an eleventh grader in a school with appropriate academic challenge, along with needed support systems.

Paul's courses were standard for junior year, his textbooks were on grade level, and he couldn't have been more serious about doing well. Concerned about Paul's lack of academic preparation, I hired a St. John's College student to tutor Paul in Algebra a couple of days a week after school. This turned out to be a good thing. Paul strengthened his skills and loved this young man, Michael, whom he looked forward to seeing and with whom he formed a genuine friendship. When we'd go out to dinner, or have a family gathering, Michael was included.

As Paul took on the challenges of higher expectations, I wondered if he may have been a bit overly focused on his school work and putting too much pressure on himself. When the first-quarter report card came out, he was disappointed. I did my best to convince him it was good, which I'm not sure he accepted entirely. In terms of grades, he received the following:

Algebra	B-
Marine Science	A
British Literature	C-
American History	C-
Art	B
Physical Education	B-

I told Paul that doing your best is what matters, and a "C" is average, and average is just fine.

Thankfully, the report card didn't curtail Paul's continued effort. Considering all the years he'd suffered school-related humiliation, followed by years of being underestimated, his self-worth was on the line. This was his proving ground.

One evening at homework time, Paul was frustrated because he didn't understand a math problem. Keely was home on break and jumped in to help. I overheard her working with him and thought she did a great job, patiently providing a clear and sensible explanation of how to do the problem. An hour or so later, after Keely had gone out and Paul had finished his homework, he and I were talking.

Paul looked me in the eye and said, "I don't care if I live or die."

I didn't think he was serious, but I knew I had to call the psychiatrist's office. And, frankly, I knew it because the psychological testing results had alerted me to Paul's depression and his bottled-up negativity about himself. I told Paul I was going to place the call, and he understood.

A few minutes after leaving a message with the answering service, Dr. Crain called back. She spoke with Paul and then me, instructing me to take him immediately to the nearest hospital, where she would arrange for the doctor on duty to speak with Paul's psychiatrist. I took Paul to Anne Arundel Medical Center, just a couple of blocks from our home. After seeing a doctor, who had talked with Dr. Felt, Paul was released to my care with the condition that I assure his admittance to a mental health facility first thing in the morning.

The next day, Paul was admitted to a psychiatric hospital in Delaware.

Chapter 6

THE HOSPITAL

Back then, my nighttime slumbers
still comprehended into unbearable nightmares,
which seemed to cripple me in a paralysis,
always leaving me a few thresholds away from my mother's arms.
It was then I clung to my sheets in fear,
while my boundless imagination clipped its own wings,
and subjected my body to terrible hallucinations
and ultimately a fear of dreaming....

I DON'T KNOW where or how to begin. After all these years, I am baffled still. You might think reliving it, reading through my notes of the daily back-and-forth communication, could provide some clarity. But the truth is, even in hindsight, there's little about this experience that makes sense to me.

Paul was in the adolescent ward of a psychiatric hospital, which I didn't see coming, and my focus was on understanding what to expect. Instead, I spent that first day, and then some, on the phone trying to understand the insurance and knowing Paul's treatment was at a standstill as a result.

"Is the hospital in the network? What about the doctor? Is the doctor in the network?" I was asked these questions and told this needed to be coordinated between the insurance provider—one office for the hospital and another for the doctor—and the hospital's business office. Everyone I talked with gave me a different answer.

I was asked what I wanted.

"I want the doctor to be in touch with Paul's mental health providers in Hyattsville, Maryland," I said.

"But there is no doctor," I was told. "The business office is waiting on the insurance."

"Get Regina to coordinate with Michelle," somebody said.

"No, it's Sherry who handles that . . ."

"I've called them," Sherry said, "but they haven't called me back."

I was told of two probable doctors. "It looks like Dr. Franklin is in the network," Regina said. "But Dr. Spencer is in the same group as your Hyattsville doctors. He's more expensive though."

"You need to get something in writing from the hospital to the insurance company." someone said.

"No, get something in writing from the insurance company to the hospital," another voice piped in.

"Dr. Franklin goes on leave in a few days; you better go with Dr. Spencer. Insurance will pay eighty percent of his daily fee," Regina told me.

"What is his daily fee?" I asked.

"Not sure."

I decided on Dr. Spencer before all this was resolved. Even after I thought it was resolved, it wasn't. In reality, it was never entirely resolved.

I asked if I could speak with the doctor and was told he would call me after he had seen Paul. *Reasonable*, I thought. I was given the name of the social worker with whom I would meet twice a week. I learned visiting hours were in the evenings from 6:30 to 7:30.

Considering rush hour and getting through the inevitable Chesapeake Bay Bridge traffic, I allowed two hours to get there that first evening. But I didn't anticipate getting lost, going the wrong way on the correct exit. I arrived at the hospital at 6:35 and, because parking was a challenge, I didn't enter the lobby until 6:45.

I was rattled enough without being late. But, as it turned out, I didn't lose any time with Paul. Visiting parents had been corralled but were still waiting. After my identification passed muster, and my pockets and handbag were duly inspected, I was herded with the others, shoulder-to-shoulder on the crowded elevator, then through the double doors—unlocked to let us in and relocked behind us—into a common room where our loved ones were ushered in.

I was so glad to see Paul's face.

"I spent half the day in a room by myself but I just talked with a doctor who is changing my medication," Paul told me.

Before I could say anything, he continued, "How long am I going to be here? I'm worried about school."

"I called the school and you don't need to worry," I said. "Your teachers are more than happy to help you when the time is right."

In what felt like mere minutes, it was time to go. Paul asked me to bring his books and said he wanted to go home. I kissed him goodbye, and we parents were herded out. We weren't to be trusted; that's how it felt anyway. We were part of the problem, if not the whole problem. The experience was humiliating. *If it feels bad to me*, I wondered, *how does Paul feel?*

I talked with Dr. Spencer the next day. He told me the combination of medications Paul had been taking often stimulates depression, obsessional thinking, and suicidal ideation. I couldn't help but wonder—assuming this information was accurate—why in the world this combination would have been prescribed for any child, let alone one who was at risk. Was this inside information that Delaware had yet to share with Maryland?

The doctor said he'd started a mood stabilizer, Zyprexa, after which he would consider adding Lithium or Depakote. He said several medications were often needed—one to treat depression, one to help with disorganized thinking, and one as a mood stabilizer. I asked about Paul's attentional impairment. Dr. Spencer told me that the mood had to be addressed first and that Paul's inattentiveness could subside if his mood was properly treated. I could accept mood stabilization taking priority, so I chose not to tell him Paul's attentional issues wouldn't subside. The fact is, the only reason Paul had been on medication in the first place was his lifelong attention deficit.

Dr. Spencer said Paul would be able to come home once his mood was stabilized. At the end of our conversation, he asked me if Paul had been happy when he was young.

"Yes," I said. "Paul was a happy child."

"Good," he said. "It's easier to return a patient to that state than it is to create something that never existed."

The following day, Keely and I met with the social worker, Joanne, and Paul was able to join us briefly, but he didn't say much. In the hallway, we saw a young man who was near hysteria with several nurses struggling to restrain him as other patients gathered around, looking on with varying degrees of apprehension and despair. This scene upset Keely, but we were both on edge, more fragile than usual.

Anguish permeated our world.

The daily visiting hour provided no interaction with the staff, other than what I had taken to calling "the inspector" and "the herder." My routine was to get feedback from the nurse by calling during the day and then to visit with Paul in the evenings.

Usually a couple of days elapsed between conversations with the doctor. In our second discussion, he told me the illness that brought Paul to the hospital was "unfolding fast," and was "severe and getting worse." I didn't know there was an unfolding illness. I'd been thinking the medications Paul had been taking were responsible for his hospitalization.

"Does the illness have a name?" I asked.

Dr. Spencer said, "Paul has a mood disorder with psychotic symptoms. The onset of schizophrenia often occurs in the late teens, but I can't be more specific at this time."

He then told me Zyprexa was most often used to treat schizophrenia.

This information was disturbing to me. None of the recent professional assessments had foreseen this. Then again, if this was the onset of the illness, maybe it wouldn't have been apparent. I tried to grasp whether my own thought process was muddled. In any case, I knew I had much to comprehend.

Within a few days, Paul complained about gaining weight, something that was noticeable. In a conversation with the nurse, Jane, I mentioned his concerns. She suggested he get more exercise and did tell me weight gain is a side effect of Zyprexa.

In following up with the doctor the next day, I asked if the weight gain was temporary. He told me he was going to start Paul on Topamax right away and then could add Depakote rather than Lithium because it could counterbalance the weight gain. He said he'd ask Paul which he'd prefer, given the side effects, telling me Lithium dehydrates, makes acne worse, upsets the stomach, and may make his tremor worse; Depakote causes nausea, vomiting, doesn't cause weight gain, and may or may not exacerbate Paul's tremor.

No one would choose either of these. Furthermore, I was pretty sure Paul would not discern the difference.

I called the unit the next day to see how Paul was faring. Another nurse, Ken, answered the phone.

"He is opening up with his peers. He cries but that's good because he's not afraid to cry," Ken said. "Paul has conquered wanting to hurt himself and is showing good insight into issues and gives good advice to his peers."

He's never been afraid to cry. Plus, I didn't really think he wanted to hurt himself but, if he did, *how is it that they conquered it already?*

Paul's father came to join me for my second session with the social worker. We met in the hallway outside her office. Don hugged me and asked how I was holding up. I don't remember my reply, but I remember appreciating the question and the hug. In the meeting with Joanne, to my surprise, she told Don that he didn't see Paul enough, "which is a source of great pain for Paul," she said. I hadn't mentioned this to her and, as far as I knew, Paul hadn't either. Then again, maybe he had. And, I realized, she did have Paul's records.

Don said, "That is going to change, starting now."

Christmas was a few days away, and we had no idea what to expect. On the 23rd, Jane told me Paul might be able to get a four-hour pass to come home on Christmas Day. *Perfect*, I thought. We could drive by our house, see the Christmas lights, and return to the hospital. We wouldn't have to be inconvenienced by getting out of the car. My sisters and I talked about taking Christmas to the hospital on the 24th or 25th so we could all be together, even though briefly.

Jane also told me Paul had written an excellent paper, portraying his good value system. "You must have taught him well," she said. She was nice, I thought, but patronizing.

Dr. Spencer called in the morning on Christmas Eve to inform me that Paul was stable enough to be discharged and that I could pick him up right away. I was floored, but really happy. The doctor told me to get a blood test Monday and fax the results to Paul's psychiatrist, Dr. Felt, with whom we should meet as soon as possible for medication management. Dr. Spencer had started the Depakote, and the blood work would inform the decision about next steps. Also, he said, therapy with Dr. Crain would be needed.

Using a roll of shelf paper, Keely and I made a huge sign— WELCOME HOME PAUL!!!—in red and green letters that we stretched across the outside front of our house. I then made what I thought would be my last drive to Delaware. After I left, Keely took our holiday decorating to a new level, tying bows on everything— lamps, doorknobs, candles—and otherwise making up for Christmas preparations that may have been somewhat half-hearted due to Paul's situation. Keely was obviously excited that her brother was coming home.

My family's annual routine included Christmas Eve at our house. On the drive home from the hospital, I told Paul it was up to him whether or not we would have the whole family over that evening, explaining that everyone had agreed to be "on standby" and to let him call the shots. Paul didn't hesitate—he wanted our gathering to be just as it always had been. In fact, he said it was important to him.

A few hours later, as we sang Christmas carols with my parents, sisters, brothers-in-law, and, of course, "the cousins"—with Paul joining in—I felt like the worst Christmas ever had transformed and, despite the uncertainty before us, I counted my blessings.

I do not remember if this anecdote pertained to this particular year's singing, but from the time Paul was little through his teenage years, his version of the lyrics to the Christmas standard, *Rudolph the Red-Nosed Reindeer*, went like this: "Red nose the red-nosed reindeer . . ." No matter how many times we told him it was "Rudolph," he'd sing the song his way, and at the top of his lungs. That tune and *The Chipmunk Song* were his seasonal favorites—funny because it was impossible to miss the similarities between Paul and Alvin.

Paul slept most of Christmas Day but remained happy to be home and was enthusiastic about joining the family again that night at my parents' house, another annual tradition. Fortunately, I had given him nice flannel pajama pants and a sweatshirt, size XXL, as none of his clothing fit. I can see him now—sitting on my parents' couch and barely saying a word. He didn't seem sad, but he wasn't Paul either.

*

SCHOOL RESUMED IN early January, and Paul returned to Chelsea. His teachers worked with him, helping him prepare for the first-semester exams, which he managed pretty well. But it wasn't long before drowsiness—resulting from medication increases—challenged his ability to stay awake throughout the day. Even with twelve to fourteen hours of sleep per night, Paul would fall asleep on the bus going to school or fall asleep in school. One time, the bus driver didn't realize Paul was sleeping, or even on the bus for that matter, and dropped off the other kids, continuing past the school with Paul still aboard.

Paul always had a slight build, yet now he was considered borderline obese. I decided to get a family gym membership, entering a world that was new to me, and quickly realized that Paul would need a trainer. We went three times a week, two of which Paul worked with his trainer, Heather. He moved slowly, and his coordination was compromised, but he tried hard. He was eating salads and highly focused on losing weight, but nothing seemed to make even the slightest difference.

We met with Dr. Felt. I told her I was confused about who was in charge of Paul's medication, what the next steps would be, and whether feedback from Paul and me was a factor in the medication decisions. She said she was in charge, although she was following Dr. Spencer's plan and would likely increase the Depakote after reviewing the next blood test results. I shared concerns about Paul's slowed state, his falling asleep in school, and his weight gain, along with my overall lack of understanding about his diagnosis and its implications for the future.

She said he had schizoaffective disorder or possibly another non-specified mood disorder, that the weight gain would level out and, over time, he'd acclimate to the drowsiness. When I mentioned the stress created by not knowing whether to send Paul to school or keep him home, as well as the hardships of managing my professional responsibilities in the face of this uncertainty, she suggested I look into the possibility of taking medical leave.

For how long? Where's the damn light at the end of this tunnel?

She spoke so casually, as though my taking medical leave would be easy—bringing to mind that I didn't trust this woman's investment in Paul, much less me, from the get-go. I wished *she'd* take medical leave.

I spoke briefly with Dr. Crain and learned she was not comfortable providing Paul's therapy, given his diagnosis. I appreciated her honesty, and I didn't doubt the professionalism behind it, but this was not good news. When you get right down to it, Dr. Crain was the reason I had been able to hang in there with Dr. Felt, who suddenly I found myself wholly dependent on, and in a time of dire crisis.

The medication increased and so did the side effects. Paul could not go to school until he could stay awake. With little to no faith in Dr. Felt, I had to turn to Dr. Spencer. Aware that his bedside manner held zero promise, I had to forgo any expectation of reassurance for my sake, but I couldn't forgo alerting him to Paul's escalating needs. I called Dr. Spencer several times over the course of the week, leaving messages expressing the degree of Paul's suffering and the diminishing quality of his day-to-day life. He did not return my calls.

Paul was unhappy on multiple levels, all of which seemed related to his coping with the medication side effects. His frustration regarding the list of things he couldn't do, such as playing his guitar, was mounting and, as of the first of February, he was readmitted to the hospital.

I knew I needed to be more aggressive this time around. I just didn't understand enough to feel comfortable. But I also needed to be strategic, more clinical than motherly. I was well prepared for my first meeting with Dr. Spencer, arriving early with my list of questions in hand. But, as I wrote his answers in my notebook, he said, "You are as obsessive as Paul."

Paul was miserable. The first night during the visiting hour, he cried and begged me to get him out of there. He asked me to write down his questions so I could relay them to the doctor. I did as he asked, telling him he could ask the doctor as well. But he needed me to literally write out his questions, so I obliged. They were:

Do you know why I am in the hospital?

Do you know why I am depressed?

Do you know about my obsessive thinking?

How long will I be on these medications?

In my follow-up conversation with Dr. Spencer, he told me Paul was in the hospital to enable them to monitor and adjust his medications so his stress could be reduced.

"That makes sense," I replied. "But his medications seem to be interfering with his ability to live his life."

"His worry over the side effects is greater than it needs to be," Dr. Spencer said.

I didn't see how his response was remotely helpful, for Paul or for me. Do I wave a magic wand to make Paul's worry disappear? Or maybe I just tell Paul that he shouldn't worry about being obese. And that he's making too big of a deal of not being able to attend school or participate in any activities. *I see. That should do it.*

I can handle bad news and am pretty good at accepting that which I cannot change. But I'm terrible at being kept in the dark, particularly when my earnest attempts to understand are met with glib remarks. I was dumbstruck—a state I initially chalked up to being caught off guard by a "rapidly unfolding and severe illness"—but I was starting to get angry. Initially, I reserved judgment, but it was becoming clearer to me that Dr. Spencer was arrogant. And, with our lives on the line, I didn't see any excuse for it. Whether or not he was competent in managing Paul's treatment, I had no way of knowing. I could only hope that he was, and I clung to optimism. But he certainly didn't have the capacity for, or the interest in, helping someone in my position.

I felt like saying, "Try to refrain from being a pompous ass when I seek information about my son and his suffering. I'm not stupid; I'm confused, which I would think would be expected. And even if I were stupid, I would deserve better." But I knew that approach would set me back with a man like Spencer, a man who, for now, we needed.

Rather than confront the doctor, I turned to the social worker, Joanne, telling her of my and Paul's frustrations. She wrote down and handed me the name and phone number of another psychiatrist who she believed would be more helpful. Having her empathize with my position was somewhat satisfying, but I was surprised by her suggestion and didn't know what to do. The doctor who she recommended had no affiliation with the hospital nor was he located near Annapolis. I felt as though her concern was genuine, and I sensed she wasn't a fan of Dr. Spencer. But her advice, as well-intentioned as I believed it was, only contributed to the whole "magical mystery tour" feeling I had about the place.

During the next visiting hour, Paul was rocking, swaying, moving his head in a circular motion, then stamping his feet. He was nearly impossible to talk with but said he felt good and wanted to go home. He told me he attends a class during the day and because he is so sleepy, they make him sit on the floor—reducing the risk of injury from falling when he nods off.

A couple of days later, Paul said to me, "You don't want me home; that's why you won't help me. I am not telling anyone about my obsessive thinking because I need to get out of here."

After three weeks as an inpatient, Paul was discharged to the hospital's day program, which provided a school-like setting with teachers as well as mental health professionals. In theory, Paul's transition from inpatient to outpatient represented progress—a logical conclusion on the surface. But for me, it was a nightmare, one I endured while Paul's suffering was as dramatic as ever.

I had to orchestrate getting Paul to Delaware and back each day—representing four trips—and care for him in the evenings. And I seriously do not know which was worse. I rallied reinforcements to help with the transportation, with my brother-in-law being a godsend. But I made many a trip myself. On more than one occasion, Paul tried to get out of the car while I was driving on the highway and otherwise was prone to hitting his fists against the passenger side window, a challenge that presented itself for me and, scaring me even more, for Keely.

On the homefront, Paul was not the boy I had known. He was feeble, a status that applied to both his physical and mental capacities. In addition to being dramatically unhappy, he seemed at times to be losing touch with reality. One evening as I said goodnight to Paul, he asked me to get his CD wallet out of his bedroom. His sense of urgency prompted me to accommodate his request without hesitation. I picked up the wallet and walked toward the door.

"WHAT are you going to do with it?" Paul demanded, with his voice and facial expression revealing his panic-stricken state.

"I am going to take it into my bedroom," I replied.

"NO!!!" Paul cried out. "PLEASE. DON'T DO THAT! THEN IT WILL HURT YOU!!!"

Another evening, Paul smashed his electric guitar on the floor. Immediately remorseful, he cried and said he couldn't handle the frustration of not being able to play it.

I left a voicemail message for Dr. Spencer: "Paul is out of control and unmanageable. I need help."

He returned my call and said we needed to increase the Zyprexa.

"Should I beep you if there is another outburst?" I asked.

"If you do, you are acting like Paul," he replied, reminding me again that I'm part of the problem. Keeping me in my place.

On the weekend days, I tried to involve Paul in simplified versions of activities he had always enjoyed. For example, we got seeds to start a garden—an idea that made him happy. But in execution—as he realized he couldn't complete any of the tasks—he disengaged. He stood in the yard and stared straight ahead for several minutes before his eyes welled up. Leaving the gardening tools in the bed we'd planned to prepare, I ushered Paul to our back steps where we sat down; he leaned on me, put his head on my shoulder, and wept. I held him, supporting his weight as his now whiskered and tear-streaked face pressed against mine. That was all I could do.

Another day, I took him to Frederick, Maryland, to an antique store that had a good-sized collection of old vinyl record albums, something Paul loved looking through and an activity that wouldn't require any skill on his part. As we approached the store entrance, Paul stopped walking forward. With his right foot pivoting in place, he took steps with his left foot, turning himself in circles over and over again.

I can still see the old marble floor and the sneakers he was wearing, which I was riveted on as I asked myself: *What is happening to us? Why don't I understand? Why am I dizzy when he's the one turning in circles?*

After looking through the albums, we found a little café where we had lunch. When Paul finished eating, he used the restroom. After waiting for him for a good fifteen minutes, I had to go in the men's room to get him, where I needed to zip his pants, something with which he frequently needed my help.

Paul's difficulty in the school portion of the program stemmed from his stupor-like condition. When I picked him up at the end of the day, he would tell me everyone thought he was stupid, usually adding that he thought they were stupid too.

There was a disconnect between the day program and the hospital. I had to ask at one point if Dr. Spencer was still involved. The adults with whom Paul worked seemed unaware of his background, with one teacher asking me if Paul had ever had psychological testing. I was speechless. I mustered up a "yes," but I was too weary to elaborate or, more to the point, I didn't expend the energy because I didn't see what good it would do.

Working with the day program education director, along with Anne Arundel County, next steps were explored. I knew Paul couldn't return to Chelsea, even though he had made the honor roll for the first semester—with one A and five B's—something I often told him, and showed him, when he was discouraged.

After considering a couple of options that could provide the level of support Paul needed, it was decided he would attend Forbush School, located on the campus of Sheppard Pratt Psychiatric Hospital in Baltimore, Maryland. Paul started the twelve-month day school at Forbush in late April. And, with that, the months of what I then considered the innermost circle of hell came to an end.

*

AFTER ELEVEN WEEKS of the drive to and from Delaware, nine of which entailed two round trips per day, it was a relief to have a county bus provide Paul's daily transportation, even though I felt more than a little sorry for him in being the only student on a full-size school bus for more than an hour's ride, morning and afternoon.

At Forbush, Paul was assigned a psychiatrist and a social worker, both of whom I met with every week, and for whom I developed high regard. While Forbush was a good hour's drive from my office, juggling my schedule seemed easy relative to the recent past. And, in the same vein, I was ever grateful for my confidence in these professionals.

By July, the psychiatrist, Kevin Harrison, was able to summarize his thinking about Paul's overall condition and dramatic cognitive decline, which he said boiled down to one of two things. As he explained each one to me, I jotted down his words as well as I could:

- A regression due to a nervous breakdown (in layman's terms), which occurred because he was overwhelmed, he collapsed, couldn't keep his head above water; the loss of health brought about a severe depression. With a respite from the stresses, he can recover. Tinkering with medication may bring about a return of the functioning he lost; however, his learning disabilities will make the recovery more complicated.

- An ongoing process of a degenerative nature; a cerebellar dysfunction that will continue to decrease his ability to function. He does look like there is some degree of dementia going on, but will need MRI and CAT scans to show the physiological functioning of the brain.

I was frightened, and I could see that my state of perpetual worry about Paul had shifted over recent months without my putting it in words. But sitting there that day, it hit me—my worry had evolved to fear.

In light of Dr. Harrison's uncertainty about these two possibilities, it was easy to understand his reluctance to take further steps with the medication. To rule out a degenerative brain disorder, which I perceived he was leaning toward, he asked me to obtain a specific kind of neurology report.

I ended up taking Paul to Johns Hopkins Hospital for an evaluation with Joel Goldman, a neurologist Dr. Harrison helped me select. After the assessment was complete, as Paul and I were about to leave, Dr. Goldman invited me into his office, where he told me what he felt was critical. I will never forget this experience.

As he shook his index finger close to my face, he spoke slowly and with passion. "You nor I would function any better than Paul if on the dosage of the medications he is on. There is no need for any further testing. Paul's condition is not cerebellar. His cognitive slowing is one hundred percent due to medication. Topamax is the biggest culprit in reduced functioning and the medications have exacerbated his tremor. He is on too much Depakote; it doesn't matter what the blood work says. Depakote is probably also causing the weight gain. They've taken his life away and there is no excuse for it!"

He was angry, but not with me. I took comfort in his words.

The neurology report, written by the assisting physician and signed by the doctor, arrived a few days later:

The patient is an obese 17 year old. . . . Since his depressive episodes in December and again in February, he has been placed on multiple medications including Topamax, Depakote, and Zyprexa. We feel his current cognitive decline and exacerbation of his tremor are secondary to his medications especially with the high doses.

We suggest the following changes in medication: Topamax is currently at 600 mg a day. To our knowledge, we do not know of any psychiatric treatments that have responded to Topamax. In this light, since he does not have a seizure disorder, we feel he needs to first wean then completely taper off the Topamax. We have chosen this medication first because of the side effects of cognitive decline and confusion. The second suggestion is that his Depakote, which is very high at 2000 mg a day, be tapered off as much as his mood can tolerate. Depakote has a well-known side effect of exacerbation of underlying tremors as well as development of new tremors. We also feel this will help with his weight control.

The overall impression is drug toxicity.

After months of anguish over the quality of life with schizophrenia, or worse yet, schizoaffective disorder, followed by a degenerative brain disease, this was good news. When Dr. Harrison explained the lengthy sequential process for weaning Paul from the medications, I knew we were in for a long haul. Even so, my spirits were lifted by newfound hope.

As is often the case in life, "when it rains, it pours." As I was grappling with Paul's mental health and the associated stress, I was also dealing with my mother's diagnosis of Alzheimer's Disease and her gradual but continuous loss of functioning. In one week's time, it wasn't unusual for me to drive north of Baltimore to Forbush School one day and another to the inner city of Baltimore to take my mother and stepfather to Johns Hopkins Hospital for her regular appointment with her neurologist.

By the fall of what would have been Paul's senior year, we knew he would stay at Forbush for that year and the next in order to finish high school. In the scope of all the hardships, I saw this as a blessing of sorts. Forbush was a safe and caring place, and Dr. Harrison was focused and capable, advantages for Paul that I didn't take lightly. Paul, however, found little to feel good about, and his prevailing sense of inferiority bumped up another notch when he learned he wouldn't graduate on time.

Paul's weight continued to upset him. His pants size increased to 38/30, impossible to buy in any of the stores we frequented, or even those we didn't. He had not come out of the fog enough to place in the academic track he desired and had to choose between food service and landscaping for his school focus. He lamented this to me along with the facts he had no friends and his teachers didn't understand him. He no longer wanted to go to the gym with me because he said it didn't change anything, an attitude I could more than understand. In fact, he was right.

*

SARA CONTINUED TO be Paul's girlfriend, and his best friend, but her parents were no longer in support of their seeing one another, something I surmised was due, at least in part, to Paul's challenges.

Even though I am not one to actively nourish a teenage romance, I wished this could be different, for Paul's sake. But as parents of these two kids, we didn't confer on anything philosophical. Sara's parents pretty much called the shots, and I didn't make any attempts to insert myself or even share, much less try to impose, my thinking. It probably wouldn't have made a difference anyway.

One constant was the fervor of Sara's commitment to Paul, giving way to her relentless pursuit of ploys to see him on the sly. While this enabled an occasional few minutes together, the relationship no longer provided the regular camaraderie Paul had enjoyed a couple of years before. This represented another loss for Paul, as did the twelve-month school schedule that precluded the fun and social aspects of summer activities.

My weekly meetings at Forbush throughout Paul's first year had been focused on weaning him from the medications and the ongoing assessment of his abilities, as well as his mental health status. This was a slow and agonizing process. But one year after Paul's arrival at Forbush, we had finally eliminated the Topamax and substantially reduced the Depakote, a process that would take another couple of months to complete.

On a positive note, I did begin to see the Paul I knew reappear. I remember telling Keely, when she moved home again at the end of the academic year, that she would be amazed by his progress. While he continued to have trouble with anxiety and bouts of perseverative thinking, he was more successful.

As Dr. Harrison got to know Paul in a more realistic light, he asked me if "something happened" to him earlier in his life. I told him Paul's stepfather had been verbally abusive. But Dr. Harrison was getting at something more, trying to uncover the root of Paul's disproportionate negativity about himself.

I was sure nothing had happened to Paul other than the ego insults he had repeatedly endured. I did think back, but only fleetingly, to a similar concern revealed by Dr. Crain's psychological testing a few months before Paul was first hospitalized.

Paul completed a driver's education program in Annapolis and went on to get his learner's permit and ultimately his license. This whole process was a bit unnerving for me—bringing on flashbacks of sailing camp with higher stakes—but over time Paul actually became a good driver. I think his visual spatial strengths served him well in this regard.

Years later, just two years ago, I was driving on the Washington beltway with Paul and, as we took an exit ramp, he said, "Mom! For God's sake! You need to speed up and use your mirrors—you're scaring me!"

Even though I knew he made a fair point, I said something defensive like, "I'll have you know my driving record is perfect." In pondering how we had gotten to the point where *I* scared *him*, I thought but chose not to say, "At least, I'm not trying to get out of a moving car!"

As we headed into Paul's final year of high school, he once again made the case for taking more academic classes. Because his guidance counselor didn't agree, I intervened in support of Paul's wishes. In response to my initial request, I was told their hands were tied on the grounds that Paul was not eligible for a high school diploma but instead—not unlike a good portion of their population—would get a certificate of completion.

In learning about the long list of requirements Paul would have to meet in one year's time, I could understand their hesitation. But as I reviewed the list carefully, I could see they were unaware of some aspects of Paul's record, including: Paul's hours of volunteer work at the SPCA in Annapolis, sufficient to complete his community service requirement; his two passed competency tests in English and Math (meaning he need only to pass the Citizenship test); and the half credits earned in all his academic classes at Chelsea School.

In a letter to the guidance counselor, I substantiated this information and included Paul's cognitive testing from before his hospitalization, predicting—although with fingers crossed—his gradual return to that baseline capability.

After meeting with the teachers, Dr. Harrison, and the guidance counselor, the decision was made to put Paul in the required academic classes, all of which he had to pass.

I was, and I remain, grateful to Forbush School.

In June 2002—the year Paul would turn twenty—he crossed the stage in cap and gown, receiving his high school diploma with an entourage of loved ones cheering him on.

3-year-old Keely, 6-month-old Paul, and me

Keely and Paulie on beach

Paulie, almost 2 years old

Matching nightshirts

Paul with Granddaddy

Paul's second grade school photo

Keely and Paul with Ruff-Ruff

Playing guitar at age 12

Christmas 1995

Keely and Paul dancing

Paul with his sister, last day of sailing camp

Paul with Calvin and Hobbes in shirt pocket

Sara and Paul mark one year "anniversary"

Paul at 16, skimboarding

Hospital homecoming

Home from hospital for Christmas

Chapter 7

WEIGHT OF THE WORLD

I want to sing and climb on stars, gravity.
I want to do a handstand on the moon and dip my feet in the pacific.
I want to cover miles to grasp a notion of what infinity means.
I want to cover my dreams in ink and repel you with my pen.
I want to hide in my poem and sleep with my own inspiration.
But I'm stuck here with you gravity,
And I'm bearing your weight for you.

ON BALANCE, I probably rely on navigating one day at a time more than mapping out the future. Maybe this is a lifelong pattern that explains why I don't readily challenge the status quo. Or, let's just say, I don't instinctively seek change.

After all, I was in the same job for thirty years and have lived in my house more than forty. For fifteen years, Keely went to the same school where—after a hiatus that included college and graduate school—she returned to teach.

But life with Paul was full of change, usually imposed by forces beyond my control and often my ability to foresee. I don't remember a time without worry. Even during a period of relative smooth sailing, I was waiting for the other shoe to drop. Nor do I remember a time without hope. Based in part on faith and also on my belief in Paul, I knew we would see a better day. I remember thinking I'd usher him through, whatever that means, and my life's purpose would be enshrined forever on some tablet somewhere.

But enough about what I don't know. Here's what I *do*: Transitions were never easy for Paul.

Maybe I didn't plan well enough—didn't consider all the pitfalls of Paul's transition from life at Forbush School, with its structure and safety, to life after graduation. I can rationalize, telling myself there wasn't much I could have done differently. But in my heart, I know otherwise. It could be that my autopilot reliance on a "wait and see, hope for the best" mindset was wishful thinking, born out of a degree of negligence on my part.

Paul was able to continue with Dr. Harrison in his private practice in Ellicott City, Maryland, an hour-long drive from Annapolis. We agreed to monthly appointments, enabling Dr. Harrison to address Paul's ongoing medication needs and support his progress. The thought of finding the right psychiatrist was not only daunting but also subject to failure, and Dr. Harrison's expertise, as well as his investment in Paul throughout a difficult time, made this a welcome option, if not a blessing.

Paul wanted to take classes at Anne Arundel Community College in the fall. For the summer, he worked four or five shifts a week as a stock boy at a local grocery store where we shopped and knew the manager, giving Paul a leg up in being hired. As well as I could, I explained Paul's disabilities to the gentlemanly manager, something that was always a challenge for me when Paul entered a new arena. Be it summer camp or karate or a visit with a friend's family, I consistently tried to balance imparting an understanding of Paul's differences with expedience so as not to be a burden.

Paul remained in good standing at his job that summer, but his behavior at home regressed. His mood was erratic, with some good days, but mostly he was irritable and defiant. Not only was he rude to me and to Keely, who had graduated from college and moved home, but also he was argumentative. I noticed, too, that he was less able to sustain focus and seemed disinterested in former pastimes offered by his computer or playing his guitar. Adding to the disquieting mix, Paul wanted to be responsible for taking his own medication, which I doubted would be consistent and could compound his difficulties. In sum, the quality of life in our house was poor.

In an email to Dr. Harrison, I provided some details:

Paul had two good days last week in which he not only was pleasant but also made a list of the graduation gifts he received and wrote thank-you notes, all very sweet and done independently while I was at work. For the most part, however, he has been quite difficult over the last several weeks.

Paul came to the dinner table last night and complained that I didn't cook the meal correctly, that there wasn't enough food; he continued to argue despite my explanation that there was more (plenty). As he carelessly served himself at the table, he dropped his serving and, when I corrected him, he put his hand in the food and told me I was uptight, which was the source of all his problems.

When Paul behaves like this, I know how much pain he must be in, and I work to set limits while remaining unflappable. Mostly, I worry for him; but I also worry about the effects he is having on Keely and me. In short, he makes problems where there are no problems, and I do not know how to help him or get relief from him.

I received an email from Dr. Harrison right away. "I suspect several factors contributing to Paul's regression of late," he wrote. "Certainly the transition he is dealing with creates a lot of uncertainty for him. While he talks about wanting independence and 'freedoms' that come with graduation from high school, Paul lacks the maturity and self-discipline to navigate this successfully, and still needs you to provide limits and structure for him."

When Paul left Forbush School, he was taking a low dose of Zyprexa for mood stability, Adderall for attentional problems, and Luvox for anxiety. Because we believed Paul's anxiety was at the root of his negativity, and probably even his struggle to focus, Dr. Harrison increased the Luvox twice over the next couple of months. By August, Paul was functioning better.

Paul took placement tests at AACC, scoring nearly average in English and at the seventh-grade level in math. One of the impressive features of our community college is the availability of appropriate classes regardless of ability level. Paul was placed in remedial pre-algebra, a class I thought would be perfect for him.

Initially, we thought that his taking three classes and dropping back to three shifts at the grocery store would be the best overall plan. But after learning that Paul's continued health insurance coverage was contingent on his taking a minimum of twelve credits (this was before Obama Care), I had a change of heart. In addition to the math, he registered for American Studies, Fundamentals of Music, Art, and PE.

Paul met with an advocate for students with learning disabilities, who seemed dedicated to helping him succeed. Unbeknownst to Paul, I had paved the way for this, providing background information in a meeting beforehand.

Because Paul qualified for extra time on exams, he could take tests in the library without a time limit. On the day of his first math test, he went to the class and was told his test was in the library. He promptly reported to the library, where he worked on the test for about an hour before realizing it was time for his PE class. He went to PE and returned to the library to resume working on the test, only to be told that in leaving the library he had relinquished further work on the test. Instead of saying he had misunderstood, or in any way trying to advocate for himself with the library staff or his teacher, he said nothing and the test was submitted.

Days later, Paul learned that he had failed the math test, undoubtedly because he hadn't finished it. He knew the material, but he didn't know how to navigate the process, a troublesome fact inasmuch as it applied to countless situations. I knew that this handicap contributed to Paul's insecurity, which in turn compromised his self-advocacy. There was much about the world he just didn't get but, for him, seeking any clarification would risk acknowledging what he was desperate to hide.

I could tell when Paul's school experiences became stressful, if not demoralizing, because he would turn on me again. "You won't let me grow up," he said in one such instance.

Then, even though he hadn't missed a class, he wanted me to believe he didn't have homework—which I could see by the course syllabus wasn't right. Paul had always taken homework seriously, and I felt badly for him. But the whole situation was a trap. He hadn't gotten a footing and needed support to do so, but he wanted to be "normal" and therefore manage without help. As much as I wanted to be a resource, he was outwardly resisting me, resenting just about anything I said and letting me know with frequent declarations such as:

"Don't come in my room."

"Don't say 'hello' to me when you walk in the house."

"You are stupid, and I hate you."

I was raised in a harmonious home where a few words—beyond taboo—were just off limits. No one questioned such things. Among these were: "shut up" and "hate" and "stupid." A curse word here and there was okay, but these words were not. So, for me, hearing Paul speak this way—directed toward me no less—was cringeworthy. Yet, as much as I instinctively wanted to promote the values so ingrained in my being, I had to choose my battles. Sometimes I would say, "You cannot talk to me that way." Other times I just let it go in the name of a higher priority. I see this as an example of yet another complexity in raising a child with so many challenges. You learn you can't rely on instinct alone, even when you know your instincts are good and have served you well. There is no pattern set for you. The pieces don't fit together.

*

FAR FROM WANTING to confide in me, Paul shut me out when he needed me the most. I worried that he would fail everything, even though I knew he was capable of successes. Meanwhile, it was easy for me to imagine what he was thinking: *Why risk trying and failing? I'll just blow off everything and everybody. I hate myself because this is too hard for me, and I hate everybody else too.*

I told Paul he had choices, that we could explore his living elsewhere if he believed I was preventing him from growing up. In wanting to give Paul more than a hypothetical option, I did ask his father if he could live at his house for a period of time. But Don said no, something I never mentioned to Paul. Regardless, I thought that my suggesting options would convey to Paul that I had heard him, and that I would step aside with his interest at heart, letting him grow up. I also thought it could possibly free him from digging in his heels. In other words, his knowing it was okay with me could soften his adamance.

Instead, with his insecurity getting the best of him, he concluded that I wanted to get rid of him, and his anxiety grew. With Dr. Harrison's help, I began looking for a therapist that Paul could see weekly in Annapolis.

Paul was seeing Sara, who was in her second year out of high school. Their relationship was uneven and not entirely healthy, a situation for which I thought they were equally culpable. Sara had become overly dependent on Paul for rides, which he accommodated with seemingly little concern for whether doing so made him late or otherwise unprepared for his obligations. Also, Sara wasn't always in good standing with her parents, and Paul felt some responsibility for that. My take was that Paul's having been the "forbidden fruit" for so long fueled Sara's focus on him in general. In any case, neither of them seemed able to put their relationship in the proper context with regard to life's other priorities.

Six months after his graduation, Paul was no longer in school, having passed only PE, and had walked out on his job.

It's easy to imagine that Paul had brought some of the strife at work on himself. However, the store manager who hired Paul and understood his disabilities had left, and Paul had to contend with two younger managers who, from what I observed as a shopper, had little interest in niceties. One evening as Paul was loading stock onto a conveyor belt and a container fell, a manager asked Paul, "Do you even know your name?"

I'm pretty sure that was the last straw. While I would bet that Paul's emotional vulnerability compounded the situation, I could sympathize with his challenges. Furthermore, I always knew that Paul reserved his worst behavior for family members and was otherwise appropriate and polite. Although I knew, too, that his inattentiveness could be mistaken for rudeness.

Paul was earnest in looking for a job and came up with nothing. As Christmas neared, he spent time at his grandparents' house, with whom he was always sweet, helping them in general and putting up their Christmas tree. My mother was declining, but luckily my stepfather was devoted to her and, even though a few years older, was still capable of managing her care.

In January, I contacted a counselor at the Maryland Division of Rehabilitation Services (DORS) about the programs they provide to help people with disabilities find or prepare for work. I was most interested in the career assessment offered at their Workforce Technology Center in Baltimore. I learned the assessment of aptitude and abilities would take from one to three weeks to complete, during which Paul could stay in their dorm. If an area of strength aligned with a career of interest, DORS could either provide, or help arrange for, appropriate training.

Paul expressed an interest in Computer Assisted Design, which I supported in view of his visual spatial strengths along with the fact that, despite his fine motor difficulties, he was pretty good on the computer. CAD was one of the careers for which DORS provided the training, making this choice even more attractive to me. I was pretty sure Paul's interest in this field was inspired, at least in part, by his father's being an architect. Paul admired his father's work and would have liked sharing a common pursuit.

Paul spent a week in the dorm in Baltimore for the career assessment with results that surprised and disappointed me. The testing did not reveal any strength in visual perception, a fact that, combined with his weakness in math, ruled out training for any sort of CAD career.

I was deflated and felt like telling the woman who tested Paul: "You are stupid, and I hate you," but refrained, realizing I had clocked too much time with Paul. Paul must have been disappointed as well, but he often internalized anything that even remotely hurt his ego.

Paul was assigned a DORS counselor in Annapolis, who was very nice but never came up with an alternative beyond those targeted by the assessment: auto mechanics, which Paul had no interest in, and sound engineering, which he did.

I took Paul to see the sound engineering studio that had been recommended for training in Rockville, Maryland. It was easy to see why it appealed to him—it was hip, it was exciting, and it was all about music. It appealed to me too! But I believed he would fail at it, to the tune of $9,000 for a nine-month block of courses. Not only was the material complex and dependent on agile response time, but also the mainstream setting provided no accommodation for learning challenges. Paul's DORS counselor agreed with me, but Paul was fixated, making me wish we hadn't gone to see it. I ended up telling him we couldn't afford it, which I thought was better than saying it would be too challenging for him.

Paul continued to look for work but was disadvantaged by not being able to fill out an application, not knowing basic things like dates of former employment, and not having the confidence or the verbal skills to hold his own in an initial conversation. I knew he was employable but believed he needed a connection to land a job.

I contacted everyone I could think of, including my friend, Ross Dierdorff, who was compelled by Paul's story and took him on as an assistant in a project he was working on: an analysis of proposed public transportation in Baltimore City, for which Paul lined up aerial photographs with maps to enable a coding system for gathering pertinent data. Ross, a brilliant, benevolent, and, I think it's fair to say, somewhat eccentric guy, took a liking to Paul—understood him—and they became an unlikely team. The work was not full time, but Paul enjoyed it and benefitted from the respect Ross afforded him. Ross even gave Paul a car, an old Volvo wagon with nearly 100,000 miles on it, which Paul was quite happy to have. Ross actually loved the car but said his wife would consider it a gift for Paul to remove it from their driveway!

The car enabled a second part-time job for Paul, thanks to our dear friend, Maureen Sullivan, who hired him as a driver. A crony of mine from my years as an academic librarian at Maryland, Maureen became family to me, a relationship undeterred by the divergence of our career paths, with mine being stalled and then redirected by motherhood. While I was wiping up rice cereal and whatnot, Maureen was further honing her skills in organizational development and strategic planning, catapulting her into a national arena as an in-demand consultant for research libraries throughout the country. When she came up with the idea to employ Paul, Maureen was serving on the faculty for the Leadership Institute for Academic Librarians at Harvard and needed transportation between her home in Annapolis and the Baltimore Washington International Airport (BWI), in Linthicum, Maryland, where she had departing or incoming flights several days a week. Paul jumped at the chance to both drive and spend time with Maureen—a lifelong pillar in his world. I was grateful for the benevolence on her part, only to learn that she found the arrangement far superior to her former reliance on a cab, telling me Paul was always on time and she enjoyed their uninterrupted conversations.

By May 2003, we settled on a therapist, Steven Kellogg, whom Paul would see weekly. This was an opportunity Paul was eager to get in the works, telling me the night before his first session that he knew he needed help with his anxiety and its effects on his behavior. In setting up the first appointment, I was able to share a brief history with Dr. Kellogg, who said I could provide information but, given Paul's age and rights, he could not reciprocate.

*

THIS WAS THE beginning of my years of being kept at arm's length with mental health providers, a phenomenon I had to accept but a detrimental one, particularly in light of Paul's delayed development, the complexity of his needs, and his frequent denial of both.

Despite Paul's money-making endeavors, he lacked structure and consistency in his life, and I continued to hope for full-time employment. His work with Ross took a few hours a day, and his driving for Maureen was lucrative, but in a week's time he made only three or four round trips to the airport just twenty-five miles away. With too many loose ends, and no future direction, Paul's self-doubt reigned supreme, making him more susceptible to poor judgment and destructive behavior.

I noticed empty beer bottles stashed under our back deck and asked Paul if he knew anything about them. He said he had been drinking beer, something he was quick to defend. "I bought it myself," he said.

"I am fully aware you bought it yourself," I replied, "given that none of my forty-ounce beers are missing."

"And," asserted Paul, "drinking is 'normal' for twenty-one-year-olds."

"Is it 'normal' for these mature, of-age drinkers, to hide their empty bottles under a deck?" I asked.

On a more serious note, I told Paul I was concerned about the effects of alcohol on his medication, on his driving, and his over-all health. But what bothered me the most, which I had to broach carefully, was his motivation. Was it peer pressure? Or in any way related to socializing? Or was it a way to alleviate his anxiety? He wasn't straightforward in this type of conversation, which I chalked up to his resistance to authority combined with his own inability to fully grasp, or want to acknowledge, what I was getting at.

I struggled to exert the controls I could. I didn't allow Paul to have anyone in the house while I was working, and I restricted his use of the car to work-related needs. I shared my concerns with Dr. Kellogg and Dr. Harrison, saying I felt as though Paul's life was disjointed and in a downward spiral with the stakes getting higher with each passing week.

Dr. Harrison concurred. "You are absolutely correct," he said via email. "Paul is going to flounder and feel worse about himself as he continues to lack structure and direction. There is not a simple solu-tion to suggest for you to prevent self-destructive tendencies on Paul's part. This is a particularly vulnerable time for you, so a good time to get a family therapist involved."

Medication changes were ongoing. In an effort to gain more control over Paul's anxiety, Dr. Harrison had us wean Paul from the Luvox and begin Paxil—a change that Paul said increased his tension and his worries. We then substituted Celexa for the Paxil, and Paul reported feeling relief. At the same time, the Adderall was replaced with Strattera in hopes of addressing Paul's attentional problems without exacerbating his tremors.

One mid-summer evening, my family was gathered on the screened-in porch at my parents' house as my stepfather started to behave strangely, petting a dog that wasn't there—and never had been in my memory. We called an ambulance and, just before it arrived, Paul walked in. Dad said, "Hi, Paul," which were to be the last words he ever spoke in that house.

As the paramedics carried Dad off the porch, I prayed he would rebound. But he had suffered a stroke, and he died in the hospital a few days later. Even though Dad was in his early nineties, I was shocked by his death. His general good health and sharp mind—not to mention his multiple older siblings, all of whom lived to be 100 or close to it—had made me think he would easily outlive my mother.

A few months earlier, I had argued with him—the first and only time—about getting Mommie into adult day care; eventually I convinced him to let me take him to see some places, one of which he reluctantly agreed to. As the two of us were driving back home after registering her, we talked about the free time he would have and how he would use it. He said he would go to the library and read, and in the nice weather he thought he might walk to the City Dock and read the newspaper there.

I was pleased because the program had activities my mother would likely enjoy, and Dad would get a break and still have her home, as he wanted, in the evenings. But after a few days of my mother's attendance at the program, Dad decided she would not return. He had paid for a month, and I think she went for three days.

"WHY?" I asked—I was furious with him.

"She doesn't like the van driver," he said.

Good God! Talk about the sandwich generation!

In addition to our grief in losing our beloved stepfather, my sisters and I had to forge a plan for Mommie, who was unable to do anything for herself. We continued her in-home care provider during the day, and the three of us took turns spending the evening and staying overnight with her. As we did this, still with our own families and careers, we looked into assisted living facilities. As focused as we were, it took months to find the right place and take care of the logistics, not to mention moving her out of her home of twenty years.

It wasn't an easy time for any of us, and leaving Mommie that first day in a new place was heart-wrenching. But she adjusted well enough and, since the facility was about five minutes from my office, I was able to visit her every day after work.

*

PAUL DECIDED OVER the summer that he was interested in plumbing, and we began making phone calls and submitting applications. In the fall, he had an interview and was hired on the spot as a plumber's helper for a small company in South County. Just before this good news, I had written to Dr. Harrison to provide an update:

Paul is doing well relative to the last year or so. He has not had any bouts of losing his temper or inappropriate interactions with me this fall. I see signs of maturity—he does not overreact to disappointments or stressful situations—and a more cheerful demeanor in general. I can't help but think the medication is better addressing his anxiety, although his inattention doesn't seem to be changed by the Strattera, which probably isn't as high a priority given the total picture.

Paul never missed a day on the job. In fact, he was very serious about being on time and having the right supplies. He started to go to bed at 9:30, telling me he liked the feeling of waking up early, before the 6:30 alarm went off. I was proud of him. But after a couple of months, he started telling me the people he worked with made fun of him and said he wasn't learning fast enough. Even though he never missed a beat and the consistency of his mood and demeanor continued to reflect general stability, I noticed increased anxiety on Sunday evenings.

One day at work, Paul went out to his car to get his lunch; when he returned, the door to the shop was locked and he couldn't get in. He could hear laughter inside, and he tried the door a few more times before getting back in his car and driving home. In telling me about it, he was calm. "They didn't want me there, Mom," he said.

Paul asked his father for help, which paid off in short order. Thanks to Don, Paul started a new job at Exotic Lumber, a specialty lumber yard in Annapolis that sold fine wood obtained from all over the world with a clientele that included cabinet makers, boat builders, and other craftsmen. Paul was one of three people, joining the owner, Bill West—a South African with a big heart and a colorful personality—and a young college graduate.

Paul's work included loading and unloading lumber and moving pallets of wood with a forklift. He also learned to use the saw and help customers. Paul liked the work and appreciated being in a more genteel environment. He also felt good about his father's help and wanted to put his best foot forward to earn his father's respect.

Working all week from 8:30 to 5:00 provided the needed routine, but even so there were challenges. I didn't know whether Paul's drinking or his overall anxiety was the bigger culprit. Looking back, I realize they were intertwined.

Paul was doing well at work, and Bill West took him under his wing, enlisting Paul to join him in projects around his house during non-working hours. Fortunately, Exotic Lumber was less than a mile from our house, meaning Paul could easily ride his bike to work, which he needed to do since his sporadic behavior had prompted me to take his car away. He was rational and civil most days, but not reliably so.

One evening, I could hear Paul on the phone arguing with Sara. I went upstairs to tell him to keep his voice down and saw that he was in the shower with the cordless phone.

I did raise my voice: "Get off the phone," I said, "or get out of the shower! NOW!"

As I turned to leave the bathroom, the phone hit me in the back—Paul had thrown it at me. I wasn't physically hurt, but I was angry. I had had it.

After a few minutes of collecting my thoughts, I decided to call the police. I calmly told Paul I had done so, explaining that he had crossed a line and people cannot live in a situation where they aren't safe. He was sitting on a bench in the bathroom and started to cry, saying he was sorry. I knew he meant it. But I also knew I needed to let the police come, to send a strong and memorable message about behavior that plainly could not be tolerated.

As far as calling the police goes, I would advise a parent in a similar situation to do the same. But I regret the decision I made in the minutes that followed.

A young officer came to the house. Together we went upstairs where Paul was still sitting on the bench, hanging his head and tearful. After saying a few words to Paul, and listening to Paul's respectful reply, the officer took me into the hallway. He looked at my back and said he could see a red mark where the phone had hit me, and he wanted to photograph it. I told him that was unnecessary, it wasn't even sore. "I didn't call the police because I was hurt," I said. "I simply wanted to teach my son that his action was unacceptable." He asked me if I wanted to press charges, and I said I did not.

"If you *really* want to teach your son a lesson," the officer then said, "you will let me take him to the station. We won't keep him there long, and you can pick him up when we call you in a couple hours."

I said I didn't know if that was a good idea. The officer, who looked to be about Paul's age, said, "He will remember it more if he goes to the station. We will not mistreat him."

I reluctantly agreed.

After three hours had passed, around 10:30, I called the police station and was told that Paul had been taken to a room in the basement of the courthouse for sentencing, and there was no way to make contact with anyone there.

"Sentencing? What do you mean?" I asked pleadingly.

I was dumbfounded, and foolishly continued, making multiple statements:

"I was told to pick him up at the police station . . ."

"He is on medication and it's critical that he not miss a dose . . ."

"He has a job and it's past his bedtime."

None of this mattered to the person on the phone.

I called my friend and lawyer, Alan Legum, who explained there was nothing I could do other than contact a bail bondsman.

"Bail bondsman?"—these words had never crossed my lips. I had enjoyed fifty-five years of ignorance of such things. But Paul needed his medication. And he did not need to be in jail.

By 3:00 a.m., I was meeting a total stranger in the parking lot behind the courthouse. I paid him $500 in cash in exchange for Paul, who had been arrested. There would be a court date.

A week before Paul and I had to appear in court, my mother was taken to the hospital, where my sisters and I spoke to the doctor and learned that she had a strangulated hernia. It was a condition that, as the doctor put it, "was not compatible with life." We were told she would live no more than two days, so the three of us settled in for the duration, making sure her living will was honored and she was comfortable and knew we were there.

Each day, for what ended up being fourteen days, we thought was our mother's last, with the day of Paul's hearing being no exception.

Paul and I entered the courtroom and sat down. I had typed a formal letter to the judge, which I passed up to him before the proceedings began, asking if our case could be heard on the early side of those on the day's docket, explaining that my mother was on her deathbed at Anne Arundel Medical Center and I wanted to be with her. I included her name, the name of her doctor, and her hospital room number to help substantiate the information.

Then I sat there for *hours*, desperately wanting to be in the hospital, and without the ability to use my phone and therefore to know if my mother was still living. I felt like a caged animal. I was trapped in this courtroom, and in this state of mind, as the cases dragged on, ours being among the last to be heard. In hindsight, I guess protocol would suggest that it's inappropriate to ask His Honor for favors—yet another world unknown to me at that time. But, at least, Paul was given probation before judgment, and thus the assault charge would not remain on his record.

I must say, I resented that cop who flat-out lied to me, and whose veiled agenda trumped our well-being, inflicting unnecessary harms on both Paul and me. But life goes on and I didn't look back.

My mother died a few days later at the age of eighty-eight. Even though she had gradually declined over a handful of years, we didn't escape the sorrows of her death. Never again to see her face or hold her hand seemed unimaginable. In all, I knew I had been blessed with three wonderful parents, but my sisters and I had suddenly become the family's lead generation. The cushion provided by all who came before us was completely gone.

*

PAUL CONTINUED TO enjoy working at Exotic Lumber, but his behavior at home was increasingly unpredictable. I told Dr.

Harrison that within a six-week period, Paul's drinking seemed to have become a "need" rather than a choice. Paul did agree to attend AA meetings but was often agitated, a feeling he complained about, saying it had *encouraged* his drinking. As a result, Dr. Harrison eliminated the Strattera and increased the Zyprexa. Paul's weight, which had remained a problem for him, began to climb, and thus the Zyprexa was slightly reduced.

It wasn't long before a relatively new drug, Abilify, was prescribed in place of the Zyprexa. Abilify addressed Paul's overall stability with reduced side effects—one of which was weight gain—representing an improvement for Paul. All in all, Abilify turned out to be a much better medication for Paul and, while more expensive, it was worth it.

Unfortunately, Bill West and Paul began to clash, eventually resulting in the termination of Paul's employment at Exotic Lumber. I can see Paul now, furiously pedaling his bike up the street toward our house with tears streaming down his face. When he came inside, a puddle in my arms, he recounted what Bill had said: "I can't be your psychiatrist!"

I didn't know any details, but I sure didn't harbor any animosity toward this man who had employed Paul for nearly a year and taught him so much. I was sorry, though, to see it come to an end. In spite of their parting, Paul considered Bill West a friend for the rest of his life.

After being unemployed for about a month, Paul got temporary work with a friend of mine, Jim Praley, whose law office was converting paper records to digital and needed someone to scan documents. After a few months of this, Paul's father came through again. Paul was hired by California Closets, where he operated a beam saw with a Windows operating system to cut custom closet components, a job he would have—although off and on—for three years. The franchise where Don had connections was located in Arbutus, Maryland, about thirty miles outside Annapolis.

With Paul's work life feeling secure, he and Sara and another friend moved into an apartment in Eastport, an Annapolis neighborhood just a couple of miles from home. Paul's routine, which worked quite well, was to come home in the morning to shower, get his lunch, and take his medication. I got the sense he knew he needed this touchdown, and I was happy to have it too. Overall, I was comforted by this milestone in his growing up.

After his ninety-day trial period at California Closets, Paul achieved a more permanent status that included benefits, prompting Paul and Sara to sign a lease for a nicer apartment, without the roommate. Paul was very excited about the prospect of their having their own place. About the same time, we started seeing Gail Martin, a family therapist in Glen Burnie, Maryland, on Saturdays, and we liked her very much. Things were looking up.

Then Sara announced that she was pregnant. She told Paul she would have the baby, but she couldn't honor their pending lease because she was moving home to live with her parents.

Chapter 8

SO STRANDED, WE SIT

Our feet and hands are restrained by the
Humility of watching the world
Move freely below us in swift movement;
With camouflaged work attire
And batons concealed to briefcases,
Ready for the battle of youth.
We, however, came unprepared;
Meeting the dawn with our eyes
But brains still stuck in their wet,
Midnight slumber… searching.

IT'S NOT FAIR. Young people without handicaps like Paul's get the gift of a buffer between high school and figuring out how to earn a living. I know this isn't universally true, but in my world it is, and always has been.

College is that buffer.

Make no mistake: College is a gift. Kids get to break away from their parents' rule—which, developmentally, they need to do—but with a safety net. They have expectations to meet and rules to follow, along with a network of caring adults who are there to counsel, teach, and otherwise support the discovery of interests and the shaping of futures. On top of all this, there are peers who, from classes to parties to dorm life, provide camaraderie, inspiration, and challenges—all packed full of lessons about life and how to manage it.

But by the luck of the draw, Paul didn't get any of this. And absolutely everyone else in his family did.

While Paul didn't expect much, and didn't ever resent those who had more, his needs weren't met. He was too smart to be satisfied with a lifetime of menial work but seemingly saddled with too many differences to avoid that sentence, a sentence that included poverty-level wages.

And he was isolated. Few knew how smart he was.

For years, I've looked at parents of Down's Syndrome children with envy. Ironic, isn't it? What you fear most at the outset of motherhood can look so good. Those kids are content.

*

WITHIN TWENTY-FOUR HOURS of learning Sara's news, Paul moved home. It was a Sunday. He cried most of the day. It was clear he was trying to reckon with his role in it all. And he was sad to have lost the apartment. I sensed he was overwhelmed with the short- and long-term considerations.

I started by explaining why Sara's wanting to be at home made sense. Furthermore, I told him, "You have no choice but to accept the fact that any decisions are Sara's to make."

"I'm worried about her," he said.

"I know you're worried about her, and I don't blame you, but you have to recognize that her position in this is harder than yours."

"But I feel helpless," he said. And after a few minutes of silence he added, "I'm afraid, Mom."

I couldn't refute that. I was afraid too—for him. But I couldn't let him know how much. I did my best to guide and support him, but it was evident that he was poorly equipped to handle the sweeping uncertainty, not to mention the gravity, of fatherhood.

The harmony of recent months deteriorated fast. Paul and Sara saw one another frequently but were prone to disagreements. Stress was in the air. I took them to the new apartment complex, where the three of us met with the manager, who released them from the obligations of the lease agreement they had signed, providing a little relief.

As Paul's anxiety grew, so too did his disregard for me—met by increasing toughness on my part. As much as I understood the strain he was under, I just couldn't let him take it out on me.

One evening, I made him sleep on the screened-in porch, telling him I didn't want him in the house until he learned how to be consistently respectful. I held the line too. I did give him a pillow and blanket, but I locked the door and turned off the inside lights. There would be no negotiating.

I was surprised by the extent of his regression. Having seen signs of maturity setting in, I had thought we were over the hump. I know growing up is two steps forward and one back—it sure was for me—but this was more like two forward and three or four back.

Other unacceptable behaviors caught me completely off guard. One morning, I noticed my lawnmower was missing. After checking with my neighbor, I mentioned it to Paul in passing, telling him it must have been stolen and I was going to report it to the police. After a staring spell that concerned me for unrelated reasons, Paul looked at me and told me he had sold it.

I was flabbergasted.

"You *what?*"

"I'm sorry, Mom. I shouldn't have done it, but I needed money to help Sara and I don't get paid until today."

"I'm speechless, Paul! What on earth made you think this was okay?"

"I'm sorry. I will get my check this afternoon and pay you back. You can get the mower today."

"Gee, thanks." I was pretty near the end of my rope with him.

This would be my foray into the world of pawn shops, an experience I could never have imagined in the life I was supposed to lead.

I left work and drove to the pawn shop, located along a busy four-lane thoroughfare with end-to-end strip centers, used car lots, and fast food joints. I don't know why I'd never noticed the place, given its two-foot-high neon letters screaming "PAWN SHOP."

As I approached, I could see that its few parking spaces were taken, meaning I had to pull into the fine establishment next door, separated from the pawn shop property by a chain link fence and some scruffy shrubs that went all the way to the road. I got out of the car and scurried around the fencing, moving quickly to avoid oncoming traffic. A little daunting, but nothing compared to my return to the car when, on top of having my back to the cars whizzing by, I was pushing my lawnmower. A proud moment for me, prompting me to be thankful my mother couldn't see me. Or I hoped she couldn't.

It was around this same time that I noticed cash missing from my purse, or I thought I did. I had never allowed either child to go in my purse. They knew to bring it to me when I was giving them money for one reason or another. I, and only I, went in my purse. Making a mental note of my suspicions, I also told Keely to be on guard. One particular evening after work, Keely and I were in the kitchen and realized we both had our purses over our shoulders. On the one hand, this was a sad picture but, on the other, Keely and I did laugh when I suggested, "Just pretend you're at a cocktail party, keeping your purse over your shoulder all evening."

On the 4th of July 2005, I was hosting a party for my family and close friends. It was early in the evening, and Paul was demanding my attention. As people began to arrive, his inappropriate attention-seeking antics escalated.

I remember this as though it happened this morning. To avoid drawing undo attention, I took him out on the front porch and gave him an ultimatum. "You cannot stay here. You are out of control, and I will not have it. You choose—and choose now—the homeless shelter or a psychiatric hospital."

I didn't raise my voice, but I was dead serious. He knew it too. He chose the hospital.

Minutes later, as the two of us were on Route 50 headed for the Baltimore Washington Hospital Center, which had the only psychiatric ward near us, Paul politely told me where to turn. As if we'd driven into another dimension, his angst toward me vanished, and all I could figure was that he must have felt relief.

It was in a small room in that hospital that night when I learned Paul was addicted to cocaine. Before any sort of assessment, he announced this to the intake nurse. I was shocked but didn't flinch. Again, he felt relief. I didn't.

I missed my party, which didn't matter. But staying awake all night in what seemed like a vault rather than a room, seated in a straight-backed chair with Paul snoring away in a deluxe La-Z-Boy made up with sheets and a blanket, somehow didn't seem like my idea of a holiday. After a few hours of sitting still in that air-conditioned cube, wearing just shorts and a t-shirt, I finally decided to take Paul's blanket. *I should've done it sooner*, I thought. The thing is, he had a sheet and he was sleeping. Seemed fair to me.

In the morning we finally saw a psychiatrist, who was inclined to send Paul directly to a rehabilitation facility. I intervened and arranged for him to confer with our family therapist, Gail Martin, after which it was decided that Paul would go to Sheppard Pratt Psychiatric Hospital. I was able to follow the ambulance, thankfully joined by my sister Erin, and could see Paul's expressionless face looking out the back window, staring right at me, the whole way to Baltimore.

My heart was heavy. As I drove under the archway of the landmark gatehouse—a two-story Tudor Revival-style fieldstone structure that distinguishes the entrance to the Sheppard Pratt campus—I thought of Paul alone on that big school bus and now alone in an ambulance making the same drive. But this time we turned toward the hospital rather than the school.

Paul was hospitalized at Sheppard Pratt for a week, during which time the doctors told me he needed a dual diagnosis program. They explained that dual diagnosis, sometimes referred to as co-occurring disorders, is a term used when someone has a mental illness and a substance use disorder and that integrated care is important but often challenging to find.

Fortunately, Paul was sent to Warwick Manor Behavioral Health, a facility in East New Market, Maryland, that provided inpatient treatment and had a psychiatrist on staff. After a couple of days of detoxification, we were able to visit Paul and attend family meetings.

With an allée of old trees creating a formidable entrance, the sprawling property and meandering 1950s ranch-style home, once a retreat facility for the Baltimore Colts, overlooks the Warwick River. After an introduction to the staff and an overview of the program, Paul and I sat outside among other families milling about. I remember looking across the manicured lawn, its greenness striking a stark contrast with the pristine white Adirondack chairs arranged in a row facing the water, when Paul said to me, "I would like to spend the rest of my life here."

I was gratified to know that Paul appreciated the care, but his words made me realize just how much he had lived life on the edge as well as the slew of worries he must have racked up without any idea of how to untangle it all. The setting comforted me on the one hand but made me feel so sorry for Paul on the other. In addition to grappling with the implications for his future, I struggled even to imagine his interactions within the world of illegal drugs.

Throughout Paul's life, he had been an easy mark in many ways. More than once when he was younger, for example, he'd walked to the corner store for a candy bar and returned home without the change. Yes, he was absent-minded, but I knew too that he was ripe for being taken advantage of.

I was inspired by the Warwick Manor staff, particularly Paul's counselor, John Carruthers, who was as kind as he was knowledgeable. I remember asking him which of Paul's dual conditions he thought was primary and he couldn't say. But he did tell me he was struck by the level of Paul's mental illness, and he worried that long-term employment for Paul was a pipe dream. Once again, I found myself confronting a new reality.

Since California Closets had agreed to hold Paul's job, insurance was not an immediate problem. Even so, coverage for this level of care would run out within a few weeks, and a clinically managed medium-intensity program would be the next step.

In the fall, Paul entered a six-month residential program located in Baltimore. Based on a twelve-step methodology, treatment included individual and group counseling with the goal of re-entry into the community. Paul's medication remained the same, Abilify and Celexa, and was administered by the program.

*

SIX WEEKS BEFORE her due date, Sara went into labor. And in mid-November 2005, Paul's daughter and my granddaughter, Kayla, was born. Paul was able to get a pass from his program and joined Sara's mother in accompanying Sara for the birth, while Keely, Sara's father and sister, and my sister and I waited outside the delivery room. Because Kayla was premature, she spent her first few weeks in the NICU, after which she went home and continued to thrive.

Paul loved her! We all loved her. She was, and remains, a delight. While my mother and father were no longer living, I thought about Kayla being their first great-grandchild—a girl no less! Some weeks later my family joined Sara's for Kayla's baptism and a gathering after. There was a lot of uncertainty regarding the future, but our collective love for Kayla was not in question.

Sara's mother made sure Paul signed paternity papers while in the hospital and talked to him about child support expectations within a day of Kayla's homecoming. Again, as parents of Sara and Paul—both of whom were in vulnerable positions—we didn't talk about the best way to impart this information to Paul, or the timing of it. But as a follow-up, with two goals in mind, I made sure to have a talk with Paul the next day.

First, I explained child support in general terms to him, emphasizing its importance and the simple logic behind the legal requirement. I told him that when two people bring a child into the world, the law is designed to ensure that those two people are held accountable and additionally are spared the stress involved in negotiating the details, explaining the standardized formula. Overly simplified perhaps, but he understood.

Next, I wanted to ease his anxiety in order to avoid his collapsing from the weight of it all. I explained that everyone wanted Paul to be productive for his sake as well as for Kayla's and, when he became able, he would want to contribute his fair share to benefit Kayla. But during the time he was unable to work due to his health, he didn't need to worry. I could see his relief.

I also wanted to make sure he didn't feel as though the law was "out to get him." Or that Sara and her parents were, or that the mother pockets the hard-earned cash of the father for her own needs, or any other scenario that his young mind might conjure up to make it all seem unfair—to make himself the victim. I knew that seeing multiple sides of an issue—even when your own best interest tempted a narrow view—helped in accepting challenging circumstances and in promoting a peace of mind about that which just *is*. In sum, victimhood—especially when self-imposed by short-sightedness—is an unnecessary burden, one I wanted to spare him.

Down the line, we would face some child-support challenges, requiring negotiation and the help of lawyers, but we all did okay.

Paul took his responsibilities seriously, regarding both financial matters and his interest in his daughter and her life. He saw Kayla when he could, wanted what was best for her, advocated for her within the family, and obviously loved her dearly.

Throughout Paul's time in Baltimore—which ended up being nearly eight years—Sara and Kayla often joined me in seeing Paul on weekends. We would usually go out to lunch and then visit a park or a museum, or simply take a walk, exploring areas such as Canton, Fells Point, and the Inner Harbor.

Even though we were making the best of an unfortunate situation, we did have some good days. But we had our share of bad ones as well. After Paul's successful completion of the six-month program, he moved into a transition house in Baltimore, where he was afforded the freedom to work and come and go as he pleased, although he did have a curfew and would remain with the counseling services. Sadly, he relapsed almost immediately. And in doing so, he went down fast. I was alerted to this dreadful news when his house manager called to tell me Paul was missing; they had not seen him for two days.

Overcome by panic, I fought to breathe but then to reason with myself. There was no time to dwell on the massiveness of the problem; I had to do something, which would require a cool head. You cope in manageable chunks.

Given my access to Paul's bank account, for which he had only a debit card and a small balance, I could see that he had made a cash withdrawal and paid for a hotel room, making it easy for me to track him down. I drove to Baltimore and found Paul in the hotel. He told me he had relapsed and didn't know what to do. I called the emergency number for his program and learned that he was officially dismissed and could not return. Pointing out his perfect compliance until that time, I asked if there was any path for restoring his relationship. Sadly, the answer was "no."

Part of me wanted to nurture and protect him, and part of me wanted to let him suffer the consequences of his decisions. I went the "tough love" route, despite my uncertainty about whether that was the right choice. Today I know I was wrong, and if I were ever to find myself in an identical circumstance, I would make a different decision. My heart may have been in the right place, but I was tragically uninformed. In truth, I believe that the people in the program, who advised and influenced me, were acting unethically. Or, maybe they too were woefully unenlightened, as I have come to know is all too often the case in countless treatment programs throughout the country. But my grasp of how to navigate in Paul's best interest was way off in the future.

I told Paul he couldn't continue to stay in a hotel using a credit card for an account in arrears. His only choice for that night was to sleep in a homeless shelter.

I drove Paul to a men's shelter where entry was permitted at a particular hour in the late evening, with a morning meal provided before the departure time. When we arrived, men were lined up to get in. Watching Paul join them, with a garbage bag containing his few belongings slung over his shoulder, was agonizing. I hesitated . . . Then I saw a policeman and lowered my window. I told him that my son was in the line and I hoped he would be safe.

"If you want your son to be safe," said the officer, "don't leave him here."

But I drove away. Somehow, in spite of my steely heart, I cried the whole way home. The next day, I called Paul's counselor, Patricia, whom Paul and I both liked. Even though he wouldn't be able to continue seeing her, I wanted her advice. She said he might be able to find long-term shelter at American Rescue Workers, a resource for homeless men where there was a twelve-step program.

When Paul called, I passed on Patricia's suggestion. He said he would consider it and let me know. I didn't hear from him for days.

When I did, he told me he had entered the program at American Rescue Workers and was staying in a dormitory over the church.

Paul spent three months in this faith-based program that provided shelter, food, and rehabilitation in the form of "spiritual guidance" in exchange for work in one of several endeavors that sustained their operation. He attended the required church service every Sunday, and I did as well, often taking Sara and Kayla. Paul wasn't happy there, and everything about it went against my grain, but he conformed to the expectations, ultimately enabling his readmittance to his former program, where he started over.

*

AFTER A SECOND successful completion of the highly structured six-month program, Paul again moved into a transition house where, in spite of the lock he kept on his bedroom door, he was robbed of the few things he had of any value. This experience upset Paul and he began to make a case for leaving Baltimore City. "I'm tired of all the rules in a program with too many people who don't follow them," Paul told me. "I don't fit here, Mom. It's not a good place for me."

Having returned to his job at California Closets, Paul rented a room in a house in Arbutus, enabling him to walk to work. The house was owned by a woman, Gloria, and her middle-aged son, Bob, both of whom lived there. Gloria liked Paul and made him breakfast before work and even started to pack his lunch, which Paul appreciated, telling me, "She looks out for me, Mom, and that makes me feel good." I went over on weekends to take Paul for groceries and to monitor his well-being.

One fateful morning, everything changed. I can't possibly describe it as well as Paul did in a paragraph he'd saved in his laptop:

The sun shown through my window and I awoke to the same bleak reality that had greeted me the previous day. Always slow to rise, ungroomed and pale, I put my shivering feet into my work boots and followed the stairs. Nothing would prepare me for what would greet me in my very next few steps. I crossed the living room floor and froze on the kitchen's threshold. There she sat lifeless, head cocked back toward the ceiling, but yet her eyes seemed to meet mine through a lifeless stare, shocking my mind in 1000 pulses.

Paul immediately awakened Bob, who called the paramedics. After their arrival and the removal of Gloria's body, Paul went on to work. But he was shaken, calling me multiple times throughout the day.

In the days that followed, his complaints shifted from the shock and sorrow of Gloria's death to the fact that her son seemed unable to function without her and was "going off the deep end." Paul seemed frightened and wanted to move, but he didn't want to give up his job. I too wanted him to move, and quickly.

I found a room for rent in a house in nearby Halethorpe, less than a mile—along a sidewalk-lined street—from California Closets. Paul and I went to see the room. We met the owner of the house, who lived in the finished basement, renting the bedrooms on the second floor. In addition to the owner, who was a paramedic, we met another tenant who was a firefighter. Both men were in their thirties and very personable, and we felt good about them and the tidy house. Paul had been drug-free for over a year and was doing well, and I thought these slightly older men with responsible, community-minded jobs would be a good match for him. A week later, to Paul's great relief, I helped him move in.

Paul was interested in taking a class, and he was looking into the offerings at the nearby Community College of Baltimore when he met a man who convinced him that enrolling in TESST College of Technology was a good idea. This man had given Paul the details of the courses and the fees, breaking down how the tuition could be covered. Paul called to share his enthusiasm with me, saying he had all the information and was very excited about it. He told me it was a nine-month program that would give him certification in HVAC.

I was more than a little dubious. But Paul didn't want to hear about any aspect of my skepticism, refuting each of my concerns. Even so, I advised him not to do it, saying the community college made more sense. But I didn't come on too strong for the simple reason that I didn't think it was a battle I needed to fight. I was confident that Paul wouldn't be able to negotiate the financial process without a cosigner.

A month later, Paul confessed. He had enrolled in the program, bought all the required textbooks, and was beginning to realize the pace and the material were overwhelming. He was despondent, stressed about the debt he had taken on, and deflated by his inability to keep up. His financial obligation was more than $6,000, and he didn't know what to do.

I was mildly annoyed with him, but I was furious with whoever had enabled this debacle. Paul gave me the name of his "friend" and I called the school, speaking first with an admission representative, then the financial aid office, and ultimately the director of education. Usually not a whole lot goes my way when I face off with an institution, particularly a for-profit one, but my fury, combined with my knowledge of ethical practices in admission and financial aid, paid off: Paul was released from any and all obligations. He was relieved but still reeling from the disappointment, on top of the realization that he'd been hoodwinked.

But my own naiveté was about to surface.

It would be several months before I knew it, but one of Paul's housemates was addicted to cocaine, a worrisome discovery that prompted me to explore recovery or transition houses in the area. Paul was just too vulnerable for me to feel comfortable about his safety. But by the time my thinking turned up an alternative, it was too late.

Once again, on a downhill racer: Not only had Paul started to use cocaine, but also, to support his habit, he had stolen $500 from a new and unsuspecting tenant in the house. Paul was arrested, charged with a felony, and was being held at Baltimore Central Booking, a notoriously brutal correction facility in the heart of the city.

I was frantic and distraught, but mostly I was afraid. Gripped by an "in-over-my-head" kind of fear, I wasn't thinking clearly. So much so, that I was momentarily conflicted about the merits of posting bail. But I came to my senses when I learned that Paul couldn't get his medications if he was detained, something I soon came to know was but one of a thousand reasons to keep him as far away as possible from any such place.

Thanks to a connection my sister Jennie provided, I found a residential rehabilitation program that would take Paul while he awaited sentencing and where Keely was able to deliver him upon his release from Central Booking. I was grateful for his immediate safety and hopeful that his placement in a dual diagnosis program would work in his favor when it came time for a judge to decide his fate. The thought of him in jail for an extended period was unbearable.

I guess the outcome of his trial could have been worse, but I didn't think so at the time. Upon hearing it, I literally fell to my knees. Paul was taken directly from court to Central Booking, where he would be incarcerated for several months as he awaited a bed in a specified residential dual diagnosis treatment program in Baltimore. He would be on supervised probation for two and a half years and was ordered by the court to pay restitution to his former housemate, which he did, and was relieved to do.

Infamous for its inhumane conditions, Central Booking lived up to its reputation. This is the big league in terms of what you do not want for your child. In reality, the place made the psychiatric hospital in Delaware seem like the information highway. Did I really complain about communication there? I may have been overwhelmed and confused, but nurses answered the phone. Ask anyone who has experience with Central Booking what it's like. No one communicates. No one is nice. Nice is for sissies. I am a sissy; Paul was a bigger one.

*

PAUL SPENT THE rest of his life as a felon, shattering his already bleak chances for employment. Just after he was given this lifetime status, Maryland law changed. A theft of $1,000 or more was classified as a felony, anything less was a misdemeanor. But the new ruling didn't matter for Paul. He was a few days on the wrong side of that change. He was a felon forever.

I know what Paul did was wrong. There are consequences, and there should be. A free society depends on it. But jail—where he couldn't take his medication and where he was preyed upon—was not the right place for him. And a lifetime as a felon, beyond challenging an uphill battle to be productive, precluded the ability to vote—a right that Paul cherished.

Paul and I were able to communicate through daily letters. Our first exchange is transcribed below. The letter from me to Paul is in my possession only because Paul wrote to me using the back side of my letter. Figuring out how to get paper to an inmate was a challenge for the days ahead.

September 2, 2008
Dear Paulie,

I want you to know I am thinking of you and hope you are okay. I know you can be strong enough to get through this and learn something about yourself and the world. Jail must be a very harsh experience, especially for someone like you, who is so sweet and kind.

But I am sure you understand our society depends on people who govern themselves within the parameters of the law, and who aren't a threat to others or themselves. I can understand your plight—and know addiction is impossible to navigate without help and that bad luck can lead to a bad decision— but the rules for acceptable and unacceptable behavior can't take individual circumstances into account. I say this just to clarify that I am on your side, I understand you, but the legal system just can't fine tune the rules. It's important for you to know you have not been singled out, and you must try hard to keep resentment from getting the best of you.

I am glad you are willing to get the treatment you need both for mental health and self-medicating. You have always wanted to deny your mental health struggles (which I under-stand) because you wanted to be "like everybody else." But you are you, and have to appreciate that you are important and worthy of respect and good care.

Having a health issue of any sort—diabetes, high cholesterol, whatever—requires a doctor's attention and careful monitor-ing. So in that way, it's a bummer, but not an embarrassment. It's not shameful. Stealing from an innocent bystander is shameful; but treatment for a health problem is not.

There is hope out there too, in the form of good people. Jerome wants you to know he got your things from BBH and will keep them for you. Jerome also said you are a "great kid." Despite the roller coaster ride you were on, he said you "have a heart of gold." No one can teach that—it's just "you" and you are worth the fight you have before you.

Win that fight, Paul, and you will be a resource to others. If each of us can do something to make this world a better place, then our lives are worthwhile.

I did learn you can't have a visitor for 60 days. I hope you are out before then. I don't have to tell you how much I love you but I will anyway: I love you with all my heart.

Your loving mother

Sep 8
Dear Mom,

Hey. I am writing in return to your letter to let you know how appreciative I am. I am using the back of your letter because I dont have paper. I love and miss my family so mutch that it makes me sad sometimes. But it totally eases my mind to hear that you understand why I've used drugs.

It's all because I've been trying to be someone I'm not and hiding who I reely am whitch is a kind and loving indevidual who was meant for great things. One of my dreams is to raise a family of my own and teach Kayla to be the best. I wish I could talk to her. I miss her allot. and allthough its going to be tough to try to father Kayla, in a way Im glad that I don't have that full burden yet because I can't take care of anyone unless I take care of my mental illness and my addiction problems first.

How is Kayla and Sara doing by the way. I wouldn't blame Sara if she had a new boyfriend. It would hurt because I really do love her. my hurt will heal in time thogh and I'll have allot of time to think about the things I've done wrong in the next couple months because my bed date for gaudenzia is not until nov 15.

I really hope you had a fun time at the beach. I wish I could have been there.

Are you mad at me at all? I really am sorry for letting you down. and myself down.

Now I'm sorry to ask but there are some things I need to be mailed to me. I need clothes. Alls I'm allowd to receve is 3 white t shirts, 3 boxers and 3 pairs of socks and the t shirts have to be white. I only have the pair of clothes I was wearing when I got here.

Also can you send me a mony order in the mail with my name and jail ID number on it? They will put it directly into my account in jail so I can buy toiletrys and food. They have at jail what is called comessary. It is a store you order food and toiletrys from. You dont have to send it, but it makes life here a whole lot better. If you do send a mony order it has to be in an envalope seperate from the clothing package, and it has to be a mony order. no checks are exepted.

They don't feed us very good meals so your always hungry. Also after you run out of toothpaste and stuff they don't give you more so please please send a mony order.

I really need clothes. But I have been washing my socks and boxers and t shirt by hand so the clothes can wait a couple days.

Now that they moved me to "N" section Im in a small cell with bars, before I was in a dorm. and I'll be here the rest of the time. They only let us out of these small cells every other day for an hour. Im not exaderating. Its miserable. but Im lucky I have a cool cell buddy.

Anyways I love you to death and miss you and the same goes for Keely. Tell her I love her too.

Im really homesick I want this to be over with soon. It all just feels like a bad dream.

Tell my cousins Im thinking of them too.

get in touch with Sara and tell her Im thinking of Kayla allot. I'm crying thinking about it. I want to get out of here.

Goodnight. Love you all.

In December, Paul was released from Central Booking, on probation, and sent to Gaudenzia, a treatment facility that specializes in mental health and substance use disorders. We were allowed to visit him on Christmas Eve for a two-hour holiday gathering with other families and the staff. Otherwise, he couldn't have visitors nor could he leave the facility.

It would be a long time before Paul was out from under the legal system, longer than I knew.

Chapter 9

TANGLING WITH THE LAW

Life is lovely when you allow yourself awareness of an alter ego,
An imaginary friend, sometimes a darker half
Who rather than imagined can be frighteningly real.
Tortured in his own right, he's experienced all the turmoil I have.
He's been there all along. I didn't give him much choice
But to tag along with me through my 10,000 hours of hopelessness
And the many bologna sandwiches awaiting us upon consciousness,
Or the bag lunches at the end of filthy lines with three teeth in all.

GAUDENZIA SEEMED LIKE a five-star hotel compared to Central Booking. In reality, it was a dreary 1940s-era flat-roofed brick building with a hospital-like interior. The residents' rooms, situated along both sides of a corridor, each had two beds and a window. After four months of not seeing the outdoors, Paul was particularly grateful for the window.

When he'd completed thirty days, Paul could have visitors during a two-hour window on weekends. Even though Sara and Paul had decided to end their romantic relationship, Sara and Kayla visited Paul several times. As a matter of fact, they saw him more than I did in the first weeks of this leg of our journey. I talked with Paul on the phone most evenings, but I needed a break from the frenzy of mad dashes to Baltimore and back.

We humans can sustain an unrealistic pace for an extended time, despite exhaustion. And then, we stop; we catch our breath. I don't believe this is a conscious decision nor do I think it is based on the degree or the duration of the overload, but rather on instinct. We stop when we know we can. Paul was safe. I could regroup and tend to the frayed edges of my life.

Breathe. Gather your reserves.

Paul's investment in the recovery program filled me with hope. Using a spiral notebook, he recorded his thoughts, wrote poetry, and wrote letters. He helped put together a flyer with program-related announcements for fellow residents and felt proud to be making a contribution—one that aligned with his otherwise hidden strengths. He also submitted a poem to a more widespread regional publication and was excited to report that it had been published.

His letters to me consistently spoke of his activities as well as his soul searching. His first letter, wishing me a Happy New Year, included:

I'm sending you a copy of the *Free State Region for Narcotics Anonymous Newsletter* for Maryland and Delaware. They published one of my poems! I was really happy about that. I thought it was cool. I'm also sending the newsletter I put together for our program here. I was proud of it. They were too. I like sharing these things with you.

I just want you to know I'm staying busy. I'm not going to give up this time and I'm very confident that I won't use drugs ever again. I know that must seem like such BS coming from me; so I'll just have to show you in the future.

After six months, the court moved Paul to Christopher's Place, a residential program designed to support the transition from problematic substance use to stable living. After a period of training, combined with volunteer work, the program would focus on finding employment and, ultimately, affordable housing.

Paul lived in a dormitory, housed in a bright and modern facility that included a cafeteria, classrooms, and a meeting center. I never saw his room, but I attended a few meetings with him and visited in the lobby, where a wide, open staircase, leading up to the living quarters, provided a view of the comings and goings of a vast array of people. Attached to the same building was Our Daily Bread, a soup kitchen where Paul volunteered, serving meals to the homeless and sorting donations of goods and clothing.

Using a computer in one of the common areas, Paul started a blog—a phenomenon then still in its early years. I think he had five followers, maybe four if you didn't count his mother. I checked it regularly and was proud of his work. For one, it was legible, and two, he used Spell Check. I wish I had printed his introduction and his posts, but I guess I thought the blog would be there indefinitely. His web address was www.blogfromthesoupkitchen.com, but sadly it is gone.

Paul's job search took him to Johns Hopkins Hospital, where he was hired to clean operating rooms between surgeries. He felt pretty good about the work, explaining to me that the lowest level of worker cleaned the hallways, a position for which there was little to no training. Paul's job, alternatively, required a high school diploma and training in the turnover and preparation of the rooms, as well as the containment and removal of contaminated instruments and supplies. Once again, Paul demonstrated his work ethic, with perfect attendance and a seriousness of purpose.

It was Paul's good fortune that Christopher's Place matched him with Ben, a mentor he loved. I think Ben's name came up in every conversation I had with Paul, and I too appreciated the friendship they formed.

Even though Paul had a disability pass for the Baltimore bus, and knew the schedule as well as anyone, he usually chose to walk to get where he needed to go. He loved to walk, and he built up surprising stamina, walking all over the city and losing weight as a result. But as wonderful as Johns Hopkins Hospital is, the surrounding neighborhood is notoriously crime-ridden. Paul often worked at night, and I did worry about his walking home. When I suggested he take the bus after dark, he said the bus was just as dangerous, and walking helped him think; he didn't want to give it up.

This walking craze would stay with him for the rest of his life. While he loved biking too, probably for the same reasons, he thought nothing of walking from Mount Washington to the Inner Harbor; or, years later, when he lived in Silver Spring, walking to the Mall in Washington, D.C., for a concert.

On a mid-December night in 2009, I got a call from a paramedic telling me Paul had been beaten up by two thugs as he was walking home from work. I was told that Paul's head was bleeding and his face was swollen and scraped, but that his wounds appeared to be mostly superficial with no signs of internal injuries. "Your son is shaken," the paramedic said. "But he's handling it well." He also told me that Paul had been forced to surrender his wallet and iPod, his only possessions other than clothing.

This was upsetting to me and to the rest of our family. In fact, Don bought a new iPod and delivered it to Paul the next day.

As streetwise as Paul had become in some ways, he didn't stand a chance if there was a physical altercation. While that was something he came by honestly, it nevertheless contributed to the long list of ways in which he felt inept, if not helpless.

This worrisome situation aside, Paul was doing well, conforming to the expectations of his program and his job. Incrementally, he was given freedoms such as overnight passes that enabled him to come home for our family events. And he didn't miss a single one.

Because Paul was working, mandated child support deducted $338 from his monthly pay, and he was "stressed out" about how he would make ends meet when his living expenses increased, which was about to happen. I knew this was weighing on Paul and felt his concerns were legitimate, but I reminded him that child support was an important obligation and, to ease his mind, said we would cross all those bridges as we came to them.

Paul's night shifts at the hospital were scheduled to cover emergency surgeries, meaning some downtime was inevitable. Killing time in a staff room that had a computer, Paul worked on his blog, joined Facebook, and decided to go on a free dating site, OkCupid.

He always managed to draw me into such things, calling me multiple times before he was satisfied.

Paul: "Which photo of me do you think is best?"
Me: "I like them both; maybe the one taken outside is better."
Paul: "What should I say about myself?"
Me: "You are good at written expression. What would you want someone to know about you?"
Paul: "I'm not good at talking about myself. I need your help!"
Me: "Don't say you are a felon."
Paul: "MOM!!!"
Me: "Just write a couple of sentences; say something about your interests—blogging, snowboarding, guitar. Maybe something about your personality, that you have a good sense of humor, or that you love animals…"
Paul: "If you were a girl, would you think I was cute?"
Me: "I am a girl. And I think you are adorable."

Conversations like this are etched in my memory due to the repetitiveness. While there was never an overarching label that summed up Paul's diagnosis, there were consistent components. In addition to anxiety, and a developmental disorder, Paul had obsessive compulsive disorder. In dealing with his OCD, I coached myself on the strategies I found most effective: (1) Provide details in your answer. You simply cannot get away with "I don't know." (2) Try to keep it lighthearted. Making him laugh—which is easy to do—eases his anxiety.

As for OkCupid, in addition to allowing you to peruse profiles based on selected criteria, like age or geography, such dating sites periodically send you a profile of an individual that their system has deemed a good "match" for you. Unlike Facebook, there are no names or addresses provided. If you choose to make contact with an individual, you can send a message using the site's platform.

I'll never forget the day OkCupid "matched" Keely and Paul! I guess you could say the system's data analytics were impressive inasmuch as these two did indeed have things in common—the same mother and father being primary! Anyway, Paul thought it was hilarious and told Keely instantly, saying he was going to post it on Facebook because it was so funny.

Keely's reply: "DON'T. YOU. DARE!"

He must have thought being matched with her was a feather in his cap. Apparently, the feeling wasn't reciprocal.

After six months in the dormitory setting, Paul was moved to a house—owned by the program—where he rented a room, a step that enabled him to enjoy aspects of life he had never known.

While there, Paul started seeing Amey, a young woman whom I met when he brought her home for his cousin Lauren's May 2010 wedding. A friendly and upbeat young woman with a lot of personality, Amey was a big hit with the family. The manager of a grocery store produce department, Amey lived in Street, Maryland, where Paul visited enough to get to know Amey's mother, Debby, who took a liking to Paul. As it turned out, Amey had a change of heart and broke Paul's, although they remained friends and saw one another again some years later. Debby stayed in touch with Paul for the rest of his life. "Paul was just a beautiful person, a breath of fresh air and such an easy boy to love," Debby later told me. "He had the free spirit of a little boy, but the depth of an old soul."

Since Paul spent his years of schooling in special education and his teenage years in an even more confined therapeutic setting, he never had much of a social life. Now nearly twenty-eight, and having ended his long relationship with Sara, Paul was entering the world of dating—in many ways for the first time. This realization crystallized for me when, by late-summer, he brought home another girlfriend, Monica, for a family crab feast at my sister Jennie's house in honor of three birthdays—mine and two of the cousins. Monica joined the whole family again in October for a celebration of Paul's birthday.

A responsible, personable and all-around lovely person, Monica was the manager of a popular Baltimore restaurant. Even though Paul wasn't in the right place to invest in a lasting partnership, I was as heartened by his choices as I was his opportunity to learn the ropes in a social realm.

*

PAUL'S EMOTIONS COULD get in his way, not consistently and not even with great frequency, but with great intensity on his part. Over the years, there were sporadic incidents of his striking out with heated words directed sometimes toward me but also at Keely and his father, and in one instance his half-sister, Annie, who at the time was a college student, living away from home, and on whom—unlike the rest of us—he could pin nothing.

In his hastily fired-off email to Annie, Paul told her he was mad and he resented her, blamed her for taking his father away from him. In true form, Paul copied me on the email. I contacted him immediately, telling him that he was just plain wrong and Annie was one hundred percent innocent. "Your pain is legitimate," I said, "and I get that. But you are not helping yourself by lashing out at Annie who bears no responsibility for your pain. Think about it, Paul. What is she supposed to do? And how do you think your email made her feel?" He heard me and expressed remorse, which I felt was sincere.

Paul's fluctuations notwithstanding, I emailed Annie myself to comfort her, telling her that Paul's anger was displaced, and she bore no responsibility for his upset. Secondarily, I wanted to provide some insight into Paul's plight—not to justify his poor behavior, but in hopes that Annie would be able to muster some compassion in spite of his having targeted her. A day later, Lucy thanked me, and we all moved on.

A situation in which Paul's feelings were hurt usually provoked his outbursts, but this wasn't always evident on the surface, nor were his words always directed to the source of his pain. When he did fly off the handle, usually it was via email, rarely face-to-face, and never with any kind of physical aggression.

More often than not, I could see an alignment between Paul's vulnerability to emotional disruption and inconsistencies in his prescribed medication regimen, and I felt it explained—although it didn't excuse—his behavior. While I could usually make sense of his anger, his reckless reactions were deeply troublesome and rarely constructive, mostly achieving the opposite of what he hungered for.

My front row view, over many a year, of Paul's ability to maintain control of his emotions, fueled my efforts to ride herd on his medications to the greatest extent that I could. But it was all a huge challenge. I knew medication was essential to his ability to manage his impulsivity and rise above his irrational approach, but I was often helpless in this regard. Furthermore, I also knew that Paul's underlying pain was real and legitimate—and deserving of attention in its own right.

Paul saw everyone's situation as better than his and, even though he always knew he wasn't blameless, he harbored resentment for things that had gone wrong in his childhood. When his fragility peaked, he would blame anyone or everyone for his seemingly relentless hardships. All these feelings festered, too, because he was isolated—not free to live where he wanted nor to interact as he wished. When I factor in Paul's life-long isolation imposed by his language impairment, it makes even more sense that his frustrations could flare.

Adding to the mix, Paul worried that once he got over the big hurdles in front of him—beating addiction and living down his legal status—he would *still* be disadvantaged by his limitations and absence of skills. On top of all this, he'd gotten a taste of what it was like to work full time and not have enough money to support himself. What did the future hold? What was he fighting for?

The thing is, I could see how his pent-up emotions sometimes simmered to a boil. And I wanted to be a resource for him as much as I ever wanted anything.

An email from Paul to me provides an example of his malaise:

You never truly listend to me growing up and you neglected my deepest needs. By taking a professionals advice over mine has led to medical malpractice and hand tremmors. By never listining to me you let me fall victem to so many abuses at home. Maybe thats why I torture you so much with phone calls because, truthfully, im mad and you. Youve never even asked me in ten years how my recovvery was going and you've never taken an interest in the things I've told you about it, that really hurts me.

i know ive caused you allot of grife and worry over the years but i want you to know that i think most of my issues stem from how ive been treated. You and keely both are now as equaly condisending as my step-father was. maybe his qualitys rubbed off on you. I can remember always feeling like an outcast in my own home growing up with no place of refuge…it's important to have refuge and I had no place to turn. i can remember him making me feel studpid for everything I ever did and you did not defend me…and life now isn't so different.

i know the decisions ive made threw things off track but i can lay all my problems and mistakes out on the table, and i can say that ive made more mistakes than anyone i have ever known. But im also more reasonable than you give me credit for. You are so unwiling to look at your own mistakes and that is deffinately a strength i have over you.

I remember thinking: *He's got to be kidding! I sacrificed my life for him! I have loved him unconditionally every step of the way. And, oh boy, did I defend him.* But in this particular case, I decided to let it go for a day rather than to react defensively.

I called Paul the next evening. And I thought about it first. Instinctively, I still wanted to say, "I was *always* in your corner," and "I'm *not* afraid to admit my faults." Both would be true statements, but neither applied one hundred percent of the time. Also, I knew better than to simply counter him. For one thing, there were undoubtedly times when I didn't listen; for another, a big part of his message rang true. Above all else, I knew that I wasn't his opponent; I was his role model, his teacher.

I can't say I didn't express any emotion, telling him his words were hurtful and he didn't mean some of the things he said. But I emphasized that he made some valid points—which I respected and would take to heart—and that I had made mistakes. Acknowledging my accountability allowed him to let his guard down enough for me to point out that sweeping statements such as "you never . . ." or "you always . . ." were not productive.

I asked him, point-blank: "Was your goal to zing me? To fire one over the bow? Or to be heard, helping me to better understand your feelings and hopefully improve our communication?"

"I just want you to understand," Paul responded. "I've never belonged, and I'll always be different, even if I'm doing well."

I did understand, and I told him so. Also, I said it was okay that we get mad at each other, but respect should be a given. "Respect is important," I explained. "Respect for me and respect for yourself—and to maintain that you have to choose your words carefully. If you don't, you cause unnecessary pain and sabotage your purpose of getting your point across."

"Sometimes I feel unimportant," he said, "and think my strengths aren't recognized enough. My life is hard and I need all my family to help me, and I want them to want to support me. I don't want to beg for it."

I understood that too. While he had been able to join family get-togethers in recent months, there had been long stretches when he couldn't, followed by strictly controlled day passes that challenged us all. Plus, it had been years since Paul had been able to join our vacations. I knew these circumstances were hard, and I always thought he handled them remarkably well.

I remembered Dr. Crain explaining that when Paul was angry, his capacity to control his impulsivity was weak, resulting in actions that could be quite outlandish. But she emphasized the importance of helping Paul handle his emotional turmoil by using strategies that would capitalize on his innate potential for reasoning, which she knew he was capable of, and I did too.

He wrote to me again, just after we talked:

im not saying ive done good things, im just saying if i could now find my place in society, things would be alot different. I just want to fit in.. I love you and keely and im sorry if it feels like im attacking you. I think you have been an amazing mother. But still, I have to get the more ugly stuff off of my chest.

One of the many things I admired about Paul was that he could listen, and he valued reason over self-defense once he knew he was on safe ground. But if I didn't keep the bar high, how was he supposed to take advantage of his better self? "If anyone knows the power of words, Paul, it is you," I told him more than once. "So try to avoid letting your emotions obliterate your intellect. You have a gift. Let it work for you!"

*

AS THE HOLIDAY season neared, Monica sent me a message, "Maybe I shouldn't interfere. Paul means the world to me, but something is going on. He called me from work, but the call wasn't from his work number. Later he suggested we see each other on Sunday, but he works on Sundays. Maybe I'm just a worry wart, and I wouldn't blame you if you told me to keep my opinions to myself."

I thanked Monica and told her I appreciated her communication. But this worried me. It worried me a lot. We'd had two years of relative smooth sailing. Wasn't this our life now?

Doubts started to creep into my thinking, and I did my best to push them away. I spoke with Paul almost daily, with my antenna up. He came home for Christmas a couple of days before we had planned, which didn't pacify my newfound unease. But he said everything was fine, work was good. He joined the family for our sit-down dinner at my house on Christmas Eve and then for a party at my sister's on Christmas night. He was home again for New Year's Day with the whole family. He still seemed okay. But maybe I felt that way because I needed it to be so. I had adjusted nicely to this otherwise unprecedented period of grace.

But I will admit I was braced for bad news. And sure enough, I got it. And it was worse than I had feared.

Late one night in January 2011, I answered a call from Paul's phone, but it wasn't Paul. It was a stranger, who screamed, "Your son is out in the middle of Martin Luther King Boulevard trying to sell his shoes!!! He gonna get hisself killed!!!"

He hung up. I felt sick. I called Paul's number immediately and multiple times throughout the night. No answer. No sleep.

Early the next day, I received a Facebook message from Paul's mentor, Ben, with whom I then exchanged information for the first time:

Hi Ms. Dunleavy.

I truly hate our first interaction to be under these circumstances, but I'm concerned about Paul's well-being right now. If you have heard from him or know anything about his whereabouts, please let me know.

What I do know is that I spoke to him last night at about 11:40 p.m. and he sounded okay. This was after a guy called me from Paul's number saying he had the phone and that it was an emergency to contact him. I just feel like something is up.

I'm happy to share with you what I know, but I realize this has to be difficult. If it is your wish that I stay out of this, I completely understand. I don't know much beyond what I've shared in this email, but if I can do anything to clarify the situation, I'm happy to try.

Again, my regrets in reaching out to you this way. I don't know who else to contact.

Regards,
Ben Ballard

My reply:

Dear Ben,

Thank you for contacting me. I share your concerns and have been worried sick since receiving a mysterious call last night.

Paul just now called me. He said he talked to Mr. Newman and is waiting for a follow-up conversation with him. They didn't do a drug test because Paul told the truth that he had relapsed. He said Mr. Newman told him to find a place to stay tonight (he is officially out of the program) and they will look for treatment tomorrow.

Jessie

I wrote to Ben again, later that same day:

I don't want to wear out my welcome with you but I did want to tell you that Mr. S. called me just now. He is with Paul, and Paul is safe for the night. Right now, that's the best I could hope for. I know I can't protect him from the reality of what he's done, but at the same time the system he may fall into is brutal, and, beyond being inclined or able to really help him, will exploit the vulnerability that his differences have dealt him. No matter what, though, having encountered a good person like you is invaluable. Thank you again, for everything.

The same day, Ben to me:

Hardly wearing out the welcome.

I had the chance to speak with Paul on my way home from work tonight. He called me and told me about what is going on with him. He confessed that he had "cultivated a little drug habit in the past week" and that he had told them. He apologized and, I think, was a little ashamed to confess this to me. I tried to be as supportive as possible; no need to kick him while he's down. I told him I'd always be around as a resource, but that he needed to focus on getting himself help for now.

I am just glad that he is safe. While I am disappointed at this blown opportunity, I think he knows that he is worth more than being out on the street. At the very least, he knows that I believe he is worth more than that; maybe if he doesn't think so, knowing someone does will help him come to that realization.

It breaks my heart to think of Paul in general population. I saw how rough the other guys at Christopher's Place treated him sometimes; I can only imagine how horrible jail would be for a gentle soul like Paul.

I know recovery is not always a linear path. Hopefully this is just a small speed bump. Please know that I always had Paul's best interests in mind and that if I can be of any assistance to you, I am always available. He's a special guy and I really hope gets back on the right track quickly.

Hopefully, sleep will come a little easier tonight knowing that he has a roof over his head and that he is with people who want to help him. I know I feel an enormous relief already.

Take care and please send any updates you have. I will do likewise.

Regards,
Ben

Regretful and afraid, Paul confessed to the director of his residential program, from which he was immediately dismissed, leaving his only option a facility with a program that would preclude his working. Because he was a month shy of completing his two-and-a-half-year probation, this decision was mandated by the court. Paul called his supervisor at Johns Hopkins, who advised him to resign and to call back when he finished the program, saying he would hire Paul again if he could.

Paul told me he had been afraid recently, referencing the "people outside his door," and saying he was "afraid to ask for help" and "afraid to tell on them . . ." I wasn't sure what he was getting at, but I hoped he had furthered his grasp of the slippery slope of one bad decision and realized that some people may pose as friends, but do so only to take advantage. While I was thankful that it looked as though he'd get treatment rather than jail time, Paul was despondent, lamenting his losses: a girl, his independence, his job, his self-respect, his family's admiration. I didn't coddle him but tried to reassure him, saying the outcome could have been worse and that people may be disappointed but they do respect him. I also said there was nothing he couldn't recover once back on the right track.

Part of him heard me. I think. I was downtrodden too and not entirely confident that my advice was the best advice, or even that it did him any good. I was also exhausted by the combination of stress and helplessness.

A few days after moving into the treatment facility, Paul left one morning to keep a coffee date with a girl he had first talked with on the phone a couple of days before his relapse. Because his phone had been locked away, he had no way to communicate with her and, not wanting to stand her up, he went.

Paul had told me about this girl, Kim, but naturally didn't tell me of his plan to meet her in spite of his new circumstances. I learned of this lapse in judgment the same moment I learned of its consequences—he was in jail, Central Booking. I prayed that his stay would be brief. With Ben's help, I tried to recover his belongings, somehow lost in the shuffle, and was never successful. Everything he'd owned was gone.

For several days, I couldn't get through to Paul's public defender, or to Central Booking. After finally obtaining Paul's address and the all-important Jail ID number, I sent him a letter along with paper and stamped envelopes. Paul's return letter to me represented the first information I'd received regarding his conditions and his plight. He wrote:

Hey Ma, I just want you to know how very sorry I am for the choices that Ive made. I agree that I don't know how to navigate. Its scarry. I don't trust a thing about myself. . . . I will stay out of your hair and I hope you will forget about me. I'm ashamed of just about everything Ive brought to the table ever in friendships or family. I love you.

Some things hadn't changed: Paul wasn't getting his proper medication, his meals consisted of bologna sandwiches with an unidentifiable drink, and he spent all but fifteen minutes per day in a cell.

A few years later, I came across an article by Jeffrey Toobin in *The New Yorker Magazine*—"This is My Jail"—about Baltimore's Central Booking and its notorious gang leaders and their management of an underground economy, fueled by the smuggling of drugs and other contraband with Green Dot cards as currency. On top of the extreme corruption, I read of its abhorrent conditions, characterized as the worst and most dangerous in the country. "Inmates spend more than twenty hours a day in their cells, which measure six feet by ten and are shared by two men. Each cell has bunk beds, a combined sink and rimless toilet, and a single dim light on the wall. . . . The facility shut down its dining room so the inmates eat in their cells. . . . The heat is balky in the winter, and there is generally no air-conditioning in the summer." Peeling paint . . . Cockroaches . . . Horrible food . . . Images that haunt me still.

And a *combined sink and rimless toilet*? *Why* did I have to read that?

Paul wrote to me about a national service called "talk to your inmate"—a phone account I could open that would enable him to call me during his time out of the cell. This being 2011, with Paul's former incarceration having been in 2008, it stood to reason that some things *had* changed. As long as I kept money in the phone account, he was able to call daily. But often the connection was so bad that we couldn't hear each other at all—not one word—which was extremely frustrating for both of us. Furthermore, the time he was permitted to call wasn't predictable, meaning he wasn't always able to reach me, especially if he called during the work day. When we did talk, Paul usually cried and always spoke of his misery as well as his regrets and his fears. While I wasn't physically there, my heavy heart was imprisoned too.

Paul had been told he would have an evaluation within a couple of weeks, done by the Baltimore Substance Abuse Systems (BSAS), which he understood would result in a recommendation to the judge prior to his court date in late February. I didn't get what the evaluation entailed or exactly how it would be used. Paul didn't either.

After Paul saw the BSAS people, he said they had told him his hearing would result in one of two possible outcomes—release to a mandated treatment program or a prison sentence. Also, he was told the state's attorney was going to press for prison because Paul had already had the benefit of a treatment program and had failed. Still confused, I asked what the evaluation consisted of, and Paul didn't know. None of this sounded very encouraging.

Paul was given a job in the jail kitchen, where he worked from 4:00 a.m. until noon for $2 per day. He was glad about this—partly because he got out of his cell, but mostly because he wasn't as hungry. I breathed a little easier myself. I had been sickened by the knowledge that he was hungry and angry that he was deprived of food and needed toiletries, on top of which I was grappling with my recently discovered helplessness. I had mailed him a "Green Dot MoneyPak," the 2011 method of sending money for the commissary. But it was stolen—grabbed right out of his hands—just minutes after he'd received it. There was no point in sending another, he told me. He didn't stand a chance.

When your child is hungry, it's hard to eat, and impossible to rest.

I was in too much despair to let profiteering occupy undue brain power, but the money-making industries like "talk to your inmate" and commissaries that force the purchase of bare necessities exploit those who are detained while outside companies with monopoly contracts make huge profits. Plus, the phone system's substandard connectivity prevented "talking to your inmate" at least half of the time. In 2011? With thirty miles between us? Paper cups and string might have worked just as well. *Greedy, mean-spirited racket.*

The outcome of Paul's hearing in late February was a disappointment. The judge postponed the decision for another four weeks, meaning Paul would have to continue to endure the inhumane conditions of Central Booking and suffer the anxiety of not knowing what was in store for him. The judge did say it was fifty-fifty as to whether Paul would be sentenced to three years in prison (mentioning Jessup, a maximum security penitentiary, as a possibility) or released to a program for a specified probation period. One big strike against Paul was the felony on his record.

The prolonged uncertainty regarding his fate seemed unbearable, as did the cruel treatment he had to tolerate. The next hearing was scheduled for March 28. On March 20, 2011, I sent an email to my sisters, providing some updated information:

Paul just called. They moved him. He is now in a cell he stays in except for a few minutes every other day and he no longer has the kitchen job. After talking to him, I feel as though I've been kicked in the stomach. He is as bad off as I've ever experienced. But I do have hope for improvement.

I was able to speak with Paul's public defender about the nature of the evaluation conducted by BSAS. Knowing it was a significant factor in determining Paul's fate, I asked if there was any awareness on their part of his mental health diagnosis or his other disabilities. I was told there was not. In considering hiring a private attorney, I sought advice from two respected lawyers in Annapolis and received the same response: Since Paul's trial was for violation of probation, it was unlikely that a private attorney would make a difference.

The thought of Paul serving a multi-year sentence in a maximum security prison scared the life out of me. They may as well just push him off a cliff. And me too while they're at it. He had made plenty of mistakes, but this was not the answer!

Feeling increasingly panicked as the trial date approached, I turned to Joan Gillece, a longtime friend to Paul and me whose professional life as an advocate for people with mental illness had involved work within correctional facilities. Joan explained that she was in a different job, one in which she no longer frequented the jails. But she did tell me about the Forensic Alternative Services Team (FAST)—mental health clinicians who work within the criminal justice system. "I know the director," Joan told me. "I can call her to share my knowledge of

Paul's condition and his circumstances." Naturally, I took her up on the offer.

Joan did place the call and leave a message the next day—the Thursday before the Monday trial. On Friday, Joan and this woman traded calls but missed one another. With time running out, not to mention my awareness of Joan having a full plate of her own professional responsibilities, I knew I needed to keep Paul in the forefront of her mind and impress upon her the urgency of the moment. So I called Joan again on Sunday. I told her I was downright scared, elaborating on Paul's current suffering as well as the agony generated by my understanding, albeit cursory, of what the BSAS people had told Paul in regard to his pending fate.

Monday came. Because Paul's trial was scheduled for the afternoon, I went to work in the morning. Joan called to tell me she had talked to the FAST director and that the conversation had been a good one. I was in a meeting and couldn't get more details, but I breathed a sigh of relief in just knowing they had talked.

A few hours later, I was in the Baltimore City Courthouse, accompanied by Paul's father, Don, and stepmother, Lucy, and my good friend and retired judge, Joe Manck. Seeing Paul in the front of the courtroom in an orange jumpsuit with "GEN POP" stenciled on the back was hard enough, but the fact that his legs and arms were in shackles was nearly unbearable and is a memory that continues to sicken me.

The state's attorney made her case for a prison sentence. The public defender shared the results of the BSAS evaluation, which concluded that Paul did not need another program. My heart was sinking fast. At that point, the judge conferred privately with another woman who seemed to appear out of nowhere—I wondered who she was. Laser-focused on the two of them and leaning as far forward as possible without falling off my seat, I strained to pick up any clues. And

I was able to overhear the judge say her name, tipping me off: Sure enough, she *was* the woman Joan had spoken with earlier that day.

The judge asked the two attorneys to join them at the bench for a discussion we couldn't hear, after which he announced his conclusion. Paul would go back to Central Booking, allowing time to obtain a FAST evaluation, the results of which would enable the judge to render a final decision.

As we were leaving the courtroom, the FAST director came over to me and handed me the business card of the person who would conduct Paul's evaluation, telling me to call to share any history I thought important. Choked-up and wanting to hug her, I settled for shaking her hand and thanking her.

As relieved and grateful as I was, I felt terrible for Paul, who had no way of knowing what had just happened and why he was once again being loaded in the armored bus to return to jail with his fate still unknown. When I explained it to him that evening on the phone, he listened, but he was too discouraged to find any comfort.

*

IT WASN'T UNTIL late April that Paul had his next hearing. Paul's cousin, Abby, accompanied me to the courthouse that day.

The state's attorney spoke. "The state hasn't changed," she said. "He was given a chance, then he violated it and walked. We say no more charity, it's not a good use of resources."

The public defender was next. "He admits to the violation," she said. "He's accepted our offer and has given up any rights to a jury trial. We have secured housing and a clinic to start Monday. He will have curfew, house meetings, therapy, and psychiatry as well as twelve-step meetings five times a week."

Once again in shackles, Paul stood before the judge, who spoke sternly. "Your counsel focused on the fact that you did so well for a considerable time," he said. "That is encouraging. But violating your probation is discouraging. If you do it again, I'll give you time. There are resources for mental health that I urge you to use. I know your mother is here and she supports you, but now you have to be all the way grown up. I am extending your probation to April 2012 and releasing you to residential treatment. No running away, or I'm going to slam the door on you."

Thank God.

I was told to wait behind the courthouse for Paul to exit, after which I was to take him to the address that would be given to me by the officer designated to walk him to my car. I didn't understand the two-hour wait that ensued and felt stressed as the courthouse closed and gradually its parking lot emptied. Nonetheless I was counting my blessings. Paul would never have to spend another night in Central Booking.

Or so I thought.

The miserable conditions and excruciating uncertainty from mid-January through April had seemed—to me—excessive for a relapse to which Paul had confessed, after two years and five months of successes. There was no crime other than addiction. And there was no victim other than Paul.

Then again, he did keep that coffee date. Foolish? Extremely. Criminal? I didn't think so. Furthermore, I wondered if Paul's poor judgment wasn't indicative of the ways he just didn't comprehend the world. I could've been wrong, but as I tried to imagine Paul's plight, I was sure the "glitch"—as so many called it—in his brain added an overlay that could make it impossible for any of us to put ourselves in his shoes. I knew this much: There had been many ways throughout his entire life that his neurological differences had separated him from others, including me.

Finally, Paul was escorted to my car. We found the address. It wasn't a house, as I had expected. Instead it was a door between two dilapidated retail stores. Seeing that it was a bad neighborhood, I waited on the sidewalk until Paul had made a connection. The man who greeted him explained that he worked for the program's intake office and would assure Paul's transportation from there.

I heard from Paul the next day. He described his routine, which he took seriously as he did his commitment to following all the rules. He had met and liked his new therapist and was relieved that the nightmare of Central Booking was finally behind him, a nightmare I knew only partially. For one, I hadn't lived it, and two, he had yet to tell me the full extent of his suffering, which tragically included his being exploited, and in multiple ways.

Paul's initial challenge was navigating a new neighborhood and getting from a meeting with his probation officer downtown, to his therapist in Canton, and back to North Caroline Street for a house meeting. Luckily, Paul was familiar with both Baltimore City and its bus system.

One day during his second week, Paul reported on time to his probation officer, who was late for their appointment but regardless kept him for their full allotted time, meaning Paul was behind schedule when he left her office. Sure enough, he was twenty minutes late for his house meeting. His penalty? A sanction was imposed—two weeks back in Central Booking.

Several weeks later, a similar miscommunication among those in charge landed Paul back in Central Booking yet again, this time for six nights. It was torture. And I seriously started to believe someone wanted him to fail. Paul was overwhelmed by fear, and I was gravely worried that his terrified state was going to do him in, one way or another.

In a letter to me from Central Booking, Paul wrote:

Jun 22 2011
Hey Ma,

I'm a little frustrated right now as you can imagine. At this point, the judge and the state know that I'm no threat to society but they continue to harass me and waste my valuable time. My reports have been perfect.

Anyhow I'm in this cell for 22 hours a day. You have no idea how embarrassing this all is. To be 28 years old and be in a recovery house and then go in and out of jail.

I wish I would have been born with a better head on my shoulders. You don't deserve any of this. I love you so much though.

If by chance I go back to the same house, I am going to need extra money. Those people take our grocery money but don't buy enough food. In fact, they haven't done any of the things they promised.

I know I shouldn't be your responsibility but know that I have so much gratitude for all the support you give me.

I love you.

I couldn't help but notice that Paul's handwritten letter, still hard to read due to his penmanship, was remarkably free of spelling errors. I guessed this was due to his year of frequent computer use, with the Spell Check feature serving to reinforce his awareness of proper spelling. And, he had plenty of time to make it right.

I conferred at length with Paul's public defender, whom I did respect, and told her I felt as though he was being targeted and that neither he nor I knew where to turn. Looking back on it, I wonder if someone in the chain of command had resented what may have been seen as "strings pulled" on Paul's behalf. In any case, after that conversation—for whatever reason—things did settle down and, thankfully, Paul had finally seen the last of Central Booking.

Then Paul received a notice, mailed to my address, saying that he was in arrears in his child-support payments. Since Paul hadn't been able to work for the past six months, we foolishly had been unaware of his accruing debt. Engaging an attorney, and informing Sara every step of the way, we worked through it. And while I more than appreciated Sara's position, I empathized with Paul over the stress this imposed on him.

Paul loved his therapist, Wendy Silber, but was not happy in the residence, a row-home with two managers whom Paul didn't trust. In addition to his suspicions that they were skimming money from the residents' contributions to shared expenses, he felt that they were as inconsistent in conveying expectations as they were with enforcing the rules. He told me they routinely threatened residents with sanctions that didn't seem warranted.

Oftentimes, Paul was more focused on the way they treated others than on the way they treated him. He spoke of an older man named Lenny, whom he thought was unfairly victimized—even being deprived of food. Paul stuck his neck out and talked to one of the managers about his concerns. But he was warned to stay out of it and was told that Lenny wasn't rational. While this didn't ease Paul's distress, and he tried to help Lenny on the sly while continuing to tell me about the unjust conditions, he did learn to adopt a low profile.

In the fall, Paul took a class at Baltimore City Community College (BCCC)—Sociology 101—and did well, sending me his papers to edit, all of which demonstrated his investment in the work as well as his evolving skills. And when Paul wrote about social inequality, it wasn't just theoretical. Not yet eligible for full-time employment, Paul was seeking part-time work. I contacted DORS again and learned that their criteria for "disabled" had changed, and Paul no longer qualified for their services. Even though his disabilities precluded his getting a job, he wasn't disabled *enough* to qualify for job-seeking support.

By November, Paul asked the court for permission to move, a request I supported and which ultimately he was granted. He was on the home stretch with his probationary period, and the house he found was a halfway house in a somewhat better neighborhood, with rules that were equally strict but where he believed the communication regarding the expectations would be more consistent and those in charge more humane. In committing to the increase in rent, I shared insights with his public defender:

> I do not expect this new program to be problem free, nor do I think Paul won't introduce his own challenges in working with and relating to others. On balance, with Paul as my only source of information, I do believe this setting will provide more stability as his own mood swings seem to be exacerbated by those in authority in the current setting.

My friend Joe and I helped Paul move to the halfway house on Cloverdale Road, where he lived for several months without incident, seeing his years of probation through to the end.

Chapter 10

OVER THE THRESHOLD, INTO A NEW DAY

In her arms I've again found refuge
And above my sorrows, I will recognize
This city's streets have new meaning
As I again take notice of constellations in the skies
To me they resemble all I've found this December
Inspiring emotions I once chalked up to lost
And here in this room above Mount Washington
Lying on peddles, she's strewn across

THERE IS NO such thing as a perfect parent—I let myself off the hook for that so long ago that I can't remember. But I do believe there are two fundamental components of good parenting: unconditional love and wisdom. For most of us, the former is a given, innate to the human condition. We start this trail-blazing journey with that in place.

If my father said it to me once, he said it a hundred times, "I'm on your side, Jess . . . Rob a bank, and I'm on your side."

Not that many years ago, an acquaintance said to me, "Wouldn't your father's words have encouraged wrong-doing on your part?" *Wow* is what I thought, and who knows what I said. Something benign and socially gracious, I suppose. I knew the philosophical divide was too much to take on at that moment—or ever, for that matter.

My interpretation of my father's words when I was young was, simply, "He loves me no matter what." As an adult, and a parent myself, I know that he was also saying, "If ever you're in trouble, don't be afraid to come to me."

Wisdom comes over time and through experience, and even so it can peak and wane based on circumstances. Beyond life lessons in humility and acceptance, being Paul's mother strengthened my ability to keep cool in a crisis, remain above the emotional fray even when frightened, and provide constructive feedback and guidance without expressing disrespect.

Kids try to bring you down to their level, especially when they're hurting, and they're very good at it. But this is the precise time they need you not to go there. My advice to another parent would be: When your child gets on a roller coaster ride, don't buy a ticket. After all, if the car goes off the rails, you need to be on the ground.

*

WHILE IN THE home stretch of his time in the halfway house, Paul met and fell in love with a successful and grounded young woman named Casey, who lived in Mount Washington, an area northwest of Baltimore City. Casey was completing her master's degree at Johns Hopkins University, where she also worked in the admission office.

I met Casey, as did the rest of my family, on Christmas Eve when she joined us for our holiday dinner. Because the "cousins" were adding significant others to the mix, not to mention the launch of a new generation spearheaded by Kayla and followed by my great-nephew Campbell, I had eighteen for dinner that year. By adding every leaf to my dining room table, I was able to seat all of us comfortably, but passing through the dining room was a bit of a challenge—so much so that I joked with the family, saying that those who were seated on the side of the table closest to the living room should enter the house via the front door, and those on the other side should use the kitchen door. An exaggeration I found funny! It was a wonderful evening. Kayla was so happy and so good, and Casey fit right in.

As Paul's extended probation was coming to an end, I hoped he would stay put, taking the time to consider his options. He wanted to take more classes and, as much as I loved his finding pleasure in learning for the sake of learning, I knew he needed to work. He said he could do both, and would, and was eager to do so, just as he was to live without "rules." I believed there was a good chance he couldn't manage both school and work, on top of which the absence of rules could heighten his vulnerability.

He was facing a big turning point, one he understandably welcomed. And while I applauded his well-deserved triumph and was in sync with his relief in breaking free from the criminal justice system, I had concerns. I knew there would be challenges, although I didn't think he'd benefit from my saying so. The thing is, all of Paul's safety nets were going away, and all at the same time except for Paul's therapist, Wendy, whom he wanted to continue seeing. Even this, however, would no longer be a binding relationship. In effect, Paul was now going to be free.

For years there had been oversight of his medication as well as a coordinated focus on substance-free living. Furthermore, the one job he'd gotten in the eight years since adding "felon" to his resume had been secured through a mandated rehabilitation program. To Paul's credit, he performed well during this two-plus-year stretch of his initial probation until, that is, the very end when—with increased freedom—he backslid.

It's easy to understand why he was resentful of all the controls he'd lived with during his long probation, particularly in considering the mistreatment he endured. But Paul didn't just break the law; he had trouble managing *life*, which ultimately led to his breaking the law. Making everything all the more dicey, he just didn't—or couldn't—buy the idea that any of these safety nets mattered.

In essence, Paul often appeared to have an inflated view of what he could handle. But did he really? I guess part of him was unrealistic, but another part was in hyperdrive denial. His limitations and his fragile ego intensified his feelings of incompetence, which in turn made him anxious, and anxiety was his enemy. Yet finding a job and taking on all of life's responsibilities in light of his emotional fluctuations was itself anxiety-provoking. And either anxiety or failure could lead to self-medicating.

Then there was his prescribed medication. Throughout the years, Paul had continued to take Abilify as well as an antidepressant, which had changed to Wellbutrin. He didn't like Abilify because it caused some weight gain, but at this juncture he was downright thin due mostly to his extreme walking. But he also didn't like the *idea* of Abilify because it was an antipsychotic and he "didn't need antipsychotic medication." There were times when I wished there was a patch I could slap on him without his knowing it—times when he was getting in his own way. To me it was crystal clear: When Paul took a relatively low dose of Abilify, he was even keeled and reasonable ninety percent of the time; when he didn't, it was about fifty percent of the time. None of us can claim one hundred percent . . . but fifty?

And lastly, there was me. Paul loved and admired me, and he turned to me for help and advice, but on his terms. In his heart he knew I was his best friend in the world but, for the same reasons he didn't want rules or medication or meetings, he didn't want a mother-manager. No one does, and I got that. He was nearly thirty years old, and while his development was delayed, he didn't see it that way. And he, by golly, wanted to live like everyone else.

When Paul received his official release from the court, he told me he was moving in with Casey. I suggested that he might be better able to nurture his relationship with Casey if he lived separately, reminding him of the challenges of cohabitation and the value of independence. But he couldn't resist. She wanted it. He wanted it. And so it was.

As much as I could see the pitfalls of this decision, I could certainly understand it. Not that my insights mattered.

Paul said Casey was "a breath of fresh air." From what I could gather, Casey was taken by Paul's sweetness, his insightfulness, and their shared interests, not to mention his looks, which I'm sure didn't hurt.

Casey's apartment was on the third floor of an old mansion in Mount Washington. At one time the summer home of a prominent Baltimore judge, this historic building—perched on a hill surrounded by a sprawling lawn—featured a large foyer with an old-world brick fireplace and a dramatic stairway that led up to the third floor. The condition of the apartment was far from pristine, but the original pine floors, window dormers, and access to a rooftop deck via the bedroom window added to the charm, as did the panoramic view of Mount Washington.

I do think Paul had some of the happiest times of his life with Casey. He clearly loved her and was excited about the domestic partnership—to him, a trip with her to Ikea to get a small household item was a fun outing. Having just gotten a new computer, I gave him my old one, along with a few pieces of furniture and some other decorative items that they loved.

Paul was never lazy and he jumped right into looking for a job. He felt optimistic at the start but was deflated after countless failed attempts. He did a lot of searching by walking and stopping into such places as McDonald's, Home Depot, and any other establishment he passed or thought of, including Mount Washington Hospital. If handed an application, he'd call me on the spot to ask for dates and other details. I typed a resume for him, stretching the truth where I could, and told him we needed a plan for how he would answer questions about the gaps in his work history. He found a website listing of "felony friendly" establishments, a good idea that didn't prove fruitful. I advised him to apply electronically when possible and otherwise to take the application home to have Casey transcribe his information. Reading his handwriting remained nearly impossible.

Paul qualified for cash assistance, which helped him contribute to the living expenses, and I took over the child support payments. As Paul continued to seek employment, he registered for two classes at BCCC, Social Problems (Sociology 102) and a poetry class.

From the start, Casey formed a relationship with Sara and Kayla, which was to everyone's credit and, of course, Kayla's benefit. They all had an easy rapport and got together frequently, often at my house. Paul said Kayla was one of the things Casey saw in him.

Casey was adventurous, a trait Paul embraced, and they did a lot of things on a shoestring budget. Casey had a car, allowing them to go places on weekends. And go they did. They went to the ocean or the mountains for a day and even drove to New York City, taking pictures of one another on top of the Empire State Building, in Central Park, Times Square, and FAO Schwartz, and somehow pitched a tent somewhere and managed two days of sightseeing.

They went to a driving range and to free concerts, they cooked and they cared for Casey's dog, Noah, deciding after a while to adopt another mutt whom Paul named Hobbes. They both loved those dogs, and when they visited with me, so did Noah and Hobbes.

One evening, Paul went out to run an errand and was pulled over because Casey's car had a headlight out. Unbeknownst to Paul, his license had been suspended. When the police saw this, along with the fact that Paul had a record, they arrested him. They released him later that night without giving him the car, which had been impounded along with his wallet and cell phone. It was a cold winter night. Paul was wearing flannel pajama pants, and he was afraid Casey would be upset about the car. What did he do? He hailed a cab to deliver him to my house in Annapolis.

The first I knew about any of this was when he knocked on my door. Seeing him surprised me, as did the fact that I had to pay the cab driver $100 in cash, something that required me to dash to an ATM machine. This was around 10:00 p.m. on a work night, and I was none too pleased about any of it, which I didn't hide from Paul. Even so, we chatted for a while before I drove him back to Mount Washington, a good hour away, but something I couldn't have managed in the morning. Paul gave me the police paperwork detailing the charges and the upcoming trial. From Paul's report of the events, I didn't think he'd been treated fairly, but I was confused about much of it. Overtaking my irritation with him was my worry about the outcome. I had learned to distrust the criminal justice system and, as I thought about it more, my worry grew.

Paul sent me an email first thing the next morning:

> Thank you so mutch for having me last night and for paying for that cab. I know that wasent fair but I dont know what I would have done, do you know what I mean? Im getting the feeling that you and keely are pretty mad at me right now and I understand it. I do wish you had wanted to just give me a hug last night. I know that sounds stupid and weak but I cherish the comfort you give me and I cherish your advice too, even though I repeat myself over and over and hardley ever listen to you. Im such an idiot.

We subsequently learned that the child support agency had suspended Paul's license when payments were in arrears, an oversight on their part as this had been settled by the attorneys and payments made to everyone's satisfaction. We did get a lawyer, who represented Paul at the hearing, where the charges were dropped, and who helped clarify Paul's status with the child support agency. While it all worked out, this was a bit of an ordeal, one that was stressful for Paul and worrisome for all of us.

It came as no surprise that Paul and Casey did have their struggles. Naturally, they kept some of it from me, but not always. At times, I was brought into the loop when one or the other of them needed me.

In this aptly titled piece of writing, found in his laptop, Paul provided some insight:

MOOD DISORDER

If I could only write to you a few stanzas of gibberish, or spill a few abstract thoughts on paper that could be interpreted as something other than mood, you and I could re-analyze this mess. Maybe within some spontaneous action, you and I could re-channel conflict into love and we too could find our staple in history as did the Romeo and Juliets of time. But you and I are only able to move under pressure, so just entertaining the thought may be damaging to my health.

As internal flames flair and take their shape in an array of smoldering words never meant to leave our lips, my conscience takes another small breath, then suffocates, and I am at once blinded by anger. It's not the hurtful things said that take such a bad effect, it's the unwillingness to compromise. And free from the reigns of reason, I am a ticking time bomb unable to budge in any margin of reason-ability.

And within a few short moments, I again will be out the door, beyond the lawn and down the hill, to collect what rational thought is left. The moment is seized as reality rears its head to sooth my frustration in its breathtaking draw, and once again I am alone. There is no reason that the authors I had once admired or the musicians I've idolized could inspire me enough to catapult me from this muck. I am in fact crawling for whatever scraps are left of this dying and inspiration is a dimly lit porch light, far off in the night.

*

DESPITE THEIR UPS and downs, Casey and Paul decided to drive across the country, which they did in the summer of 2013—a year and a half after the start of their relationship. They lined up hostels and traded spaces and I don't know what all, and they created a detailed plan mapped out by time and money. Their ultimate destination was a Phish concert at The Gorge in Washington State, an experience Paul talked about for the rest of his life. Although he would see this band again, it would not be in such an awe-inspiring setting.

I will never be able to view in one sitting all the photographs they took. I had thought the weekend in New York City was marathon viewing. I'm pretty sure I could string all these photos together and make a video of driving across the country, featuring highlights like the Gateway Arch, Mount Rushmore, and the Golden Gate Bridge.

Better than the photos were Paul's text messages letting me know, in addition to their precise real-time location, what was exciting and what was not. I laughed out loud as I read, "Just crossed into Missouri. Not much to this state." Nothing like sizing up an entire state after a mile on its freeway. Sorry, Missouri.

Back home by summer's end, Paul and Casey resumed their weekend activities, and in September they went camping in Harpers Ferry, West Virginia. While pitching the tent, Paul slipped on the wet ground and fell down an embankment. In recounting this, Paul told me he was lying on the ground, and when he lifted his leg, he could see his foot dangling from its end. Casey called an ambulance and Paul was taken to the emergency room of a hospital in Frederick, Maryland.

Unfortunately, Paul's insurance covered only his therapist and his medications, not hospitalization or surgery. As a result, his treatment was substandard. Instead of performing the surgery the injury called for, the doctor manipulated the bones to set them as well as he could and cast Paul's leg up to his hip. When Paul was released the next day, he was issued a walker and told to stay off his feet.

In spite of having been able to crawl up to the third-floor apartment, the challenges Paul faced were overwhelming for him and, secondarily, for Casey. For example, the walker was too wide for him to pass through the narrow door to the bathroom. Keely and I went to see him and felt the situation was untenable. I thought about bringing him home, but—on top of my long hours at work—my house is on three floors without as much as a powder room on the main living level.

Within days, Casey told me in no uncertain terms that Paul had to go—she simply couldn't manage him, and frankly I didn't blame her. Not even a little. Sara saved the day, providing a stopgap but life-saving solution. Paul moved into her first-floor condominium in Germantown, Maryland, where he slept on the couch.

Sara's generous reprieve was short lived—her parents learned of it and put their foot down. I didn't blame them either. A second temporary solution was kindly provided by Sara's boyfriend, John, who invited Paul to stay with him until we could find a more workable solution, a top priority for us both.

This move would represent Paul's final departure from Baltimore and his foray into the Washington, D.C., suburb of Maryland's Montgomery County—the one silver lining, as far as Paul was concerned, since the move also would mark the end of the relationship with Casey, something Paul bemoaned for years.

Even though Paul was heartbroken, if not crushed, he and Casey stayed in touch and remained good friends.

When Casey learned about Paul's death in May 2017, she posted the following tribute on his Facebook page:

For Paul, I hope you are somewhere dancing and laughing because you are finally free.

I've seen Paul at his best and at his worst.

The day I met him he walked at least 10 miles to meet me. He loved to walk, to be outside and to say hello to strangers on the street. I think walking and biking were his way of coping. Each foot step or mile was an accomplishment that he could be proud of. That is who Paul was, he found hope in the small things.

When we met that day I knew I found someone I would be lifelong friends with. He had an easiness about him. You could really be yourself around Paul because he held no judgments against you. He also laughed at himself, his mistakes, his bad habits, and his overall silliness. Everything and anything could and would be a joke with him. I'm sure he is looking at me now laughing at all of this. I'm sure he is happy wherever he may be as well because he could make the best of a bad situation.

It was his adventuress spirit that drew me to him and eventually led us both to drop everything and drive across the country in 2013 to see Phish. We both wanted to be free from this society and Phish offered it to us. We talked about buying an RV, making grilled cheese, and going on tour indefinitely.

It was part of his spirit to be free. And you could tell from his writing that he knew freedom.

When he wrote it was like someone inside him that could only be seen through the stroke of a pen. He was never happy with his writing and often threw out poems and parts of novels saying that it was part of the process; to write something and immediately rip it up. It was both an act of bravery and torment that he did this, I believe. I think that he felt it would never be good enough, yet he knew how good of a writer he was.

It scared me when he told me that he couldn't write anymore; the words wouldn't come. I knew writing was his freedom . . . The struggle to start writing was just as important as the finished product; both take pain and discipline. I always wished he would write a book because I knew that I would love it. He knew how to captivate people.

It's been a month since he passed, and I only now just found out. I spoke to him days before and we had planned on going to lunch before I moved. In our last conversation he said he was happy for me. He sounded happy too. He was at work and laughing. No matter how much he struggled in this life, I know he cared deeply and lived passionately. I will never forget him.

Chapter 11

THE CAGE

Perfectly imperfect; words tell stories of my subconscious
And awaken its many hidden memories of my past
And immortalize them on white tablets; unable to age in time.
Like pedophiles in trench coat stealth;
Artsy cravings study my pubescent youth from dark corners
And capture them down to a science; to a beautiful cage;
Where they can lie naked forever
For another's unprotected pleasure.

DURING THE TIME Paul was living with Casey, the year he would turn thirty, he divulged experiences he'd suffered as a young teenager.

I guess the best way to put it is that Paul had sexual encounters that left him feeling coerced and used, as well as confused and ashamed. These incidents started when he was thirteen and occurred off and on until he was fifteen. Because this happened with someone Paul admired, someone he had always looked up to, Paul went along, and he honored the secrecy pact to which he had agreed. Furthering his commitment to secrecy was his shame.

Around the same age as Paul but a lot more socially adept, Martin was a friend. While he and his parents no longer lived nearby when Keely and Paul were growing up, they once had been neighbors and remained close to us, spending holidays with mutual friends and often joining our get-togethers. Martin's friendship was particularly important to Paul. Martin was comfortable with people and made friends with ease, on top of which he was musically gifted—all characteristics that impressed Paul. I never detected envy on Paul's part, but he clamored to be like Martin, relished his attention, and felt privileged when he got it.

Paul's delayed confrontation with this segment of his life was ignited by anger, with all the ingredients in place for him to escalate the drama. His feelings had been hurt in an unrelated matter, so his anger peaked, his emotions surged, and they got the best of him. As was his pattern, Paul expressed his anger in writing—in a text message conversation with Martin.

While unknown to me at the time, the texts—which I would see some days later and are still in Paul's phone—started with Paul's inflammatory accusation of "rape," expanded to the threat of "pressing charges," with both parties then spewing nasty insults at the other. Ugly as it was, the exchange eventually took on a reasonable tone, with impressive concessions on both sides.

"I regret that," Paul wrote. "I don't think you are a rapist. That was too harsh." He continued, "I'm not going to press charges. Just false threats. I have nothing to go on. I have a lot to be angry about. Sometimes I don't make sense, but all of my pain is real. Not all of that is from you." As for Martin, he offered to join Paul for a chat with Paul's therapist, asking Paul to keep this arrangement between them.

Even though this communication had evolved from hurtful to caring, the experience opened emotional floodgates for Paul. He called me in tears, and his outpouring on the phone would be the first I knew of any of this. He was sobbing and hard to follow, but he recounted the gist of what had happened some fifteen years earlier.

I was stunned by all that Paul had just told me, but at the same time I wondered, *Is this true?* While the degree of his upset was heart-wrenching and alarming, I knew Paul could overreact. I knew he was capable of displaced anger. He could be provocative. He could exaggerate. He lied sometimes.

It's hard to explain how I felt. I was gravely concerned, but I didn't know how my concern should be channeled.

Paul told me he had talked about these encounters with his therapist, Wendy. In one session, she had told him there was no statute of limitations in Maryland for reporting certain crimes. I was shocked, not by Maryland's law per se, but by the fact that such information—still so new and unfathomable to me—had been discussed by others, wrapping in facts that could fan Paul's ire and emotion. I was at a loss. It was late when that first call came, and all I could do was try to soothe him. I was marginally successful, at best.

Early the next morning as I was about to get ready for work, I happened to see that Paul had Tweeted his declaration of having been raped as a teenager. I was horrified. I dropped everything and called him. Even though he was crying when he answered the phone and told me he had been awake all night, I was far from pampering. "PAUL!" I said, my raised voice conveying the degree of my distress. "YOU LISTEN TO ME, DAMMIT—TAKE THAT TWEET DOWN! TAKE IT DOWN *NOW!* ARE YOU CRAZY?"

"I know, I know," he said through his tears. "You're right, I'm sorry. But I'm shaking too much to work the keys, I'll give you my password and you can do it."

I deleted it while we were still on the phone. Considering it was barely daybreak, I thought there was a good chance it hadn't been seen. Even so, the experience took my breath away. I don't remember much other than telling Paul he shouldn't have a Twitter account if he didn't have the maturity and judgment to use it constructively, reminding him this was the second time he'd used social media to rant inappropriately, and shockingly so. I was hard on him, but concurrently I knew he had a long way to go before the emotional spillage was going to let up.

I called Wendy to see if I could join Paul for his appointment that week. In driving to her office in Baltimore, I thought about what I hoped to get out of our conversation. Most important, I wanted to know whether Wendy thought Paul's reports were credible and, if she believed they were, how to proceed in supporting him. In addition, I needed to impress upon her my opposition to even entertaining the idea of any sort of legal action, something I saw as calamitous for Paul. As befuddled as I was, I saw no gray area here. I wouldn't dream of subjecting Paul to any such process, no matter the circumstances. If Paul's claims had any basis, it was a terrible thing that had happened. But I wished for resolution, not war. Not only had Paul had enough of courtrooms and judges and the like, but I was feeling protective of Martin and his family.

Although I didn't learn anything in the session with Wendy that would make this road easier, I felt that the meeting was worthwhile. Most significant, and simultaneously most disturbing, was the fact that Wendy did not question Paul's account of events. In addition to the consistency of his reports, she said, Paul showed all the signs of having suffered such incidents, noting in particular his anxiety and his distorted negativity about himself.

I felt dizzy. I didn't trust my legs to get me to the car. Nor did I think I would be able to drive it safely. But I had my wits about me enough to convey there was no ambiguity about legal proceedings—further mention was not constructive, and Paul's having been armed with this idea (which he admitted to using recklessly) was disadvantageous. Wendy understood my adamance and could see that planting this seed with Paul may have worked against his greater purpose in his communication with Martin. But she explained that when she first learned of these incidents, she felt it was her professional obligation to share this information about the legal issues with Paul. Even though I was perturbed that she had done so, part of me understood.

Paul piped in, expressing irritation with me: "I already said I didn't really mean it, Mom. I told Marty it was just hot air. Your focus is on the wrong things."

He was probably right. No, he *was* right. I just didn't want Paul's ability to move forward thwarted by unproductive, hollow words. When I read the texts, later that week, I was relieved to see that Paul had been so clear. Therefore, the focus could be where it belonged: on the crux of the issue and the best way to deal with the unresolved baggage that was tormenting Paul. In reading the text message exchange, I could see that Martin also needed to work through the issue, evidenced by his offer to talk with Paul's therapist—and by his telling Paul, "I live with it too."

*

THE FIRST FEW months after Paul's disclosure were painful. As I wrestled to comprehend the gravity of it all, I became aware that in the minds of people important to Paul, *he* somehow became the offender and was unworthy of another opportunity to be heard.

Martin had confided in his parents, and I could only surmise that they had dissuaded the follow-up communication Martin had offered Paul. Admittedly, I didn't really know how this decision was reached since they had distanced themselves from me too. Nonetheless, I was pretty sure the intensity behind it would blow over.

I could fathom Martin's parents' denial. It was shocking information that landed in all of our laps; it wasn't easy to process, much less accept. Plus, Martin was a grown man at this point, a successful one. Why get caught up in Paul's emotional roller coaster? I could even get my mind around their exasperation with Paul, whose credibility could easily be dismissed given his history of mental health struggles, substance use, and legal entanglements.

But I wholeheartedly believed they would eventually come around and respond to my efforts to move in a direction that honored our bedrock relationships. Even if Paul had fabricated his story, I thought they would be supportive of Martin talking with him. After all, these people had known Paul all of his life and were among those who understood—or I'd *thought* they did—not just the hardships he'd endured but also his basic goodness, not to mention his idolizing Martin.

The outcome I hoped for was the opposite of parting ways, a fate I frankly couldn't even imagine. I wished for a follow-up conversation between Martin and Paul, with or without a therapist. Because Paul wanted the same, I tried to break the ice, reaching out to Martin and his parents in different ways, always avoiding judgment or blame, even as gradually I began to piece together the extent to which Paul had suffered. But my attempts at any sort of resolution were bitterly rejected.

As much as I was quick to correct Paul when he was wrong, something I wasn't always gentle in doing, I was mindful of his challenges. Paul's handicaps had always had him boxed in, if not trapped, and because they were hidden, he was misunderstood. He coped with this frustration all of his life. Now, in finally dealing with his bottled-up feelings over these sexual encounters, Paul's outburst of anger with inflammatory words—even though short lived—was apparently being used to marginalize him further, a realization that broke my heart.

It wouldn't have taken much time or effort on Martin's part to have made a world of difference for Paul. So I didn't get it. *Why didn't they have some compassion for Paul? Or, if nothing else, want to lend a hand to me?*

I struggled to catch my breath. Paul's years in a system ruled by indignity, where he withstood relentless humiliation and cruelty, had finally come to an end. But less than a year later, an all-too-familiar dread loomed: Paul's punishment didn't fit the crime. While it wasn't the first time, the heartache doesn't recalibrate—particularly when the "sentence" is handed down by people you love, people you turned to for affirmation when weary of injustice.

Paul knew only that Martin was unresponsive and thought time was on his side—a logical conclusion but for the groupthink that threatened it, something I kept to myself.

I gave more thought to the trajectory of Paul's development, remembering when he was twelve and Dr. Zametkin concluded his report saying: "I think Paul is doing extremely well. Given his excellent self-esteem, I am optimistic at this time." Ethna Hopper, the renowned educational consultant, said the same of twelve-year-old Paul, as had every one of his homeschool teachers.

But then at sixteen, Dr. Crain's report rang serious alarms, highlighting a constellation of symptoms, including Paul's startlingly poor self-image, common in victims of sexual abuse or exploitation.

"[Paul] maintains a state of hyper-alertness, a reaction to some concerns that he needs to be defensive and protective in a world in which he must be on guard in order to assure his well-being."

"Paul seems both simultaneously angry and concerned about being victimized himself as many of his responses involved aggressive themes and issues related to harm and potential annihilation."

"He is also preoccupied with issues of bodily concern, as his ideas of being damaged seem related to both physical and mental status."

"The level of Paul's discomfort with himself and self-negativity seems out of proportion to his abilities and his positive qualities and may be related to his suspiciousness."

"He is mistrusting of the intentions of others and feels

vulnerable in a world he views as more threatening. He is guarded and preoccupied with issues of autonomy and personal space."

Why didn't I read Dr. Crain's report and wonder about the dramatic change from age twelve to sixteen?

Paul was hospitalized a couple of months after Dr. Crain's testing, which we came to know was the result of a nervous breakdown, a collapse brought on by his being emotionally overwhelmed. Had these experiences contributed to the feelings that prompted his statement that fateful night: "I don't care if I live or die."?

When Paul was eighteen and coming out of the residual fog of his hospitalization, Dr. Harrison said to me: "Something happened to Paul."

"Nothing happened," I said. Even though I remembered a similar alarm bell from Dr. Crain, I failed to connect the two.

Paul's heightened anxiety, which in many ways dominated his teenage years, challenged his ability to cope and mine to understand and to manage. At the time, I attributed it to adolescence—something that I figured just had to be weathered—and to his unhappiness in school.

I wondered about the significance of these episodes during this turbulent time. This wasn't Paul's only cross to bear, but it added to the mix, prompting me to seek a deeper understanding of the forces at work, including my own role in it all. There was more to this unearthed crisis than the price to be paid now, a price shared by my children and me. But what was the real cost? The cost already borne by Paul alone?

*

IT TOOK YEARS for me to understand—or at least to reach as much understanding as one can regarding the experience of another— these childhood incidents in Paul's life. While still a teenager, he shared this experience with only one other person: Sara. It was when he was either eighteen or nineteen, she recently told me, just a few years after the last incident, and all Paul had told her was that when he was younger, he did things he didn't want to do with a particular person. This was a person he was trying to please and whose favor he wanted to win, but who frequently hurt his feelings anyway.

Naturally, Paul and I had several conversations following his disclosure, but there were often gaps in between. I wanted to be a resource for Paul on his terms. I certainly didn't want to swoop in and expect that suddenly he'd want to share specific information with me. I knew this might inadvertently further his self-doubt or, worse yet, contribute to his anxiety. At first, all he was able to tell me was that he had given in to something he didn't want for a friendship he never fully got. His exact words were, "I felt I prostituted myself only to be rejected the next day, and that hurt."

Over time, Paul told me a few stories. This is just one: He was thirteen. I was going to the store and asked Paul if he wanted to come along. Paul said he did. But then he was chided by Martin, who said, "Only babies go to the store with their mothers."

In recounting this incident, Paul told me, "I didn't really want to go to the store. I just knew what would happen if I stayed back." With tears in his eyes, Paul studied mine, and then he looked away. And I could see the pain of reliving it.

My head was swimming. I wanted to go back in time and save him. What were the signs? I began to wonder how I could have missed them. Then it struck me: There were some things I should have taken seriously and didn't. In truth, I turned the other cheek for the sake of harmony.

In retrospect, I could see that the same part of me that foolishly turned the other cheek, skimmed along the surface of emotional turmoil that cried out for a deeper dive. Maybe it was all too hard, and the best I could muster was going through the motions of being a responsible parent, more perfunctory than mindful. I was good about getting evaluations and therapeutic support, and I did maintain a focus on Paul's academic life even though I took my foot off the gas at times.

These efforts notwithstanding, I didn't forge a response worthy of Paul's suffering. And I kept doubling back, asking myself: *Why?*

I thought about my lifelong tendency to defer to, or accommodate, the moods of those in my inner circle. Believing that I would be okay as long as everyone around me was okay, I often prioritized the needs of others, looking out for the best interest of the group. This was neither a conscious decision nor a sacrifice. If I'd given it any thought at all, which I'm not sure I did, I'd have chalked it up to second nature—a byproduct of temperament along with the value I placed on togetherness. I trusted myself to be even keeled, and I instinctively smoothed the feathers of those more prone to disturb the balance. I was never the squeaky wheel and considered my agreeability a strength.

But I came to see the weakness in there too: Maybe one of avoidance, a reluctance to risk adversity, or even a fear of confronting an unfamiliar truth.

While the ability to turn the other cheek often reflects discipline and wisdom, it can be a convenient excuse for inaction. And if passivity is your default, you allow others to discount your needs. Maybe my passive streak explains my resistance to change. I don't know. I may not be able to untangle my own flaws, but I can't shake them off either. I know I missed important cues, impeding my awareness of Paul's peril and the advocacy he needed during these all-important years. And, I do think my reluctance to rock the boat was a factor in my failure to look beneath the surface, to take on the array of challenges involved.

Insofar as our children are an extension of ourselves, I also had to wonder about the effects of my pattern of deference. Did I sweep my own children into my persona and thereby assign a status of "secondary" to their needs within a group? A question too nuanced for a simple answer . . . but nonetheless one that I ponder.

I do know that the ways we shape and influence our children go deep, and we'd be fools to think the voids, the silences, and the unspoken realities don't rival every bit the lasting impact of our deliberate selves. Added to my reflection, then, I had to face the very real possibility that I didn't just fail to protect Paul, I modeled behavior that didn't teach him to protect himself.

I was naïve in other ways. As the mother of a disabled child, I should have been more aware of the fact that children with intellectual disabilities are four to ten times more likely than those without disabilities to be victims of unwanted sexual encounters with adults or other children. If you know what the odds are, you watch for signs. You pay attention. You almost expect it.

I read *Beyond Betrayal*, a book by Richard Gartner, a pioneer in research and clinical work on sexual exploitation of boys and a co-founder of *Male Survivor: National Organization Against Male Sexual Victimization*. I contacted Dr. Gartner and told him Paul's story. He followed up, giving me advice that I do believe was somewhat helpful to Paul—an online forum where victims of sexual exploitation can connect with others whose stories are similar. Because this group discussion was in writing, with anonymity, it was perfect for Paul. I hoped the realization that he wasn't alone in his experience would help ease his shame and his self-hatred.

I heard Dr. Gartner speak about the adult consequences of childhood sexual manipulation or abuse that are common for both girls and boys. These include depression, anxiety, addictive and compulsive behaviors, and suicidal thinking. "All these after-effects are ugly," Dr. Gartner explained. "They're not only painful for victims but also costly for families and our society."

Based on his groundbreaking research on the plight of males, Dr. Gartner described the overlay of masculine socialization, explaining that boys in our society are socialized to think there are certain things that men do and don't do: Men are resilient, they do not cry, they aren't even that verbal, and they certainly aren't victims. In order to acknowledge feeling victimized, then, a boy or man has to in some way say that what defines him "is not male." Men are therefore prone to feelings of isolation and distrust, as well as to outbursts and addiction. Those who don't get treatment are statistically more likely to end up in prison.

Also a resource for men, an organization called "1in6" helped me as I tried to comprehend Paul's past encounters and their impact:

> "Unwanted or abusive" is how we refer to past sexual experiences that can cause a variety of problems, long after they happened. The "or" in "unwanted or abusive" does not imply that any unwanted sexual experience was also "abusive." We don't believe this is true. We're just hoping that "unwanted" works well enough when it comes to describing past sexual experiences that may have contributed to problems you have now.

My guess is that what Paul experienced was unwanted, not abusive, but I will never know. Regardless, I have come to understand that no matter the label, the impact is far reaching. And Paul's being blamed only magnified the pain.

*

AFTER PAUL DIED, I set about organizing papers—integrating his with mine—sorting things he'd saved, reading or re-reading his handwritten journals. At the bottom of his trunk, which had moved with him from place to place, I found an old journal in a brown envelope with some other papers. I recognized the cover—it had an Asian motif.

I had flipped through many a journal from his youth and had pulled hundreds of torn-out pages from the trash. But I had not seen these pages in this journal, even though at a glance they looked so familiar. I knew his teenage handwriting: The blackened-out words. The periods the size of any letter, often making a hole in the paper. The absence of spaces between words. The misspellings. More than one hundred pages, so full of writings that the words spilled onto the covers, front and back.

In this particular journal I came across the poems of a youthful Paul, a boy in a great deal of pain. There was also a drawing, too painful to describe, on a page he'd folded over, which I re-folded and will not view again. A few of his writings that I could decipher were:

My flesh hypnotizes my brain
and beats down reality's door.
Hinges fly,
true perception dies
As my scars tell the story.
Now your son lies raped on the floor.
A pedifyal, dried, beat, and washed ashore
Now your son lies naked in my bed
Disgusting ritual, repetitive bastard
Disgusting ritual, its so dead

• • •

If only someone knew,
but there isn't a sound.
If only someone fucking knew,
but I like all the rest have to proceed
into a pre fabricated dream.
The doors swing open and smash against the wall
And intimidation rules me
While I the broken victory
lie naked an pinned to the ground,
Exposed to this monstar
My wounds proceed all day
And feer is shot into me again and again
Like the swift poke of an angry swordsman.
But only that wasn't a sword.
It was his cock.
It dripped and pounded on me
as if I were a bloody punching bag with a hole in it.
I know it's fucking sick,
and if you won't tell,
I'd most wonderfly appreciate it

• • •

In a cloud of loneleness,
To comprehend these destorted feelings
They force me to kneel at gods feet.
My hands tremble with fear
As i bend to commit myself to coldness.
The climbing fier of anxiety grows,
Igniting a past of shame
And leaving the ash to
Furtalize your sadistic excitement.

Whos to blame when I'm all alone
Lost in black space
No light ever shown
The bright stars burn my skin
But ive been tuchd by an angel,
Morning is still a mile away.

There was more. Much more. Another couple of lines I could read made me the sickest of all, *"I can feel it in my bones tonight, swolin flesh will be cut off with a hult, and will scease to rape my insides. We will drink so mutch whisky it will be allright."*

I shut my eyes; I closed the journal. But I couldn't shut out his words. Words of anguish—from long ago and from Paul the boy— landed in the pit of my stomach where they found a permanent home. They ache; I ache. The anguish of my boy, now mine to carry.

Had I seen these writings when Paul was a teenager, or even when we were navigating the sea of troubles brought forth, or, for that matter, at any time while Paul was still alive, I can only guess how my deepened insight could have better supported Paul. Once again, I was struck by Paul's suffering in isolation and the ways in which so many people let him down, sometimes even me.

*

WHAT I HAD hoped would blow over, didn't. A year or so after Paul told me about all this, not only was it clear that Paul's rejection was enduring but also that it included me—and even Keely— with implications that ended our relationships with lifelong friends and strained those within a wider circle. What I did not yet know, and wouldn't have believed, is that Paul would never have any further communication with Martin. That door wasn't just closed; it was nailed shut.

My instincts to protect our privacy—combined with my continued hope for a resolution—precluded my sharing it, even, at first, with members of my family. I also recoiled at the thought of others rushing to judgment, taking sides, perpetuating misinformation. Compounding my aversion to any such scenario was the thought of speculation generated solely by the salaciousness of it all. But knowing that my voice had not contributed to the impressions of others was both a comfort and a concern.

The repercussions of our being distanced—intertwined with Paul's dehumanization—seeped into every aspect of our lives, isolating the three of us, and weakening the struggle to overcome. I was as troubled by the severity of our being cutoff, as I was by my inability to affect or even to understand it. Try as I might, I couldn't construct the justification for ending meaningful relationships. Paul wasn't always stable, a fact I knew better than anyone. And, yes, he had been volatile in his confrontation, but he'd quickly recouped; Martin, to his credit, had met him halfway. So it just didn't make sense.

I longed to bring reason to the table, something I saw as instrumental to the best outcome for my friends as well as for Keely and me, and especially for Paul. I worried about the inevitable burdens of rigid thinking, and I feared the long-term harm of being stuck in it. The knee-jerk tendency to cast blame elsewhere, and its allure of self-preservation or a quick fix, can be a natural human reaction, but it fails the test of time. What seems a simplistic solution risks unintended consequences down the road. I prayed we could do better.

Knowing that our collective rejection would compound Paul's suffering, my initial tact was to shield him from this reality, disclosing as little as possible without arousing his suspicions. I felt that he was burdened enough, contending with diminishing hope for a resolution with Martin. And if he'd known the extent of the impact on my life, and on his sister's, it would kill him.

I began seeing Dorcas Gray, a therapist in Annapolis, who tried to help me as I grappled with a way forward. I knew I needed an outlet for divulging the despair I hid from others on top of which I welcomed the guidance and the grounded perspective of a seasoned professional. But what I really wanted was for someone to tell me how to undo this nightmare, to make things right. I wanted my regular troubled life—not this one! And, most of all, I wanted Paul to be afforded the respect that he deserved.

Dorcas told me early on: For me, a crisis was just "vintage Paul," and I'd weathered enough to be conditioned to apply a rational response; whereas, for those less seasoned, a more emotional reaction was predictable. While this made sense, and I wasn't impatient with an initial over-reaction on anyone's part, I didn't get why my ongoing hardships—suddenly on the rise—were irrelevant. In fact, if it weren't so sad, it would be funny: I just couldn't get it through my head that I didn't matter.

After many attempts to bridge the gap, including those Dorcas helped me devise, it started to sink in that my continued outreach could be futile and Paul's ever finding needed healing, remote. But still, I was conflicted about how to maneuver and was not quick to give up. Whether my determination was a strength or downright fool-hardy, I didn't know, but I continued efforts to combat the schism. Some things in life, I reasoned, are worth fighting for. I made phone calls and sent emails asking for the opportunity to talk, to listen, to be heard. I even sent greeting cards, flowers, or gifts for milestone occasions.

It was during this time that Paul left Baltimore, a move that ruled out his continuing with Wendy. He did find new mental health providers. But these folks were not at all interested in talking with me, given the HIPAA privacy laws, which set national standards for boundaries that protect individuals' medical records and other personal health information. I was proud of Paul for seeking help, but I was frustrated by the rigidity of their interpretation of the law, especially in light of Paul's needs and the turmoil in our lives.

Dorcas told me of a local psychiatrist, Howard Pressman, whom she believed could help Paul and would also talk with me. Even though Dr. Pressman didn't accept any insurance, I decided to take Paul to see him and did so weekly for several months. To do this, I had to leave work, drive to Silver Spring to get Paul, take him to Dr. Pressman's office in Edgewater, Maryland, and then drive Paul back to Silver Spring before returning to Annapolis. In sum, this was at least a four-hour block of time, not to mention a significant expense.

Paul liked Dr. Pressman, and I did too. He was smart, and he was confident in his ability to sensibly include me without violating Paul's rights. In addressing Paul's childhood sexual encounters, he said it was a tragedy that both participants didn't get the help they needed, as well as the opportunity to work through all the emotional disturbance. Those who do, he said—friends, families, even blended families, and neighbors—often overcome these obstacles and heal, growing closer as a result of a difficult journey faced together.

As Paul increasingly sized up the losses that had accumulated since he'd come forward, he found them nearly impossible to accept. He frequently asked—sometimes begged—me to "make things better." One day he said, "I was riding on the bus today and looking out the window, and I thought to myself that I am mad that Martin and his family dumped us. But I miss seeing them so much."

In time, I knew I had to accept my powerlessness over the lost relationships and Paul's being demonized. Keeping my own lingering sorrow in check and warding off bitterness, I gradually began to address Paul's pleas without expressing false hope. I realized that letting go of what you can't control and accepting reality—no matter how much you feared it or how brutal it is—promotes a peace of mind that is freeing. In comparison to me, Paul was behind the curve on this evolution because I had kept him there, and I knew I was denying him needed realism—the only option left for us. While I remained prone to occasional fluctuations in my thinking, I do remember a conversation in which I told Paul that there was nothing more I could do. Therefore, it didn't surprise me to find the following sad poem in his laptop, written in 2015, three years after the confrontation:

MOTHERLAND

Motherland is baron, fruitless and cold
Father is a vagabond searching for his soul
Brother who cherishes music and poems
Takes it all lightly till he has no more home
Sister is always in a state of disarray
Always on the brink of going away
So I pose the question do we cherish what's left
Is it worth the time to forgive and forget
Mother responded no with a solemn look on her face
As if the words gave her mouth a bitter taste
Now I too know of the sorrows of home
Living amongst family but feeling completely alone

In one conversation, Paul asked me, "Do they still love us, Mom?"

I thought for a minute, not knowing the answer myself, "Yes," I said. "I believe they do."

"Why do you think so?"

"I guess because I don't know where love goes," I said. "It can't just vanish."

"Do you want to know what all this makes me think?" he asked.

"Yes, of course," I said.

"It makes me wonder if they ever did." *Point taken.*

With my current access to Paul's phone, I was able to see a text message he sent Martin on June 8, 2015, three years after their only other communication. It reads:

Hey. This is Paul. I'd really like to talk to you at some point if at all possible, Just between you and me. If you can't, that's cool too.

There was no answer. But through it all, Paul longed for a breakthrough in communication, a fact I bore witness to for the rest of his life.

Chapter 12

FLOATING BETWEEN

Several bad thoughts away from the fall leave me hanging on summer's cusp.
This in between season seems to symbolize my nonexistence to the world outside,
Which does not pay mind to the grumbles from beyond their storefront windows,
From behind wet denim jackets, and mouths hung wrong,
From the bad postured bums, scraping for a meal in the downtown harbor noon.

IN SPITE OF missing Casey, Paul found some comfort in being in Montgomery County, mostly because he would be closer to Kayla but also because he'd suffered so much torment during his eight years in Baltimore that he felt his proximity to Washington, D.C., offered hope.

Paul did have a way of idealizing certain places where he hadn't lived. After all, his world was often harsh and unkind and, sometimes, rather than looking inward, he would profess simplified views. "The people in Vermont are nicer than they are here," he once told me. "If I lived there, I would fit in." In other words, his problems were due, at least in part, to geography.

Job hunting was unrealistic until his leg healed. Furthermore, I wasn't optimistic that he would find anything in short order, so we searched for an affordable room to rent. He was still receiving cash assistance, which helped a little, but otherwise I covered the majority of his expenses—child support, cell phone, and rent. Paul and I both felt pressure to hasten a solution; he was sleeping on a couch and risked wearing out his welcome with Sara's kind boyfriend.

I don't think I've mentioned how frequently Paul called me. Fueled by his anxiety and his OCD—along with the fact that I was his "go-to" person with any news, good or bad—Paul usually called me multiple times per day. If I didn't answer, he would call again within a minute or less. Sometimes he would leave a message, but often when his call went to voicemail it was inadvertent on his part, and he didn't say anything. So, in addition to dozens of missed calls, I had an equal number of voicemail recordings of him breathing.

Rather than calling me multiple times in a row, I suggested he either leave a specific message or send a text. I explained that I would return his call when I could, but seeing that he'd called me seventeen times in a two-minute period didn't help me know what I could do for him. This advice didn't exactly sink in, or he didn't heed it; while he did leave some messages and texted frequently, I continued to get numerous calls placed back-to-back.

When the mood was right, I teased Paul about the number of calls, nicknaming him "Phone Call Paul." One time I took a screenshot of my "Recents" calls—which read "Paulie (59)"—and sent him the photo, along with the caption: "This is not normal!!"

I can laugh at myself too. I wasn't happy about getting so many calls, and I admit I wasn't always immune to the anxiety they provoked. Yet, if twenty-four hours elapsed without a call from Paul, I didn't exactly like that either; it made me uneasy. In essence, he was damned if he did, and damned if he didn't!

Some of Paul's calls or messages fell into the "take action now" category:

"I left my cell phone on the bus; what should I do?"

"I'm in the ER because my blood pressure is spiking and it's dangerously high."

"I'm going to buy a bus ticket to Oregon so if you can come get my things before tomorrow night, I won't have to pay rent, which I can't do because I'm using the rent money for the bus ticket."

My favorites were the ones that began, "Don't be mad, but . . ."

For years, Paul's calls were distinguished by a ring tone I assigned to him only. And to this day, when I hear that particular ring—despite the fact that it's always coming from another person's phone and sometimes at a distance, not to mention that Paul is gone—my heart races, my muscles tense. Conditioning or PTSD? I can't say.

But we spent a fair amount of time going over non-urgent things that were on his mind, ranging from the fact that he was mourning the break-up with Casey, and did I think he would ever have another girlfriend, to a stain on his jeans. Conversations about the latter would go something like this:

Paul: "If you had a stain on your jeans, what would you do?"

Me: "I would wash them and, if that didn't get the stain out, I might try stain remover."

Paul: "And if nothing worked, would you wear the jeans anyway?"

Me: "Probably. Jeans are so casual that a stain doesn't matter that much."

Paul: "But what would you do if you had a stain on your jeans?"

Me: "I told you what I would do."

Paul: "So what would you do? Would you wear jeans with a stain on them?"

As Dr. Pressman had told him, "You suck your mother into your vortex, and she has no way out."—a statement I repeated to Paul on occasion, when doing so would be taken in good humor. In the same spirit, a couple of Christmases ago, I put a stain-remover stick in Paul's stocking. He laughed—I knew he would!

*

AFTER PAUL STAYED with John for a few days, we found a room for rent in nearby Wheaton, in a house that was on the bus line.

The opportunity to take the room coincided with a week I was out of town for a professional conference, but thankfully Don agreed to help Paul move. I went over to visit the following week to see the place and help him get further situated.

The house was inhabited by the owner, a middle-aged woman named Nan, and two young men close to Paul's age, Sam and Tim, also renters who had known each other through their work as bicycle repairmen. By the time Paul moved in, Sam and Tim were looking elsewhere due to difficulties with Nan. Paul's first reports to me were that she was moody and unpredictable, but when he told me he was awakened in the middle of the night by her loud chanting, coming from outside where she was sitting cross-legged on the front lawn, I agreed he could take the opportunity to move along with Tim, who was renting a basement with two rooms in Takoma Park. Sam had found a room in Silver Spring, just up the road, and he and Paul would remain friends. I lost my security deposit but fortunately had not signed a lease. Our greatest blessing at this point, decisively, was that Paul was in a walking boot.

I took off from work to help Paul move and, by day's end, I was downtrodden with concerns about his conditions. The good features included a kind landlord, who was a retired attorney; a safe neighborhood; an outside entrance to the basement; a good-sized room for Paul; and—even though they had to share the upstairs kitchen—the basement had a full bath, a washer and dryer, and shelves on which they could keep dry goods in an area where they could set up a small table. The bad news, however, was very bad—the basement had no heat. This was November 2013, and winter weather was almost upon us.

The next weekend, I packed my station wagon full to the brim with things from my attic, including rugs, lots of warm bedclothes, an oil-filled convection radiator heater, a couple of chairs, end tables, a dresser, lamps, and some artwork. I must have been powered by adrenaline, getting all this from the third floor and into the car, which I had to pack and re-pack for everything to fit. Paul and I worked together and did make the space look good, arranging the furniture to define a sitting area and a bedroom. Paul was very particular about things being neat and in their proper place, and he enjoyed making decisions about his set-up. I left that day feeling better.

Paul saw Kayla frequently, for which Sara deserves much credit, and they enjoyed activities ranging from sledding to cake-baking. Paul sent me a video of Kayla, who was just learning to ride a bike, pedaling with Tim's help along the street where he and Paul lived. I responded to the video, "Wow! Kayla is great!"

Paul replied:

That's exactly right. Im so proud of her. Its kind of something how much little things like just seeing her play can make me feel so proud. I havent done my best but i still feel so good about her. Such an inspiration. She's taught me so much about love. i dont quite know how to explain the kind of gifts shes given me. Its amazing the power she has over me. Im already grown and i somehow know she'll teach me more about life than anyone has. Its truly amazing.

Paul got health insurance—thanks to the Affordable Care Act—and promptly took a bus to the Montgomery County Department of Health in Rockville, Maryland, for an intake assessment. With their help, he found behavioral health providers in Silver Spring that accepted Medicaid. Since this office was only four miles from Paul's house, he was able to walk to his weekly appointments.

I took Paul to two of his sessions, briefly meeting his first therapist, who soon left the organization, as well as his second. When Paul told me they pretty much prescribed what he asked for, and that frequently it was a nurse practitioner instead of a psychiatrist providing the prescription, I was doubly frustrated by my inability to communicate with them. He was prescribed Abilify and Lexapro, and he was toying with the idea of stopping the Abilify. I didn't think this was a good move, but there was nothing I could do.

I usually saw Paul two or three weekends per month, taking care of such practical matters as getting him a much-needed new bed or doing something fun, such as going into Georgetown or having him show me nearby sites that he had discovered. Paul was attending AA meetings, where he'd made a few friends and enjoyed social opportunities—going to concerts, helping plan events, and connecting with people who gave him odd jobs. At this point, he had mastered getting around Washington and its Maryland suburbs.

In March 2014, Paul fell on an icy patch in his neighborhood and broke his leg. He was taken by ambulance to the closest emergency room, where he was given a temporary cast and a referral to an orthopedic surgeon in Greenbelt. In leaving the hospital that evening, Paul called to tell me about it.

"WHAT? YOU BROKE YOUR LEG WALKING? ON A SIDEWALK? Tell me you are not serious," I said without a trace of motherly love but at least refraining from launching the accusations that crossed my mind or revealing other suddenly racing thoughts like: *Is it possible to divorce a kid? I want off of this ride!*

Even though I didn't like him anymore, I took Paul to the orthopedic surgeon the next day. After seeing Paul and reading the x-rays we'd hand delivered from the hospital, the doctor told us that Paul's leg had broken so easily because it hadn't been adequately fixed after the initial break. In other words, it was an accident waiting to happen. Paul's surgical needs, the doctor explained, were too complicated for him, and he referred us to a traumatologist in Bethesda, Maryland.

Just as it hit me that I couldn't justify sustained scorn for Paul, my incredulousness was redirected. *Too complicated for the orthopedic specialist?* I'd never heard of such a thing. A traumatologist? Did he read Tarot Cards too?

The orthopedic traumatologist, Timothy Bhattacharyya, told us that Paul's fracture and re-fracture presented a dilemma and explained how the pre-existing deformity from the first break would complicate the surgery. He had a couple of options, and his approach would have to be determined during the procedure. Ideally the traditional rod would be inserted into the bone; however, the scar tissue could make this impossible, meaning the doctor would have to use plates and screws on the outside of the bone.

Instead of scheduling the surgery and sending us home from the appointment, as I had expected, Dr. Bhattacharyya sent us directly to nearby Suburban Hospital. He explained that we needed to go to the emergency room, as that was the best way for a Medicaid patient to get on the surgery docket. While we had to wait many hours to be admitted, I appreciated the doctor's advice. But as I sat up half the night in my work clothes, with Paul in pain, I experienced the added hardships of medical care for the disadvantaged.

In the wee hours, I was able to make the two-hour round trip—home and back to the hospital—before the surgery. Paul was in tears as he was wheeled into the operating room but was glad to see me, reaching out to give me a hug and kiss as he went by. The surgery lasted hours, and while the doctor had to resort to the plates and screws, my homework had assured me that Paul was in good hands.

Sitting in the hospital with Paul over the following days, I was consumed with worry over how in the world he would manage life in his basement room, navigating stairs at the entrance as well as to the kitchen. While scraping up ideas for possible resources—all remote if not far-fetched—and putting out feelers, it dawned on me that I should call Paul's landlord, Arnesea, to give her a head's up about his potential move. To my surprise, she suggested we move Paul to the first floor of her house where she had a spare bedroom and where there would be no steps for him to maneuver. Arnesea had developed a genuine affection for Paul, and I was beyond grateful.

My next worry was how to get his things moved in time, but I was able to recruit Maureen and her husband Jack (another of my closest comrades from my library days) to help me, something only the best of friends would even consider. Moving Paul's bed, dressers, other furniture, rugs, and personal items (none of which had been packed or organized in anticipation)—up the outside stairs and around the sloped yard, in the front door and down the hall to the bedroom, and then set up for Paul who was essentially helpless—took us the whole day. With our average age upwards of sixty-five, I was amazed at our accomplishment.

After five days in the hospital, Paul was released. He wasn't able to put any weight on his leg and was reliant on crutches to get around, something he'd gotten the hang of thanks to the attentive hospital staff. While his maneuvering gained proficiency over the weeks, it was a trying time due to other limitations.

Keely took off from work to get Paul to his follow-up appointment with Dr. Bhattacharyya, and Paul's cast was removed on schedule.

*

PAUL'S LEG WOULD never be the same. It was misshapen, painful, and he walked with a limp. But by summer, he was able to put his full weight down and resume his long walks. Thanks to his friendship with Sam, Paul was able to get a good deal on a very nice bike, which he used daily, even riding it to Annapolis one time to visit with me, a thirty-one-mile trek—one way! While he loved the bike and valued his friendship with Sam, Paul struggled off and on with depression. In a June text message to me, he wrote:

I have been feeling depressed lately. I don't know what is going to become of me. I don't want to grow older and be lonely. We used to have it all. I do wish you would go to the beach this summer, Mom. I know you like that. Please talk to me about these things.

I was struggling too, much of which I kept from Paul. But I lamented in a note to my therapist:

I am so confused as to how I can best support Paul. I need advice in terms of direction-setting. I try to balance the sacrifices I need to make with some degree of self-preservation, but I am not sure my efforts are strategic or that my thinking is clear.

He cannot get a job on his own and has gone through long periods of trying very hard to get the most menial work without any luck. The sad thing is, he's a hard worker, which he's proven in every job he's had. He would love to earn some money and has dreams of one day owning a car and functioning independently, but he has no skills, minimal experience, and difficulty advocating for himself, in addition to having a felony on his record.

I sent Don a text message that winter, and while he and I had not collaborated or strategized regarding a problem for either child, we got along fine and he was one of the only people who knew of Paul's recent disclosure and his resulting losses, although Paul told me they never had a discussion about it. So I gave it a try: "Is there a time this weekend that we could talk? I am very worried about the complexity of Paul's hardships and have nowhere else to turn."

He replied: "Sorry but no."

And that was that. It would be a couple of years before I would stick my hand in that fire again. I use that analogy only because it hurt. It hurt a lot. But I didn't dwell on it. I suggested to Paul that maybe his mental health providers could help steer him with regard to job training, but he said he'd been told they could not.

One of Paul's AA friends told him about a job in Washington: making pizza dough for Union Kitchen. While this ended up being another disappointment for Paul—he interviewed but didn't get the position—he did start thinking that there could be a place for him in the food business. He also told me that the interview had gone well, making him think they'd done a background check.

Trying to help him, I wrote to a social worker I knew through my contacts in Baltimore:

> Paul is struggling mightily. In general, I believe the issues are twofold. For one, his medication is not adequately addressing his mood disorder. Since his move, I am not in the loop with his mental health providers, and Paul adamantly denies a mental health condition, saying he has agreed to therapy again only to help him "cope with all his bad luck." I am proud of him for seeking support, but I think he needs more sophisticated medication management.
>
> The other half of the dilemma is the need for Paul to progress in his life to the extent he is capable. I have always felt, with the right breaks and support, he could function independently, but his luck seems to worsen, and I do not know of the availability of the resources he desperately needs.
>
> If you have any suggestions or knowledge of others who Paul or I could turn to, I would be so grateful. As I listen to his cries for help, I rack my brain and, in doing so this evening, I thought of you. Thank you for just listening.

While this acquaintance was sympathetic and did give me some leads—all of which I explored—nothing concrete came of it.

Paul liked the idea of a farm community, and I discovered a place called Red Wiggler Community Farm that was located in Montgomery County. I contacted their executive director, with whom I exchanged several emails. He was out of town at the time but said he would call me when he returned. I never received a call, and I struck out in reaching a live person when I phoned them. But I liked what I knew of the place and planned to follow up later.

Paul had completed an application for Social Security Disability Income (SSDI) when he lived in Baltimore, a process that had been initiated by his former therapist without my involvement. But he was confused by the mixed messages he got when he inquired about the status. I listened to his explanation but never took any action; frankly, I understood less than Paul about the process.

A room became available in the house where Sam lived in Silver Spring, and with Sam's encouragement Paul decided to take it, giving Arnesea a month's notice. Sam had agreed to help Paul move and, because I didn't think another move was going to solve anything, I was glad to be off the hook.

In hindsight, I do think the quality of life for Paul was somewhat better in this house. The owner, Jake, didn't live there but came around for repairs or to collect the rent. He was pleasant, and Paul liked him. Two other renters in the house were not very nice, Paul said, but he didn't have to interact with them much. Also, as it turned out, Sam was a better friend to Paul than Tim, and Paul had no regrets about the move.

Paul and Sam came to Annapolis for the 4th of July. After they did some fishing in the morning, the three of us went to a crab feast hosted by Keely and her boyfriend, Sean. Later we watched the Annapolis fireworks display, and Paul and Sam returned to my house and spent the night with me. I enjoyed my time with them and could see that they had fun together, which did my heart good. Sam was a father as well, and Paul was impressed by his devotion to his two children, one of whom was his biological child, and the other was the child of his former wife. Nonetheless, Sam loved both children and saw them a couple of times per week.

*

THAT SAME SUMMER I was contacted by Michael Steinhardt, the attorney who had agreed to take Paul's case in defending his SSDI application. I learned that Paul's first application had been denied, which apparently was almost routine. But an appeal had been filed and a hearing was scheduled.

Mr. Steinhardt needed documentation from me, which I provided—more than he bargained for, I'm sure. I think I made two trips from my car to his office, each time carrying several large shopping bags full of accumulated documents. At his request, Paul and I met with him a few weeks prior to the hearing, which was scheduled for September.

The SSI hearing was difficult for Paul, something I should have anticipated. This day-long process in the Office of Hearings and Appeals, in the Symphony Center in Baltimore, started with us packed into a room with others who were awaiting a similar hearing. For anyone who enjoys people watching, take it from me—this is an especially hot spot.

But Paul was fidgety. He was called before I was. An hour or so later, I was brought in to join him. We were in a classroom-size space that otherwise looked like a typical courtroom. My testimony entailed answering a multitude of questions about Paul's schooling and learning disabilities, as well as his mental health diagnosis over the course of his life—all of which I was able to address with candor.

Afterward, as we drove to Annapolis to Paul's favorite restaurant, the Mexican Café, he yelled at me pretty much the whole way. It was then that I realized he never before had heard the same degree of detail regarding his documented disabilities, the hardships his differences had presented in school, and the challenges he faced as a result. In thinking about it further, I could understand how hard it must've been for him to hear certain specifics, such as the fact that his teenage years didn't include parties or dances or football games, with socialization pretty much non-existent, and that when he turned to drugs, he was escaping his pain and self-medicating rather than partying. But to Paul's credit, he rebounded during dinner and we had a good time, after which I drove him back to Silver Spring.

I had mixed feelings about the pending outcome of the hearing, and I was mostly able to forget about it during the two months that passed before we would get the decision. When it did cross my mind, I flashed back to being a child and the way I felt watching the TV show, *Queen for a Day*. The winner, appearing so grateful but simultaneously tearful, was crowned "queen" and wrapped in a luxurious velvet cape, which I'm pretty sure was red even though our TV was black and white. All I could think at the time was that she won because the applause-o-meter told us that her circumstances were worse than those of the other contestants. So, I wondered, what did she really win? And, was that new frost-free deep freeze or self-cleaning range going to change her dismal plight? I didn't think so. And because I didn't, that show always made me sad. I even felt sorry for the women who didn't "win." Would anyone want to be first runner-up in the most down-and-out contest?

Now, although I didn't know much about SSDI, I didn't feel as though Paul stood to "win" anything from it. The whole situation left me emotionally depleted and, in many ways, sorrowful. On the one hand, I wanted more for Paul and still had hopes for his future, as did he. But on the other hand, Paul's disabilities worked against his getting and keeping a job. It wasn't as if disability income would preclude his realizing his potential, but I guess I just wasn't sure what to think.

Somewhere in this period, I heard that our attorney, Mr. Steinhardt, had told a mutual acquaintance that Paul was among the most interesting clients he'd ever worked with. Once again I was reminded that Paul was different even among the "different."

Paul came home for his birthday in October, and we had brunch with Keely and Sean, which he appreciated, but his mood was mostly somber. With my sisters having grandchildren at this point—all nearby if not under the same roof—our routines had understandably started to shift. And combined with our loss of friends, celebrations of any sort often served as an unwelcomed reminder of our loneliness, even though Keely and Paul and I routinely tried to pretend otherwise. In looking back, I can see that each one of us exercised restraint in expressing these emotions for the sake of the other two. Also significant were Paul's struggles to find his place in the world—and his ongoing hardships were not lost on Keely or me. Even so, we continued to perfect the art of a stiff upper lip.

Several weeks later, Paul was home again for a few days for Thanksgiving, a holiday that we were to spend with Keely and Sean and Sean's cousin's family, visiting from Vermont. On Wednesday evening, Paul and I were getting ready to go meet Keely and Sean at a local restaurant when Paul realized he'd planned to go to an AA meeting that same night and had arranged for a friend to pick him up in Silver Spring. Because of the holiday, Paul had gotten his days confused, which I assured him was understandable.

But he was overcome with worry. Pacing back and forth, he said he had called his friend and couldn't reach him. I suggested he leave a message, but Paul was afraid that his friend wouldn't get it in time and that he would be inconvenienced, waiting around for Paul and not knowing where he was. I don't want to belabor the details of our conversation, but there was no solution that could ease Paul's mind. He was too worried and too fixated on his worry to redirect his thinking or his energy. I was able to get him out of the house and to the restaurant, but he couldn't focus on the menu or on greeting the others who were joining us. He kept going outside to call his friend. I could see him on the sidewalk. Pacing. Back and forth.

Part of me wanted to put him in a cab back to Silver Spring—or Timbuktu for that matter—but a bigger part of me knew his OCD wasn't adequately addressed. He literally couldn't help himself. On Thursday, Paul was better. But having met some of Sean's family the night before, he was embarrassed to see them again. He said he knew he'd made a bad impression. I assured him that they were such nice people that he didn't have to worry. I meant it too, and Paul knew I did and was ultimately appeased by my words. Thanksgiving was a pretty good day.

Similar ups and downs played out at Christmas. We were invited to Don and Lucy's for Christmas night, but Paul didn't want to go. He felt no one would care if he went or not. I did my best to talk him into coming with me, but he wanted to stay home. I finally decided to go with Keely and Sean, leaving Paul my car in case he changed his mind—which he did an hour or so later. But again his mood was flat. I gave him credit for trying and knew how much of a battle it had been.

The ruling on Paul's disability application was "fully favorable," with the judge's decision detailed in a nine-page document that included:

The claimant has the following severe impairments [determined by medical evidence]: bipolar disorder, generalized anxiety disorder, obsessive compulsive disorder, history of attention deficit disorder, and hand tremors.

The claimant's ability to perform work at all exertional levels has been compromised by limitations. To determine the extent to which these limitations erode the occupational base of unskilled work at all exertional levels, I asked the vocational expert whether jobs exist in the national economy for an individual with the claimant's age, education, work experience, and residual functional capacity. The vocational expert testified that given all of these factors there are no jobs in the national economy that the individual could perform.

A finding of 'disabled' is appropriate as defined in the Social Security Act. . . . The claimant's substance use is not a contributing factor material to the determination of disability.

Paul had testified honestly about his substance use and his long periods of sobriety, which the document addressed: "The record shows that the claimant's mental health symptoms exist during periods of abstinence." As a result of this decision, Paul began receiving a monthly check and was slated to have a disability review conducted every eighteen months. Fortunately, Kayla received a benefit as well.

Though Paul needed less of my financial help, which he felt good about, his monthly check covered only half of his rent, food, and other bare necessities. He continued to look for work, interviewing at such places as Burger King and Safeway, and he checked in with old friends, like Bill West, without any luck. Eventually, Paul signed up as a volunteer participant in several clinical research trials, for which he got paid—and sometimes even put up in a hotel, exciting experiences he documented with lots of photos sent from his phone to mine.

*

IN MAY 2015, WE got the good news that Keely and Sean were engaged and would be married the following summer. Keely told her brother right away and he was genuinely happy. After they spoke, he sent me a text message: "Keely is getting married!!! I can't believe it!! I cried a little bit when she told me."

While Paul had some good days, and did many things that made me proud, I knew he wasn't happy. He tried to be, but it was hard. My lifelong friend, and best friend from my childhood, Cheryl Morgan, suggested I contact Meryl Lieberman, another friend who had grown up in our neighborhood, and whose career had been devoted to advocating for the mentally ill. Meryl had earned a doctorate in clinical psychology and was the director of Casa Milagro, a therapeutic community in Santa Fe, which she'd founded in 1999. I wrote Meryl a multi-page email in June 2015, seeking her advice and providing a detailed overview of Paul's story. I concluded with this: "My heart breaks for him but I do not know where to turn. Any advice you may have for me would be greatly appreciated. I am sorry to be taking so much of your time, but I am desperate for some direction."

Meryl replied right away:

Dear Jessie,

I have to say how blessed Paul is to have such a staunch advocate in you, Jessie. Your letter would benefit so many professionals, family members, and caregivers.

For starters, Paul could thrive in a community where he is valued for his contributions and accepted for his creative quirks, not defined or limited by a diagnosis. Unfortunately, I'm unfamiliar with out-of-state resources. I have visited Spring Lake Ranch in Vermont, Gould Farm in Massachusetts, and CooperRiis in North Carolina—all glorious, but prohibitively expensive.

NAMI should have a national registry of communities. I will be in touch again, soon, with a more heart-centered response to your brave quest.

Much to talk about. Believe me, I understand.

Much Love to you,
Meryl

P.S. I appreciate that your son carries your dad's name. Professor Dunleavy was one of my most influential mentors—I loved him fiercely and honor his memory.

I told Paul about this contact simply because I wanted him to know that efforts were afoot to help alleviate his struggles. While I was seeking Meryl's expertise without an eye toward her program, Paul ended up going on the Casa Milagro website, noticing that the residents were on SSI, and getting excited about the possibility of joining her residential community. His enthusiasm surprised me because Casa Milagro was clearly designed for people with mental illness. Nevertheless, Paul downloaded all the paperwork and the application, filling it out in detail, along with the required questionnaire, which he then gave to me to send electronically.

The questions, with Paul's answers:

What are you interested in learning, doing?
I want to be able to articulate ideas to people as well as I can write them down. I am an aspiring writer and poet and because of a long period of depression I have writer's block which I would like to overcome. I would like to continue my studies at the community college.

Do you get along with people? Does living in a group feel comfortable to you?
Yes. Yes. I would rather be with people. I want to relate and

be understood.

Describe your support system.
I have the support of my mother and sister. I have made some good connections through AA.

What are your personality quirks? How would you describe yourself in five words?
I ask a lot of questions, which people can find annoying. I can be overly anxious and obsessive.
5 words: <u>sensitive</u>, <u>artistic</u>, <u>outdoorsy</u>, <u>anxious</u>, <u>kind</u>.

What bugs you? How would you deal with rules? Routines?
Being misunderstood. Leaving social situations when I feel I misrepresented myself due to being shy. I am not a trouble-maker. I follow rules. I do best with a routine.

What else is important for us to know about you?
- I need a change. I have been a victim for so long and I need to be understood. I've made some mistakes but I've paid too, a steep price. I feel alone without a safe place to go. I am tempted to take off without a destination.
- I have a hand tremor and have all of my life but it doesn't require any attention.
- I have a daughter. I love her but I am not allowed to live with her. I see her and we talk on the phone and my mother has a relationship with her too. Her mother's mother and father take charge a lot—they love her but not me.

Childhood history:
I was born in 1982. My father left us when I was 2. I went through school in special education and had to change schools

a lot. I was hospitalized as a teenager for a mental breakdown. I was close to my sister and my mother. My mother remarried when I was 7 or 8. My step father could be mean and was mostly to me. I idealized my real father but saw him very little and he never understood me.

Trauma experience:
I was sexually abused at age 13.

Special talents:
I am a good writer. I think I have good intuition. But I don't think my talents are recognized.

Additional information:
I need support and I need structure. I am frightened of my future and I can't see a way out of the trap of uncertain living and the lack of kindness in the situations I can afford.

A day or two later, Paul sent a text urging me to help him: "Please stay on your friend about her institution in Santa Fe. I could really use the support of a temporary program and I feel like it would be the best way to make entrance to a new part of the world. I'm craving that. If you help me how I want to be helped, I won't let you down. I know that sounds selfish, but it's true. Ok, good night. I love you."

I knew this was a long shot, but I told Meryl of Paul's interest and learned that there were nine requirements for eligibility. Paul met all but one—he wasn't homeless. And this was a deal-breaker. Their funding was dependent on all criteria being met.

Paul was very disappointed but quickly turned his attention to going back to school. He checked out Montgomery College, the closest community college to his place, and decided he wanted to take another sociology or poetry class. I went over to see the school and help him with the business office portion of registration. He told me that he was excited about school—it gave him hope—and he was considering moving into a sober house with some of the friends he'd made through AA. He said he thought living with those particular friends would be more conducive to going to school.

"I should have never stopped going to school," Paul wrote in an email later that day. "I was happiest when I was at ccbc and applying myself and I never stopped doing well there. I got good grades in all of my classes and I felt important while doing school work. It really made me feel good."

The following week, Keely and I took the metro into Washington to spend the day with Paul, who rode his bike in from Silver Spring. We met at the National Portrait Gallery, where we spent several hours before having dinner in Chinatown. Paul's spirits were pretty good. He talked about the classes he was interested in and told us that Jake was going to sell the house, meaning he had to move. He said he felt lucky to have something lined up and told us about the particular house where he would live.

In thanking me for the day, Paul texted, again expressing optimism:

Thanks mom :)
I'm really putting all my focus into AA at this time, and think it's better than counseling.
I love you very much and want to bring you joy.

Late that summer, Paul moved to the sober house in Rockville, where he knew the other renters. He signed up for Introduction to Modern Poetry and Social Problems and Issues, which he would take at the Rockville Campus of Montgomery College, located on Rockville Pike. Another roommate was also taking classes there and told Paul they called the school "Harvard on the Pike." Paul thought that was funny!

On a beautiful day that fall, Paul and I spent the afternoon on the Severn River crabbing with Keely and Sean on their boat. Reminiscing about his countless crabbing escapades as a boy, Paul was an eager participant and rightfully took pride in the day's catch—a bushel of crabs. We had dinner that evening with Don and Lucy, after which I drove Paul back to Rockville. Even the hour's drive, with the two of us singing along to a favorite playlist, was fun. A few weeks later, we were together again for Thanksgiving, and all seemed well.

It was early December when I was alarmed by Paul's text message:

> I'm too depressed to get out of bed. The house is fine. School would be fine but I am going to get behind if I don't get out of bed and do the work. I really want to get up and do my school work but I can't. I stopped going to meetings too.

Obviously a cry for help. I called him and learned that he had stopped taking his medications—after which he turned to self-medicating, finding what I gathered may have been a bogus doctor. When that resource was exhausted, he turned elsewhere.

Paul was addicted to heroin.

Chapter 13

WANDERLUST

From alligator's jaws to midwest dust
Excitement, overwhelming as yesteryear
Hometown-dreams decay into dirt
Propelling my yearnings to wander languidly
Through America's many rest stops and soup kitchens

THOSE FEW DECEMBER days were a whirlwind. Paul wanted help. There was some degree of solace for him in having told me of his addiction, but the addiction itself wasn't in his control.

Knowing he needed treatment that would also address his mental health, I suggested he call his therapist. "I had to stop seeing her, Mom," he said. "After a year on SSI, my insurance automatically changed to Medicare. So I lost the Medicaid that Clinical Associates accepted."

Hmm . . . I wondered: *Why would the official status of "disabled" narrow his options?*

He told me he'd been seeking a new therapist when his depression hit. I started to get it. He lost his mental health support, which included his medications, and depression set in. This wasn't the first time, nor would it be the last, that insurance curve balls compromised his well-being.

I couldn't focus on that though. No time.

Through Paul's housemates and their recovery community network, Paul learned of two facilities in Florida with dual diagnosis programs. One place—The Willough at Naples—had an immediate opening, and Paul was admitted. My friend Maureen booked him a flight for the next day.

Paul and I agreed that he would pack what he needed for a warm climate and, once he was on his way, Sean and I would figure out how to get his furniture and other belongings into storage. Keely had had surgery the week before, and—even though we were relieved with the outcome—she was temporarily out of commission.

Paul had more to tell me. "I sold my bike, Mom. It's in a pawn shop in Rockville. I love my bike. If I give you my January check, can you get it back for me?" Before I could answer, he added this: "My laptop, and watch, and my guitar are in a different pawn shop."

He started to cry but continued. "It's cheaper to get them back this month," he said. "And a lot cheaper than buying them again. But I know you may not be able to get them. I am so sorry."

"Just give me the paperwork," I said, "and I'll think about it later." A perfect segue into the vortex, I realized as I spoke.

"Okay," he said.

Huh, I thought, *you never know.*

Paul called me later that evening to tell me he had lost his driver's license. His flight was for 1:15 the next afternoon. The closest full-service Motor Vehicle Administration was in Gaithersburg. If I picked him up at 9:00 in Rockville, we could make it to the MVA and then to BWI in Linthicum, Maryland, in time.

I was rattled by Paul's suffering, and I was tense about the day's mission. Situations like this bring out the worst in me. Driving to places unfamiliar, time being critical, leaving Annapolis at rush hour, dealing with the MVA, and having Paul—who was suffering—in the mix was as bad a combination as I could fathom that day. I know better now.

I arrived to get Paul at 9:00 a.m. sharp. He was packed and had organized a good portion of what he was leaving behind.

I knew the day was bound to induce panic and, sure enough—first stop. Upon arriving at the MVA, I learned that they no longer issue the physical driver's license on the spot; they mail it. I left Paul to wait in line for his photo and went to the main desk to ask about our dilemma. I was told if we had an airline ticket in hand, they could produce the license in a few minutes time. I did, and they did. Whew. Off to BWI.

Paul knew he was being met in the Southwest Florida International Airport by a representative from The Willough. Even so, Paul was anxious. He kissed me goodbye and got in the security line. I didn't leave until he went all the way through. I wasn't the least bit worried he'd bail; I just couldn't take my eyes off him. I wondered when I would see him next and what he would go through in the meantime. This was early December 2015, and I knew I wouldn't see him for Christmas. That loss paled in comparison to his needed treatment, but still it made me sad, for both of us. He was wearing the red Nike sneakers I'd given him the Christmas before. I watched his feet disappear as he blended in with others in the line.

I was reminded of a time when he was younger and was flying alone, and the airport let me go through security with him—something I had orchestrated ahead of time due to his disabilities. I wouldn't have even *considered* anything similar at this juncture, but I couldn't walk away either.

I didn't think he saw me, but I watched him strike up a conversation with a young man in the line who looked to be younger than Paul and was much more clean-cut, the kind of boy who looked like his mother dressed him—either that or he was off to play golf. The length of Paul's hair fluctuated, as did his weight, but at this point he was in good shape and his hair was long, allowing his still-strawberry-blonde ringlet curls to flourish. Anyway, I thought, *Aww. He made a friend.*

That night, Paul called from the treatment facility to tell me a few things. Our conversation started with this exchange:

Paul: "Did you see the guy I was talking to in the security line?" *Okay, so he did know I watched him.*

Me: "Yes. I did."

Paul: "I told him I was going into rehab. I also told him I was afraid of this mean dude, a dealer, who was after me for money and kept calling and threatening me."

Why a sense of foreboding shot through me I can't say. I was pretty sure the mean guy was in Maryland. Paul was in Florida.

Me: "DON'T pick up!"

Paul: "It's okay now, Mom. I got rid of him. The guy I was talking to in line told me what to do. And it worked."

Me: "What did you do?"

Paul: "The dealer guy called and I picked up and said, 'I just got busted. The cops are going to take my phone. Here they come now. Don't worry, I'll delete your number.' Then I hung up. He never called back."

Another lesson for me that day: Don't judge a book by its cover.

Paul's focus then turned to the things he left behind. He wanted to know when I was moving them, where they were going, and whether they'd be safe. No words of assurance eased his mind. He even got a little testy with me. "I don't have much," he said, "but I'm proud of what I do have, and I want to take care of my things. When I come home, I don't want to start over."

I told him I had arranged a day the following week when Sean and one of Paul's AA friends, Dan, were meeting me at the house in Rockville, which I had coordinated with the house manager, Austin. Sean and Dan both had trucks and, along with my car, we could get everything, which we were taking to the empty apartment in the lower level of Sean's house in Annapolis.

I wanted to know about the facility, the people, and his experiences so far, but he shifted the conversation to whether or not I was going to get his things from the pawn shop. I could see that the pass

I'd gotten to leave this up in the air was short lived. I should've known it would be. Even so, I told him I hadn't decided and, when I did, I'd let him know.

But the most critical thing on Paul's mind was his hiking backpack. He asked me to mail it to him.

"No," I said. "I don't see why you need it. Plus, it's so big—it would be expensive to mail."

He wouldn't drop it. We went round and round, but I didn't budge. He was calling from a phone in the facility, so I knew his follow-up calls would be curtailed. He wasn't happy with me, and I wasn't too pleased with him either, but there was no way I was mailing him a backpack, one with an internal frame that was hard for me to even maneuver. Furthermore, I had no idea how long he would be in Florida. This theme would dominate our conversations for the next few evenings.

Several days later, Paul began our conversation by telling me he liked his roommate—that he was a really good guy and was funny. In giving me an example, Paul told me his roommate had asked him, "So, tell me, Paul, does your life *really* depend on whether or not your mother mails you that backpack?"

This made Paul laugh—at himself of course. And even in the midst of relaying this to me, he couldn't get through the whole sentence without laughing. I laughed too. Some kind of medication was working! Or God bless the roommate! Whatever it was, I'd pay money for it. Some might say, "I'd like to bottle it." But my version of the same sentiment is, "Does that come in a patch?"

Paul told me he was taking Suboxone, a drug frequently used to treat opioid addiction and relieve symptoms of withdrawal as well as cravings, and Ativan, which he was told would treat his anxiety. He said he felt better as a result. He mentioned that they had considered clonidine. Hearing the word, I flashed back to Paul in the first grade—this was the medication that had caused him to pass out on our bathroom floor. I could still see my frail little boy lying there on the tiles.

Paul would be in the unit for twenty-eight days, he said. After that, a decision would be made about next steps. He told me about another program in the area that might offer a good transition.

The weather in Naples was beautiful. Paul said his only flip flops had a hole in the sole and he'd like some swimming trunks because on Sundays they would get to go to a nearby beach. This was perfect information for me to pass on to Don, who was always thoughtful and generous regarding Christmas gifts. Paul also asked if I could mail him a blank journal, which I found in my dark heart to do, and which I now have back in my possession, full of his notes. It includes what he ate for meals, his thoughts, his regrets, and, of course, his poetry:

NAPLES
Access Florida through barren channels in Naples
where white sandy beaches have no waves
and the town, no access to worthy resources.
I'm told these can be found, though,
up the road in Golden Gate,
which shines like a whistle but
crackles like bacon in soup kitchens for the wealthy.

Over from the city lights and asleep under stars,
in what could amount to communities,
the midnight oil burns away parasites.
Beaten down in their tiny tents,
hand in hand, they've built tyrants out of clay
with a toyish idealism that lacks machinery.

Off to its left, the widows sleep alone,
with goodness nailed to a cross for all to witness.

Sleeping in the wild and sheltered by a canopy of cypress
the amounting of nothingness fills the breadwinner's heart.
Beside him a child weeps alone,
praying for sacrifice.

Tomorrow the city beneath reaches judgment;
no one is ready.

*

WITH PAUL IN a regimented program where the profession-als didn't want to talk with me and where weekend visits weren't in the cards, I now had time to think, to focus without interruption. I wanted to learn more about Paul's plight. Just the thought of heroin addiction was frightening, and I knew my emotional self wasn't going to be the best resource for Paul.

In spite of an abundance of conclusive scientific data, our soci-ety's grasp of addiction is woefully poor. Pervasive misunderstandings include: (1) People suffering from addiction should be punished and shamed; (2) Addiction is indicative of a character flaw or a moral failing; and (3) Addiction comes about strictly from drug use, that all people who use are equally vulnerable. Despite bearing no resem-blance to the truth, this sort of thinking underpins societal attitudes and, in turn, shapes our drug policies.

Though not recent, the rat studies grabbed my attention. In the mid-1900s, laboratory experiments provided caged rats two options for water—one plain drinking water and the other laced with an addictive drug. The drugged water was favored, and the rats returned to it so frequently that they eventually killed themselves. Because these animals lost control of their behavior to the point of their own demise, the conclusion was twofold: the drug was irresistible, and it was lethal.

In these lab studies, each rat was isolated in a small individual cage. Years later, another scientific experiment—dubbed the Rat Park—provided a large cage to house multiple rats, along with wheels and tunnels and space to explore. These rats were given the same two choices for water but favored the plain water. And none died of an overdose.

Even more telling, and actually amazing to me, this study then moved isolated and addicted rats into the Rat Park and found that they eventually stopped drinking the drugged water in favor of the plain water and a normal life. These findings reveal that it's not just the presence of drugs, or the extent of their availability, that drives chronic use.

Obviously human beings are more complex, and no two cases are identical. But studies concur that most people—eighty to ninety percent—who use potentially addictive drugs do not become addicted. And this is not because these people are morally superior or have supernatural willpower. It is because addiction isn't the result of what you consume but instead comes from the reason you consume it. It makes sense, then, that the quality of life plays a significant role in separating those who use drugs and walk away, or even outgrow problematic drug use, from those who succumb to long-term chronic addiction.

Upon its release that spring, I read *Unbroken Brain*, a book by award-winning neuroscience journalist Maia Szalavitz in which she brilliantly intertwines her personal story of addiction with her subsequent thirty years of research, deepening the understanding of substance use and debunking the myths that cripple needed reform. Widely respected as a leading voice in addiction science and policy, Szalavitz contends that the two conflicting schools of thought about addiction—that it's a moral failing, or that it's a disease—both fall short. She maintains that addiction is comparable to a developmental disorder or a learning disorder and that understanding the context for the behavior is vital to promoting effective recovery. Highly engaging and full of compelling information, the book illuminates the emotional wounds—from childhood trauma to deprivation—that lead to addiction, and it drives home the tragic impact of our drug policies—from their racist roots to their relentless focus on punitive measures as a solution.

I wrestled to understand how it is that we continue to justify incarceration as a viable method to combat addiction. I read a very different book, given to me by a friend, that also provided perspective on the hardships that undergird addiction—and it was written twenty-five years earlier. While not science-based or policy-focused—*Blessed are the Addicts* by John A. Martin—instills nothing but empathy for those afflicted with a substance use disorder. Devoting the bulk of his career to counseling people with addiction, Martin writes from the heart, and touches yours, as he shares his analysis of the commonalities among those who fall victim and his conclusion that addiction begins long before drug use.

> But for anyone who has had [addiction], all one has to do is look back on the early childhood and on the growing up years and I believe they will concur . . . the symptoms of the spiritual pain, of the pain of life, began at that time, persisted through the years, despite tremendous efforts to deny and resolve it, and intensified with the passing of time.

> It is therefore no surprise that the first manifestation of . . . addiction is a kind of disconnection that is deep, persistent, and progressive. The alienation is embedded in the being of the person.

> Finally, the discovery of the drug gives hope. . . . It is the hope that he, too, at last, can maybe live like everybody

else—carefree, creative, and even loving. . . . He feels more at one with the world than he ever did in his life.

[He] genuinely thinks that his renewed zest for life is rooted in the real "him." This is the beginning of the lie, of the tragedy that spawns so much future pain . . .

With a couple of books and a handful of articles under my belt, I was just scratching the surface and, if truth be told, down the road I would double back and re-read *Unbroken Brain,* comprehending so much more and becoming a steadfast follower of Maia Szalavitz, whom I would meet. I would come to admire the work of Sarah Wakeman, an addiction-medicine physician at Mass General and a national thought leader in treatment for substance use disorders, who would be kind enough to answer my questions. I would read *In the Realm of Hungry Ghosts* by Gabor Maté, *High Price* by Carl Hart, *Outgrowing Addiction* by Stanton Peele and Zach Rhoads, and more. Also in my future, I would devote myself to sharing my increasing insights in any way I could devise.

But even with my cursory understanding, I was able to clarify much of what instinctively I knew but couldn't articulate—Paul's life experiences had set the stage. It made me sad but, in another way, it gave me hope.

*

BY THE END of Paul's first month in treatment, the Suboxone was reduced from 8 to 1 mg, and he was also taking Lexapro, Anafranil (for OCD), and Propranolol (for blood pressure, tremors, and anxiety).

Paul was given the option to go into a long-term program nearby, which he decided to do. I knew I wouldn't hear from him for a while because such places do not allow the use of a personal cell phone and typically don't permit any calls during the early weeks of adjustment.

So when my phone rang, and I saw that the call was from Paul's cell phone—just a week after he'd entered the new program—it scared me.

I answered, "Hello? Paul?"

"Hi Mom, I left the program. Don't worry though. I'm going back to Willough. Right now I am standing outside a Dunkin Donuts, waiting for the van to pick me up. I can stay there another month and they were happy to take me back."

"Okay," I said. "I'm so glad you lined up something; that was smart. Why did you want to leave?"

"I tried to like it, Mom, but I didn't fit in. For me to stay I would have to pretend to be someone I'm not. It was too hard to do that and focus on my recovery too."

Paul explained to me that the program's emphasis on religion was overbearing. While spirituality was an important component of Paul's life, he was repelled by anything he perceived as judgmental. In this case, he said there was no tolerance for differences. They promoted one way of thinking and one way of behaving, which made Paul feel obliged to conform at the cost of "being real." With Paul's need—often desperate—to connect with others, I could appreciate his feelings. In fact, I was impressed. Rather than go along—sacrificing his identity as he had done in so many settings in his life—he valued himself enough to go against the tide. And he did so in the name of authenticity, something he had learned was needed to make meaningful progress.

Thankfully, Paul was welcomed back to Willough, although he was assigned a different psychiatrist. The new doctor prescribed Klonopin (for anxiety), Lithium (for bipolar), Risperdal (an antipsychotic), and 2 mg of Suboxone. All my information on the medications came from Paul and, frankly, I had a hard time keeping up with the thinking and what felt to me like a lack of consistency. However, Paul did seem to feel good and to relate well to those around him.

Giving me some insight into Paul's experiences in Naples is a Facebook message I received several months after Paul's death from a person otherwise unknown to me, Larry Letchworth:

Hello, my name is Larry. And you don't know me but I knew Paul (your son, I think, and sorry if that's incorrect).

Granted I didn't know him very long, probably a few months. But he really was an amazing guy and we had a lot of good clean fun times together. I still have a video in my phone of us jumping off a bridge here in Naples and into the ocean. We were with a couple other buddies really enjoying the warm gulf water and laughing.

I don't know why but I just felt compelled to tell you about that, and the rest of our time together, which was a lot of bike riding in nature and hanging out at the beach. He was a really awesome guy and always had a happy demeanor about him as you probably already know. He didn't always say a lot but when he did speak, it was deep, meaningful, and when the setting was right, funny!

I know he had a passion for music and more importantly a passion for his daughter! And I just wanted to tell you that, even though it was a short time, I knew and felt he was a great guy! And I am so terribly sorry for your loss in his passing. I'm sure he's greatly missed based solely on how great of a personality he had. I just wanted to share that with you and maybe, hopefully, bring a smile to your face. I wish you and yours the best. God Bless.

Paul's nightly calls to me were increasingly focused on his thoughts about next steps and, as his plans took shape, the logistics. He decided he was going to Colorado Springs, Colorado, to be part of a non-profit community, Springs Recovery Connection. He had been in communication with the director of the program, whom he liked. He had found a room to rent in a nearby recovery house and had looked into bus transportation, which he could afford without my help. He felt good about his decision because "the people in Colorado are nicer," and he was philosophically aligned with this organization.

I found the following in his journal:

COLORADO DREAMS

For what my freedom is worth, I'll climb the highest ledge imaginable. I'll hang on to the galaxy's stars and let their fervent heat burn off excess emotion. My timing is short and within the near future I'll be high upon that mountain . . . The one I saw last night in my dreams. I can hear eagles cry and my voice echo over the landscape. I see it so plainly, even here and now, in my chamber, waiting to explode. I see revised poems and chicken scratch transformed into meaningful prose. I see Colorado cradling my dreams in its topsy-turvy mass. I see myself gliding down slopes into valleys with a large smile on my face. I'll give up the ocean and my childhood dreams to sail with the world. At least for the time being . . .

Paul left Naples on February 29, 2016. It would be a long bus ride, and he would change buses in several locations. The end of the line was Denver, where he would get a city bus to Colorado Springs. Throughout the trip, Paul called, texted, sent photos, and we played Words with Friends, which was all fun until he started again on the backpack—something he would obviously "need to survive" in Colorado.

Paul hit the ground running, volunteering in the Springs Recovery Connection office, then joining forces with a couple of other young men to start a chapter of Young People in Recovery, or YPR as he called it, which was under the auspices of Springs Recovery Connection. It wasn't too long before they gave him a key to the SRC office, which he manned by himself from time to time when needed to help the director, Cathy Plush, whom he came to love. He spoke to me often about Cathy during his time there, mentioning something she had said, or how she dressed, and one time saying, "You would like her too, Mom." To him, she was living proof of how very nice the people in Colorado really are.

I never had occasion to interact with Cathy until she reached out to me after Paul's death:

My heart is broken.

Paul spent many hours volunteering at my office. He was such a sweetheart and always willing to help. He was working on writing some blogs for our website. He was trying so hard and was doing so well. I started this non-profit after my own son's addiction kicked in. I thought of you often during my conversations with Paul.

He was a good man. I saw that in him and so wanted to support his efforts to get well. I knew you were very special to him. He loved his family especially you and his sister. He spoke so kindly of you.

I'm so sorry!! My prayers are with you and your family. Much love to Paul.

I've stayed in touch with Cathy since and, even though I have not met her, I consider her a friend.

*

ONE DAY PAUL called me from Colorado to say that he was going to L.A. to visit a friend, and then he planned on returning to Colorado. "Do you remember me talking about Shaun," he said, "a really nice guy I met through AA meetings when I lived in Montgomery County? You know, the one I told you was in the D.C. area for graduate school at American University?"

"I'm not sure if I do," I said.

"Yes you do, Mom. Remember me telling you I was sorry to see him go when he finished school and went home to L.A., the place he's from?"

"Yes, I do remember that."

"Well," Paul said, "he has a good job now and said he would love to show me around L.A. because I showed him so much when he was in Maryland. His sobriety is important to him, and I want to keep the friendship. So I'm going to go. He offered to pay my airfare, which he was able to get cheap on Spirit Airlines."

I wasn't thrilled about this trip but understood Paul's enthusiasm. I also understood that it wasn't my call. Be that as it may, change— which isn't my thing anyway—and Paul were a combination that inevitably tampered with my heartsease.

From what I could tell, Shaun was a good host as well as a good influence, showing Paul some pretty amazing sights. In one photo Paul sent me, he's standing on a trail off Stunt Road in the canyons between the San Fernando Valley and Malibu. He looked good. Really good—standing tall, with that "large" smile, and his long hair blowing in what looked to be a gentle breeze.

I will never know exactly what happened, much less why, but one day while Shaun was working and Paul was on his own, Paul used drugs. Knowing that this was a brush with disaster, Paul confessed to Shaun that evening. Shaun was able to get Paul into a short-term recovery program in Riverside, California.

During his week-long stay in the program, Paul met and fell hopelessly in love with a woman named Kimi. While Paul's impulsiveness reigned supreme, drugs would not be a part of the picture.

Chapter 14

BACK TO MOTHERLAND

My peace of mind is captured so effortlessly.
I wish all moments could be as eternal as love.
Come back to me in echoes
and repeat to me what you said,
the time before you left,
when I said I didn't care.

KEELY AND SEAN'S July wedding was fast approaching. And even though they were committed to a low-key event, I was focused on my contributions to their big day and on spending time with Keely, helping with inevitable details or just being together, doing nothing.

I missed Paul. And frankly, I liked it better when he was in arm's reach, but if there was any silver lining to his nomadism, it was timing. Keely's wedding could take center stage, and my days could be predictable. Always welcome and mostly a novelty for me.

It wasn't lost on me, nor on Keely for that matter, that her position in the family—as the sibling of a child with special needs—had an impact on her development. As a matter of fact, the Keelys of the world struggle with often overlooked emotional issues—ranging from guilt and over-compensation to isolation and anxiety—that can have lifelong effects. I wasn't going to make up for this reality in my role as mother-of-the-bride, but I liked being free to focus on her. And free I was, due to my recent retirement—something I generally had mixed feelings about but was nonetheless thankful for the alignment with this event. I missed my work and my colleagues, but I did not miss that way-too-familiar "burning the candle at both ends" syndrome. Not even a little.

We had originally wanted, and planned for, Paul to be at Keely's wedding—in fact, he had a role in it. But because he'd had a setback and was in California, Paul and I had agreed there were too many hurdles to getting him home and that we would celebrate with Keely and Sean as soon as he was back in Annapolis. Paul was okay with that. He never was comfortable with big social events; furthermore, he had Kimi as a distraction.

Funny enough, both my children were in love: Keely with a mature and stable man she'd known for several years and Paul with a woman he'd known for a couple of weeks and who left rehab prematurely to be with him, despite this rendering them homeless. I didn't have much to go on in the Paul scenario, but I did my best to put the speculation, as well as the worry, in the back of my mind.

I was good at compartmentalizing. Really good. I could detach with the best of them. Until the day Paul called and said, "Kimi just got money from her divorce settlement, and she felt sorry for me missing my sister's wedding so she bought us bus tickets from L.A. to Baltimore. We arrive on Tuesday!"

The wedding was Saturday.

With my mind flipping through a number of responses, I said, "Where are you and Kimi going to stay? I have house guests and am having a dinner party Thursday night for Keely and Sean with Sean's family and Dad, Lucy, and Annie."

"We're staying with Sara and Kayla," Paul said. "They're excited about it and we can all come to the wedding together."

I felt like saying, "You tell your sister," but I didn't. There was nothing I could say. The fact is, I quickly regrouped. I wanted to see Paul, and I did have his wedding clothes ready.

His call provided me a little more information about Kimi: Besides some kind of substance use issue—none of Paul's other girlfriends had had that—she was also divorced. Far be it from me to pass judgment on either, but I started to anyway. Then I caught myself. In addition to resisting blatant hypocrisy, I questioned myself further. *Wasn't I supposed to be enlightened regarding substance use?* After all, I had been moved by the personal stories of others, and it wasn't a stretch for me to embrace the value of compassion over judgment.

Okay, I thought. *Shift gears. Hope for the best. Look for the good.* One way or the other, I figured, Saturday would come and go, and Keely and Sean would indeed be married and off on their honeymoon. And no matter what, my fantasies of a simpler life had enabled a restful stretch. I was prepared.

The world travelers missed their connecting bus someplace in Utah, slowing their arrival to Tuesday night, after which another bus they boarded ran out of gas and was stranded in some other state for I forget how long. If Paul hadn't sent me photos of the bus on the side of the highway and the guy arriving with the gas, I would not have believed him. Nor would I ever have believed this same guy fashioned a funnel out of a McDonald's cup in order to pour the gas into the bus's tank—a sight worthy of more Paul photos than the Rocky Mountains!

This mishap pushed their Baltimore arrival to Wednesday. From there, they would get a bus that ran every day from Baltimore to Annapolis, which they'd looked into before leaving L.A.

Only, it ran every day except Wednesdays.

At 5:30 Wednesday evening, Paul called. "Hi, Mom. We're in Baltimore and just found out there's no bus to Annapolis today."

I suggested they take Uber, but Paul said they had no money. "How can you have no money?" I demanded. Somewhere mid-country, while they were sleeping, Kimi's wallet was stolen. Great. *Homeless girl, not too smart either.* Who knew what we were in for! But I caught myself again, remembering *homeless boy* was roughly fifty percent of this particular brain trust.

I put out an all-points-bulletin text message to Keely, Sean, Don, and Lucy: "Paul is on Russell Street in Baltimore, and there is no connecting bus to Annapolis tonight. Any ideas about how to get them? I suggested Uber, but they have no money."

Sean instantly sent an Uber, using his account, and relayed the information Paul needed. That night, Paul told me when he went up to the car to verify the ride, the driver said, "Your brother-in-law sent me." This brought tears to Paul's eyes.

"He called me his 'brother-in-law,' Mom."

I had second thoughts about Paul and his girlfriend staying at Sara's. Not only did Sara live a good ninety minutes away, but she had trouble being on time—a fact that could be stressful for her—and I was uneasy about her driving in such circumstances. Furthermore, Paul would need to be at the rehearsal on Friday. I decided it was probably best for everyone, including Sara and Kayla, if Paul and this Kimi-person stayed with me through the wedding weekend.

I ran to the grocery store to get extra food for them, and by the time I got home they were on my front porch. Paul looked fabulous. He was trim, and tan, his hair was cut short, and he looked remarkably healthy and rested. I was so glad to see his face. And then there was Kimi. A beautiful girl with a quick smile, who hugged me and thanked me and hugged me again. No one looks like she did after just crossing the country on a bus! Or him either. Then again, I had to admit, he was a sight for sore eyes.

Okay then. Let's have a wedding!

First thing in the morning, Paul sold his favorite guitar so he could get Kimi a dress. There was something about being on the front end of this pawn shop thing that went down a lot easier. Or, maybe I was finally seasoned, at home with the whole concept. Who knows?

I will go so far as to say that Paul and Kimi were assets to the dinner party. Paul was genuinely glad to see his family and was attentive to Sean's. He and Kimi helped Sean's mother on the stairs, and Kimi offered to take family photos and helped with the clean-up. In a conversation with Don, Kimi realized she knew the principal of the architectural firm where Don worked years before in Georgetown, a man from L.A., which explains why his name came up. Kimi was impressive—pretty and socially gracious, prompting Don to jokingly ask me, "What does she see in Paul?" To which I said, "Look at him!" He really did look great.

Kimi had never been on the East Coast and fell in love with Annapolis, which Paul was proud to show her. Our neighborhood is a few blocks from the heart of downtown and the City Dock and a stone's throw from favorite restaurants and shops. We walk to almost everything, a phenomenon unknown to those in the sprawl of Los Angeles. I think the only drawback for Kimi was the heat. To be expected. It was July in Maryland.

Friday afternoon, as we were on our way to the rehearsal at the historic Annapolis Maritime Museum, where both the ceremony and the reception would take place, Paul told me he was too nervous to be in the procession. After making sure he didn't have a trace of ambivalence, I told him I wanted whatever he wanted, and there was no need to fret. I had a Plan B.

After a quick walk-through, we went to Don and Lucy's for a crab feast, hosted by Sean's parents, for family and out-of-town guests. Paul was happy to be there, really glad to see his cousins, his aunt, and other family members, and outwardly pleased to partake in Keely's festivities. And, for me, it was an occasion for counting my blessings.

The day of the wedding, July 23, 2016, was the hottest of that summer—over 100 degrees—but for me it was all pretty perfect. The stunning and happy bride made her approach, flanked on either side by her father and me, down the dock to the small beach on Back

Creek where friends and family were seated. The marriage was officiated by Keely's and Paul's and my very good friend and retired judge, Joe Manck, whose humor and blessings were in perfect balance. I was, and remain, so very thankful that both my children were together for this milestone occasion as we witnessed this union and welcomed Sean into our family.

The reception took place inside the Maritime Museum, once home to the last oyster-packing plant in Annapolis, located at the mouth of Back Creek overlooking the Chesapeake Bay. A large awning-covered deck provided an outside option and a view of the water with the slew of boats, moored or docked or passing by. Sara and Kayla were there but arrived late. They had fun, and Kayla was adorable. And I was glad about all the decisions made.

Keely and Sean had, as Keely would put it, "a blast" and went off on their honeymoon. Their happiness was contagious.

My honeymoon, however, was about to wind down.

*

PAUL TOLD ME he and Kimi had decided they wanted to stay in Annapolis. They were going to get jobs and find a place to live. I asked Paul about Kimi's rehabilitation and why she had been in treatment. He said she had a drinking problem, but she'd been in a bad marriage and was on the upswing.

Her issues aside, I was in a bind.

As my focus shifted, allowing more clarity on the matter at hand, I realized that sending Paul—with a girlfriend—to stay with Sara and Kayla in tight quarters, away from needed resources without a car, was beyond a bad idea for all involved. It was untenable.

I really liked Kimi. She was warm and polite and genuinely wanted to please. She often spoke of her family members—her mother and father and her four siblings—with love and pride. However, I thought the chance of a lasting relationship between Paul and her was nil, and obviously Paul was my first priority. But Paul's singular focus was on being with her. After several lonely years, he was again in love.

My goal was to see Paul get appropriate mental health care, and I realized that his being in Annapolis was an opportunity. I could help him think through options and then support the consistency needed to form a meaningful relationship, which I saw as crucial to his overall well-being. So I used it as leverage. "You can't stay here, even temporarily," I told him, "if you don't line up a therapist and a psychiatrist now." Paul had held it together admirably for three days of wedding events, and that must've taken some hard work on his part. His efforts to impress Kimi *did* help keep him on his toes, but his insecurities—along with the challenges of a relationship—added a layer of stress that he didn't always manage well.

We looked online for mental health resources. Paul called Arundel Lodge, a facility about five miles away, where he hoped to schedule an intake appointment and be seen on a regular basis. He learned that he needed a Maryland driver's license and a Medicare card to initiate the process; he had a Colorado license and had lost his Medicare card. Neither of these obstacles was insurmountable, but with visions of the half-hearted support he'd gotten in Silver Spring, I started to think he might be better off in a private practice.

We printed out the names and numbers of a dozen local doctors who accepted Medicare and split the calls. Some no longer took any insurance, and others weren't taking new patients. Paul placed the call to David Kolsky, a psychiatrist whose office was a couple of blocks from my house and who had an opening to see Paul that week. While Dr. Kolsky did accept Medicare, there would be a steep co-pay compared to Arundel Lodge. Regardless, I thought Paul stood to get more sophisticated medication management, and the location was ideal.

I was hopeful too that such an arrangement would provide more flexibility in wrapping me in, à la Dr. Pressman. I didn't want to insert myself every week and certainly not at the cost of Paul's independence.

Still, I saw my input as an important component of optimizing the most effective medication and otherwise getting and keeping Paul on solid footing.

It was an open and shut case: Paul was better off when he took a low dose of Abilify along with an antidepressant. From our long history, I knew this medication helped reduce his more severe anxiety and helped him maintain the rational thinking of which he was capable. Otherwise, he was more prone to inconsistency, with any sort of stress exacerbating his tendency to hit the panic button. The Lexapro helped with his mood and somewhat with his anxiety, but his obsessiveness and his overreaction to certain circumstances were not adequately addressed. Furthermore, I could see the established pattern: When he didn't have needed mental health support, he slipped into risky behavior.

Paul and I went together to his second appointment with Dr. Kolsky. We agreed that I would sit in the waiting room and play it by ear to see if maybe I could meet Dr. Kolsky when their session was over. But as the doctor ushered Paul out of his office, he avoided making eye contact with me, which I took as a sign that he didn't want to talk with me—not at that time anyway. Although, Paul did start an ongoing relationship, and I was glad the therapy and medication management were bundled together. Dr. Kolsky prescribed Lexapro, as Paul suggested. Some weeks later, he would prescribe Adderall for Paul's attention deficit, which I could have told him would do no good—a conclusion Paul himself reached shortly thereafter, complaining profusely about the side effects.

Kimi went out each day to look for a job. She had a college degree but was looking in shops and restaurants. It wasn't long before she was working, waiting tables full time at an Irish restaurant in the heart of town.

Several months earlier, I had gotten Paul's bike from the pawn shop in Rockville, which turned out to be a blessing. I took him over to Sean and Keely's to get it while they were still on their honeymoon. After Paul obsessed on taking inventory of all his possessions—a long and painful process for me—he rode his bike home.

Paul got employment applications from a few places, which I helped him complete. I don't know at what point stretching the truth becomes a flat-out lie, but I'm pretty sure we crossed that line. Extending the dates Paul had been a driver for our friend Maureen was an example of the former; saying he worked for a company owned by Kimi's father in California was unquestionably the latter. While Paul had made some money here and there over the years, he hadn't been officially employed since January 2011, a fact that would be hard to explain in an interview, particularly hard for Paul.

But by mid-August, Paul had a job. He was hired as a bicycle delivery driver for Jimmy John's, a sandwich shop on Main Street. He was proud of himself and genuinely excited. I was happy too, but I didn't yet know it would turn out to be the perfect job for Paul.

He was given a company T-shirt, which he was to wear tucked in, with khaki shorts or pants and a belt. Understandably, Paul was very serious about this. He had a couple of pairs of shorts, one a greenish khaki, the other a darker khaki. Neither would do.

"Paul!" I said. "They are both khaki. You are colorblind." Which he was. But they weren't "khaki enough," as he put it. Old Navy saved the day. And after he settled down on that front, he had three pairs of work shorts. Doing laundry in preparation for an upcoming shift, however, took on an importance akin to, I don't know, oxygen.

Both Kimi and Paul worked for tips and because they were committed to saving for a security deposit and a month's rent on an apartment, each of them gave me the bulk of their cash at the end of every shift, and we all stayed on top of the running tally. They were being frugal as well as conscientious about looking for places, with the first of September as their target date.

In some ways, I saw Kimi as more capable than Paul—she was a year older and certainly more worldly—but there were times when I noticed a helplessness that surprised me. She lost her phone, for example, and didn't seem motivated to do anything about it. After several days, Paul bought her a refurbished phone on eBay. The day the new phone arrived, I took Kimi to the AT&T store where, after a lengthy process of getting access to her family's account, we learned that her latest-model phone—an iPhone 6 Plus—had been insured. When I told Kimi she should file the claim to get it replaced, both she and Paul looked at me as though I had two heads—until I explained the obvious: "Paul saves $150, and Kimi gets a much better phone!!"

But my biggest challenge during that particular episode, other than wanting to spend my time doing almost anything else, was Paul's anxiety. He couldn't stay in one place and was pacing back and forth. Then, while I was trying to help Kimi—talking with her mother on the phone and the AT&T rep simultaneously—Paul came in and out of the store repeatedly, each time asking me to step outside to talk with him.

"NO!" I said, wishing I had a stun gun or, better yet, the supernatural power to have the earth open up and swallow him whole.

When we returned home, I helped Kimi file the claim for the phone, affidavits and all. That same night, Paul wanted me to fill out applications for apartments, but again his anxiety, manifesting itself in one way or another, precluded much progress. There was no anger, just extreme OCD.

It wasn't many days before Kimi and Paul were in conflict. Typically, she came home from work around 6:00 p.m. and fell asleep. Paul worked until 2:00 a.m. or later and, by the time he got home, she was wide awake. It wasn't unusual for them to argue, awakening me in the night.

From what I observed, they were equally at fault. Paul was substance free but anxiety ridden. Kimi's drinking, newly evident to me, made her a management problem for him. He loved her in an obsessive way and their arguments, which she didn't always seem to remember, terrified him. They had some good days, but the situation was unsettling.

By mid-August, I sat them both down. "You two should not live together," I said. "I can't control what you do outside of this house, but I can control what happens here, and you are no longer welcome here." I said they could move out together or she could find a place, adding that if she wanted to return home to L.A., I would book her a flight at my expense. I told them I needed to be able to sleep through the night. While they were respectful toward me, they had no immediate solution.

After a couple of days went by with no turning point in sight, I did book her a flight and told them I had done so. They came to me later the same day and said they wouldn't argue anymore. They loved their jobs and they loved each other and were actively looking for their own place. She did not want to go back home. I reluctantly canceled the flight.

The thought of renting an apartment myself and giving them the house crossed my mind inasmuch as *anything* seemed preferable to the status quo. And even though they took my warnings to heart and were more mindful of my needs, I felt infringed upon in multiple ways. Things that weren't even their fault started to get under my skin.

*

I WANTED TO communicate with Dr. Kolsky, and I left him a voicemail message to no avail. I asked Paul if Dr. Kolsky had access to his medical history, and Paul said he had signed a release form to enable the doctor to get records from the hospital in California—a place that in my book couldn't have had a full picture. I looked online for an email address for Dr. Kolsky and saw only a pop-up box that said, "send a message to the doctor"—a resource intended, I'm sure, for a prospective patient to initiate contact, not for the mother of an existing adult patient to put in her two cents. I used it anyway. The box allowed a limited number of words for the message.

On August 23, 2016, I wrote the following, in three consecutive messages:

> I am Paul's mother and understand your reasons for not wanting to talk with me. At the same time, I would like to share some information. Paul and his girlfriend have been living with me since their unexpected arrival in late-July and, while there is good news in the fact they both have gotten jobs they seem to be handling well, their relationship frightens me. They argue, triggering his irrational and obsessive . . .

Your email to Dr. David Kolsky, MD has been sent.

> thinking. Paul and I have worked with many doctors but, since becoming an adult and moving frequently, his treatment has been inconsistent and his medication sporadic, making him vulnerable to feelings of hopelessness, and to poor choices. He needs so much more than he is able to admit, including an antipsychotic medication. I want to help him keep his job (the first one he's had since 2011) and live a stable . . .

Your email to Dr. David Kolsky, MD has been sent.

> life. I am sorry to misuse your email system, but his most recent place of treatment (for a week), has no history. As a child: ADD, LD, and PDD but unable to remain in any special ed setting due to severity of attentional issues (seizures r/o) and resulting emotional overlay. Diagnosis: Autism spectrum, OCD, mood disorder, anxiety, substance use. On SSI

due to documented history. I defer to your judgment.

Your email to Dr. David Kolsky, MD has been sent.

I never heard from Dr. Kolsky, something I realized I didn't exactly request, but even so, I never even knew if he received my messages.

If my assistance was needed in Paul's and Kimi's apartment search, I was happy to provide it, in part for self-preservation. I probably wanted the apartment for them more than they wanted it for themselves, even though I knew that in some ways I was throwing them to the wolves.

Paul and I went to see two places, leaving my stomach in knots. In one case, safety was a big concern. While the apartment was in a safe enough neighborhood, getting there—if on foot or a bike—required traversing a notoriously high-risk neighborhood. Naturally, Paul's traveling by bike with cash in the wee hours scared me. The other possibility had a somewhat safer approach but was more expensive, and I was concerned about Paul being able to afford it on his own—something I saw as important. My trepidation notwithstanding, we submitted applications.

Paul and Kimi looked at yet another small apartment over a store on Main Street, a perfect location. But the landlord was a nightmare, something I'd gathered from living in this small town, and an impression confirmed by a long list of negative online ratings. I couldn't throw them to the wolves to *that* extent. It would come back to bite us all.

As Paul was on his way home one day, he saw a "For Rent" sign on a house just two blocks from his work and equidistant from Kimi's. He called the number and arranged to meet the landlord and see the place. While there, he called me to come see it. Kimi and I were there in two minutes.

The apartment was in the historic district on Conduit Street in a three-story house built in 1912. The owner, Buz, was a gentleman in his eighties. Buz lived on the first floor and had converted each upper floor to a single apartment. When Paul inquired, both apartments were available. Paul liked the third-floor apartment best. I did too.

While nothing had been updated or much tended to in years, it was charming. In addition to a kitchen, living room, bedroom, and bath, there was a deck, albeit primitive, that overlooked the back of the house and the neighborhood's abundance of old trees. Paul was so happy with it, and I was as well. It was literally two short blocks away from his work and couldn't have been any safer. Moving all his things to the third floor, up an old narrow staircase, made me wish I'd voted for the second-floor apartment. It was hard work, but we—Paul, Kimi, Keely, Sean, and I—pitched in, and they were settled within a couple of days.

Having them out of the house was a huge relief, and a step in the right direction, but I knew this chapter of troubles was not over. The fact is, in some ways, it was just heating up. Paul used much energy in trying to limit Kimi's drinking. The responsibility was too much for him, and he was unraveling under the pressure. About two weeks after they'd moved into the apartment, Paul came over one night and told me he didn't know how to handle her. He said she was often drunk when he got home and was demanding and unreasonable. And he said she was spending too much money—hers and his—on alcohol. I knew categorically that he was a co-pilot of this ship of doom, but I also knew that managing Kimi's condition would be an overwhelming challenge for any of us.

The next day, while Paul was at work, I talked to Kimi and told her she needed to get into treatment or go back home, where her family could take care of her. She said she wanted help and my heart did go out to her. I helped her look into several options for rehab in or near Annapolis, without success—for one thing her insurance was

Blue Cross and Blue Shield of California. I booked a flight for her for the following day, September 16. The three of us agreed I would pick her up mid-morning and drive her to the airport.

When morning came, it was a new day for the lovebirds. And they decided to put up a fight. Paul let me know that he had changed his mind and they both wanted her to stay. Furthermore, he declared, they weren't going to let me in and Kimi had lost her passport—her only form of identification.

All this came to me via multiple text messages around 7:00 a.m. It wasn't a new day for me. But, resisting my every instinct, I did not respond to his texts. I figured if they didn't have me to turn on, they'd be more likely to turn on each other, and the three-hour block of time before our slated departure was ample for them to do so. I was dead set on following through with my plans. My anxiety was high, but I was playing it cool.

This was among my most challenging feats ever, but I prevailed. Powered by some otherworldly force, I let myself into the apartment, said very little to either of them, packed Kimi's things, demanded that Paul surrender her passport—which he sheepishly produced from behind the dresser—and got her in my car. As I was backing out of the driveway, Paul hopped in the back seat. I didn't want him to ride along but quickly decided I'd let it go since I had achieved my primary goal. At least we were on our way, even though Paul was crying. But as we passed the Annapolis Mall, about five miles from downtown, and Paul hadn't stopped crying, I pulled over and told him to get out and walk home. I had enough to contend with without his crying. He did as I said.

Kimi and I arrived at the BWI airport. I parked the car, walked Kimi inside, saw her to the security line, and said goodbye. She hugged me, said she loved me, and I wished her nothing but the best.

Chapter 15

APRON MAN

I fell to my knees, not in gratitude
but in prayer that I not forget this dream
and in turn forget the miracles it foretold.
To retract my pen is to converge inwards.

THE JIMMY JOHN'S where Paul worked was in the heart of Annapolis with bicycle-only deliveries in a given radius, wrapping in downtown and its immediate neighborhoods as well as the Maryland State Legislative District, the United States Naval Academy, and St. John's College. My notion that the delivery cyclist job was perfect for Paul jelled as I listened to his tales of challenges and triumphs.

The company prided itself on super-fast, high-volume delivery or—as emblazoned on Paul's T-shirts—"Subs So Fast You'll Freak." Paul's primary responsibility was delivering sandwiches in a safe, courteous, and timely manner. When no delivery was scheduled, he worked in the shop, taking orders and making sandwiches.

The first delivery he made was to an office on St. John's campus. When he arrived, the woman who placed the order exclaimed, "Oh, boy, that was quick!" In telling this to me, Paul said, "That made me feel so good." I realized that recognition for a job well done, no matter how small, is important for all of us but had not been routine for Paul. He was buoyed by it.

In explaining details of the job to me, Paul said he would enter the store through a back hallway where he'd leave his bike; then he'd watch a computer screen for the location of needed deliveries, tapping the ones he would take. He felt he was good at this because he knew the area so well and could opt to take several deliveries at once if doing so made sense geographically. His question to me was: "Should I worry about the other delivery guys or should I just take as many as I can, as fast as I can?"

Good question, I thought, and one that, for Paul, would require time to answer well. I explained that he had to balance the importance of his individual accomplishments with teamwork, and looking out for others was critical. He had so many specific questions about how to best manage what he saw as competing needs. But this was the kind of conversation in which Paul did listen carefully. He wanted to know more about what didn't come naturally.

I've never liked the word "normal," particularly when referring to people. Even so, I use it sometimes and will here: People with "normal" development infer information that is not explicit, but inferential thinking can be challenging for a person with Paul's disabilities. This was one of the ways Paul needed to break down social behavior into smaller parts in order to understand and gradually learn.

There's no doubt these job-related experiences were good for Paul, and I believe he worked hard at navigating the complexity of unwritten rules, vexing as they may have been. Yet these challenges were beautifully balanced by his getting outdoors, on his own, and moving. The fact is, the combination of fresh air and physical exertion was the perfect antidote. And this was an aspect of work Paul was innately good at, aided by his keen sense of direction, his lifelong knowledge of Annapolis, his physical stamina, and his love for his bike. Paul also had a remarkable ability to tolerate extreme weather conditions, which came in handy as he flew around town in every possible climate—four seasons' worth—that Maryland dishes out.

Part of the conundrum in trying to understand Paul was in the nuances of his condition. Not directly related to work, this anecdote comes to mind: Paul could navigate that bike perfectly, as he could a car, but walking next to him on the sidewalk was a challenge for me. He could not stay in his personal space. In fact, for thirty-some years, he stepped on my feet, or bumped into me as we walked together, prompting me on occasion to say, "Let's walk single file."

Another one of life's unwritten rules—let people get off a bus, train, or elevator before you get on—had to be made explicit for Paul. This wasn't because Paul lacked empathy, something he had in abundance; it related more to social cueing—that which I suppose the unwritten rules depend on.

Paul achieved enough social comfort at work to laugh at himself, which he did even in telling me this story:

When I'm not making a delivery and need to work up front, I take my helmet off and put on a Jimmy John's visor and an apron. Then, if a delivery comes up, I take off the visor and the apron and put on the helmet. It's hard sometimes to remember all this when I'm also thinking about the delivery and being quick. So one day, I took the visor off and put my helmet on, but I forgot the apron; then I biked over the bridge to Eastport for my delivery. When I came back to the shop, another delivery guy who had passed me on the bridge said my apron was flapping in the breeze! He thought it was so funny. I laughed too. And now they call me 'Apron Man,' which still makes us laugh!

Every pair of pants or shorts Paul wore to work had a big ink stain on the front. This is because he would write down an order and put the uncapped pen in his front pocket, where it remained as he rode his bike. Someone gave him a retractable pen, which made no difference at all, as he would not click it closed before putting it in his pocket.

I loved the way he would tell these stories about himself with good humor.

It wasn't long before Paul was working six days a week and had the busiest shifts, including Fridays and Saturdays from 4:00 p.m. until 3:30 a.m. These eleven-plus-hour days concluded with the "bar shifts"—as they called the stretch from midnight to 3:00 in the morning. Because the shop was open for business during this block of time, but no longer making deliveries, Paul waited on customers.

He entertained me with countless stories of these late nights. The clientele—having departed the downtown bars at the 2:00 a.m. closing—were mostly intoxicated and, to Paul, amusing. He said oftentimes they would order one thing and you could give them another and they wouldn't know the difference. He laughed about one guy who said, "Just give me something good," and Paul kiddingly suggested roast beef and bacon, which the guy thought was brilliant.

Paul's other job-related observations:

- The St. John's kids tip better than the midshipmen, but when either school is on break, income goes down.
- The power boat people are more generous than the sailors.
- Delivering a catering job is hard, juggling shopping bags of food on each handlebar, but usually there is no tip because the person receiving the delivery isn't the person who placed the order.
- There is a cute girl who lives on East Street!

Once every week or so, I would order a sandwich from Jimmy John's, sometimes prompted by a text from Paul; otherwise, I just called and, more often than not, Paul answered the phone. Each time he'd say, "I don't want a tip from you, Mom."

"No worries," I would say. "I actually think you should tip me!"

Not surprisingly, Paul pined away for Kimi. He was sorry he'd let her go, regretful that he couldn't have helped her, and ever hopeful that she would get the treatment she needed and come back to him. But I was proud of him for finding as much pleasure in life as he did. Seeing his ability to put his problems in perspective, and not be all consumed by them, filled me with hope.

*

IN ADDITION TO his job, Paul absolutely loved his apartment. In the past, he had rented only a bedroom, but now he was otherwise starting from scratch with several rooms to furnish and a kitchen to equip. This called for creativity on our part, which we enjoyed. Also we were lucky. My friends Barbara and Frank gave him two good-sized bookcases, a desk, a table, a chest of drawers, and dishes. Jack and Maureen gave him a futon and frame that he used for a sofa and lots of kitchen things. And Keely, Sean, and I filled in with a coffee table, end tables, lamps, and other household necessities.

Paul was a big fan of Goodwill, where we went together probably once a week over his first couple of months as an apartment dweller. He usually had one thing in mind and did have good luck, spending only a couple of dollars. Over time, his Goodwill "finds" included a teapot, a shower caddy, a drawer organizer for kitchen flatware, and a dish rack. He also got magnets, which I noticed he used to affix things such as Keely's wedding invitation and a note from Kayla to his refrigerator.

Buz sent Paul to get new mini blinds for the windows that needed them. Paul asked me to take him to Home Depot, but said he didn't need my help. After he made the selections, we went back to the apartment and he carefully installed the blinds, then made sure they were uniformly adjusted. Paul was neat and cared about how things were arranged—even the shirts in his closet all hung facing the same direction.

Buz—strikingly handsome and equally personable—was a character, and the relationship he and Paul formed was fodder for a sitcom. Fondly referred to in the neighborhood as the "Mayor of Conduit Street," Buz would sit on his front porch and read but was always quick to put down his book or newspaper to chat with neighbors and other passersby. Some years ago, Buz got widespread acclaim in Annapolis and beyond for his bakery on Main Street that featured anatomically correct gingerbread men and women. Buz got on Paul's nerves sometimes but, more often, he delighted Paul with his stories of sailing and women and life in general.

One time, Paul asked Buz, "When you stopped seeing a woman, did it take you a long time to get over her and find another one?"

"No!" said Buz, in a second flat.

Another time Paul asked me, "Is it okay, Mom, that Buz comes into my apartment and gets me up because he needs my help with something?"

"What time?"

"9:30 or 10:00 in the morning."

"Yes, it's okay," I said.

I explained that Buz was old and sometimes needed the help of a young man, and that Paul had to take the bad with the good. To say that Buz was persnickety and set in his ways would be an understatement, but he did let Paul keep his bike in the first-floor foyer, no small convenience given Paul's work. Most important, Buz was a good person and, as a landlord, a much better match for Paul than someone from a management company might have been.

One day, Buz fell and was taken to the hospital, where he remained for a week. Paul was worried. After buying a card and some flowers, Paul asked me to drive him out to the hospital where we visited with Buz, who did look pretty frail and wasn't exactly sure how he had fallen. Paul and I chuckled on the way home at Buz's explanation that some "young person on a skateboard" must have knocked him over.

We didn't think so. But the good news was that Buz rebounded and returned home, seemingly no worse for wear.

Paul was proud of the apartment and liked to show it off. In addition to the obvious—Keely, Sean, Sara, Kayla, and me—visitors included Sam, who came from Silver Spring to spend a couple of days; Cheryl Morgan, who visited with me; Paul's photographer friend, Joseph, and several friends Paul had met at work. One night Paul prepared dinner for Kayla, telling me he served lemonade, popcorn, pizza, and ice cream. Perfect.

Paul took a video of the apartment—walking from one end to the other, panning each room—which he then sent to me with a text message: "I love my apartment. Thank you for helping me make it nice."

He had two keys to the apartment. One opened the massive old door inside the first-floor vestibule, a door that locked when it closed behind you; the other went to the door at the bottom of the stairway to the third floor, which Paul rarely locked. He gave me a set of keys just in case.

One night, Paul returned home from work and realized he'd locked himself out. He didn't want to awaken me in the middle of the night, so he rode over to my house, left his bike in my backyard, took my extension ladder from under the deck, walked back over to his place, put the ladder up to his third floor deck and, after climbing up, pulled the ladder from the ground to the deck for safekeeping. He did this three different times.

I applauded his efforts to avoid disturbing me, yet I could not picture him walking six blocks in the middle of the night with a twenty-two-foot extension ladder. But he didn't seem to think much of it.

Paul continued to give me cash to save for his monthly rent. Even though I saw him a few times a week, we set up a system. I kept a stack of small envelopes under a rock on my front porch. When Paul got off work, he would put cash in one of the envelopes and slip it through the mail slot in my front door. When it came time to pay rent, I would write the check using his money. He also paid a small electric bill and bought food.

Paul thought nothing of biking to Safeway to get groceries, or walking there for that matter—six miles round trip. But sometimes we would go together, and he started saving the stamps they gave out as a promotion, which could be accumulated and exchanged for Farberware. Eventually he collected enough to get a stainless saucepan with a glass top, which he really liked. Seeing the pleasure he took in small things contributed to my optimism about his future.

Paul helped me routinely. He cut my grass, raked my leaves, cleaned my gutters, and changed outside light bulbs in fixtures I couldn't easily reach. And otherwise, he came around regularly just to talk or sometimes to watch TV with me. While I did my best to let him know he didn't need to worry about me, he did anyway. He worried about my physical health—for no good reason—and my happiness. He said I was alone too much, I needed to make different choices, and I was too picky when it came to men—prompting me to think to myself: *obviously, not picky enough!* And, if I even mentioned I had a doctor's appointment, he would say, "WHY?" Then, no matter my answer, he'd grill me further.

I enjoyed his company most of the time and started to think of him in some ways as my closest friend. I say this due to the frequency with which I saw him and the consistency of his concern for me. Despite my being long-conditioned to associate Paul with some form of uneasiness, I found him to be a pleasure more often than not. I can see him now, looking through the glass of my back door as he knocked, holding up a container of Ben and Jerry's ice cream that he'd picked up at 7-Eleven as a bribe for me to sit and watch a movie with him, a ploy he'd discovered worked like a charm.

*

SOME MONTHS INTO working for Jimmy John's, Paul met some people who offered him a second job, working for Harry's Lunch Box, which he fit into his schedule when he could. This work entailed food preparation as well as working in the cafeteria at St. Mary's Elementary School. He started to say he liked accumulating money more than he liked free time, adding, "The little kids are so cute!"

A few days after Thanksgiving, Kimi was released from a treatment program in L.A. and decided, in cahoots with Paul, to return to Annapolis. I didn't share Paul's optimism. But his excitement was palpable, evidenced by his preparations for her arrival—cleaning the apartment (with a sudden burst of interest in the exact purpose of each vacuum cleaner attachment), buying groceries, and borrowing my slow cooker to make a pot of chili.

He knew better than to ask me for a ride to the airport—I'm good for *departing* flights only—and even seemed to enjoy the independence that Uber afforded. The next day, he told me that when he first saw Kimi, his heart melted. "I felt like a million dollars, Mom, just walking beside her. Her beauty actually scared me. She's out of my league." I was moved and couldn't help but, in some way, to share—although vicariously and ever so fleetingly—the wondrous state of being in love, but I couldn't shake my trepidation either.

But even with my healthy dose of skepticism, I wouldn't have predicted that things would go as badly as they did as quickly as they did. Kimi resumed drinking within twenty-four hours of her arrival, and she hit bottom fast.

It was interesting to see Paul in the role of caretaker, to witness his dogged attempts to curb or prevent Kimi's drinking. Focused as he was, his tactics were not what I'd call strategic. For example, he poured out her bottle of vodka before he left for work, which simply meant that she would use his money to buy another. But he persisted and the increasing volatility of the situation had me on edge.

Paul didn't want to give up, which he talked about one day with my friend Cheryl, who listened to him and said she thought he expressed himself well and seemed to have a good handle on the complexity of the problems. Basically, she understood his frustration, which Paul appreciated, prompting him to tell me the next day that Cheryl had a better grasp of the situation than I did, and he would listen to her from now on. I felt like saying, "Fine. Call Cheryl to bail you out when you get arrested for disturbing the peace!"

Early one afternoon, Paul brought Kimi over to my house. Paul was dressed for work, where he needed to be within the hour. He hadn't given me a head's up, but I quickly figured out that I was an unwitting accomplice in his scheme to control that day's drinking, something that was well underway.

Startling me, they simultaneously dove for her purse. I watched as Paul outmaneuvered her, seizing the bottle of vodka and holding it up over his head and out of her reach, causing her to lunge at him. The next thing I knew, they were in a scuffle on the floor, and the bottle shot out from under them, skidding across the wood floor before slamming into the wall at the back of the china cabinet. As my luck would have it, the damn thing didn't break.

Caught off guard by this whole scene, the likes of which belonged in a bad movie rather than my house, I nevertheless was able to take possession of the near-full bottle. I hadn't thought through what good this would do, but they each wanted it, so I was compelled to exert my prowess. But this triumph didn't change the basic facts: She was drunk. And he was mad. A frightening combination if ever there was one.

Paul yelled at her, "I'M NOT USING MY DRUG OF CHOICE, SO WHY DO YOU HAVE TO?" Seeing the futility in his input, I told him to get the hell out of my house and go to work. I fought with him momentarily as he tried to peel my fingers from the door latch, but he gave in and left. I'd always had some power—when the chips were down—over him. But now, I turned to face an unknown opponent. Rational thought was useless, and that was pretty much my only tool.

I was relieved when Kimi flopped down on the couch, getting my hopes up that she would stay put so I could collect myself. No such luck. She bounded up, decided she was angry with me and, while spitting nasty nonsense, staggered toward the door without her coat, which she refused to take from me. It was thirty-five degrees and pouring rain. I called my sister Jennie for advice, but I had to abandon the phone as Kimi came at me. I didn't know what to expect as we briefly engaged in a physical altercation, but her limbs were like jelly. Her mind, on the other hand, was more like a steel trap, and her only aim was to share her displeasure with me then leave. I put her coat in a plastic bag and followed her outside, forcing her to take it, and I watched her as she headed down the block.

My nerves were shot, but I was worried about her, even though our neighborhood is safe, with lots of open shops and even social services a block over, and it was daylight. I don't know how she spent the day, but I do know that about 10:00 that night, Paul got a call from the Maryland Inn, an elegant hotel and historic treasure in the heart of town, where Kimi was a less than welcome fixture in the otherwise dignified lobby.

Paul told me he was reluctant to go get her at first, but then he buckled under. Days later, he did laugh as he recounted their walk back to his apartment, telling me that she was tipsy and kept accusing him of steering her toward my house—a ruse she was determined to outsmart, even though he was doing no such thing. I refrained from asking him if he'd been overwhelmed by her beauty after she'd been sloshing around town for hours on end.

I investigated local treatment for Kimi again, with her blessings, but to no avail. Even though she and Paul were an accident waiting to happen, I had affection for her and very much saw her as a victim of an insidious condition. As it turned out, Kimi was in Annapolis about two weeks before I booked her a flight and took her to BWI—this time with less resistance from Paul who was, in truth, at his wits' end. I gave Kimi some money so she wouldn't be penniless for the long trip and, once again, I saw her to the security line—only to find out a day later from her mother that she hadn't boarded the plane.

When I learned she'd been turned away by airport personnel for being intoxicated, I instantly regretted having given her cash. For several days, neither her parents nor Paul knew her whereabouts, and all of us were worried sick. While her safety was the overriding concern, Paul was undone by the thought of her being drunk and turning up at his work, something that had occurred before her departure. Within the week, Kimi contacted her mother from a hospital near the airport and was able to get on a flight home—a huge weight lifted for all of us.

Paul understood that Kimi needed more help than he could provide; nonetheless he was despondent. I didn't realize the extent to which he had held out hope all along, hopes that were suddenly dashed with a new reality hitting him hard. I was relieved to know that she was safe and not an immediate threat to Paul's well-being. But I did understand, for better or worse, sensible or not, that he was in love with her and that he wasn't one to move on any too soon. Those who can't relate to the pain of a broken heart must have memory failure.

I found this poem in Paul's laptop:

MY STONE
All I have to remember California is in my pocket.
In a stone I found at the beach where we lived.
And a palm tree's shade that somehow missed me,
As a reminder to always wear suntan lotion.

If it weren't for losing things constantly
the last few months wouldn't have been so bad.
But I never found anything I lost before I met you.
And you've been picking up after me since.

And if I hadn't lost my wallet in Venice,
we may have ended up taking a plane.
Losing my mind in Utah was a doozy
but you helped me find that in other states.

Most of our possessions are gone now
but the thought that's lurking in my mind:
Wherever you go, I'll direct you
and whatever I lose, you will find.

It's winter here but for you the sun is still shining
Warming the many spaces that we called home.
It occurs to me now to take off and go running
but to do it without you wouldn't be worth it at all.

My sunburn is gone but I still have my stone,
it reminds me of all that we overcame.
Those pigeons did get the best of us…
But you and I, we'll take that to our graves.

It was mid-December when Kimi left, and I gave Paul credit for handling Christmas as well as he did. He bought gifts, mostly for Kayla, of course, but also for Keely and me. He even decorated his apartment with a little tree and lights, and he enjoyed time with us while continuing to perform well at work and avoid drug use.

His OCD was not in check, however, which created some problems. One evening, Paul, Kayla, and I went out for dinner and I took photos of the two of them. Later that same night, he was obsessed with cropping the photos and sorting them—deciding which ones he would send to Kayla and which ones he would post on Facebook. It was not a happy undertaking, as he was unreasonable. I told him I couldn't help him any longer, that I would email all the photos to him, and he could go home and figure it out by himself. In short, he was making something that wasn't a problem into an overly tension-filled, no-win exercise. While this behavior was sporadic, it disturbed me.

On Christmas Day, Paul didn't like it when he learned that I wasn't going with him to his father and Lucy's house for Christmas night, as had been the case in recent years.

I explained that it was an off year, most likely due to his father's recent cancer diagnosis and upcoming treatment and emphasized that I was fine; in fact, I told him, I planned to stop by my sister's. Regardless of my multiple attempts to redirect Paul, his ruminating persisted throughout the day.

We were all worried about Don's diagnosis and prayed for his full recovery. And while that seemed a reasonable hope, thankfully due to early detection, we were also sorry Don had to cope with the uncertainty as well as the treatments. As it turned out, Don was declared cancer free later that spring, something Paul did not live to see.

The most recurring heartaches that surfaced for Paul, however, were related to the past and the turning point brought on by his bringing up the unwanted sexual encounters he'd experienced as a boy. He had pretty much given up on getting any closure, but he never adjusted to being blamed. If anyone knew that life wasn't fair, it was Paul; but somehow he believed that some form of consolation was out there somewhere.

One day, Paul came over and told me that he'd seen Martin's father, a person who had severed all ties with us and who I guessed had pretty much stopped visiting the area. Despite the loss of the relationship and the absence of any sort of reciprocal affection, Paul was happy to see him, even from afar. "Mom, I saw him," Paul said, with genuine enthusiasm. "He didn't see me, but I was glad to see him because he looked so good. He didn't look any older. I worried he'd have a lot of gray hair and look different but he doesn't. He looks really good!" Paul's kindness touched me deeply.

A reference to this situation came up time and again in Paul's writing. The very last entry in which he mentioned it was in what he called "Ongoing Journal," and was written some weeks before he died:

I didn't follow in the footsteps of my family. This is regrettable. My mother only ever wanted what was best for me. I can't stand that I disappointed her. And whether she knows it or not, I do, and it's heavy on my conscience. I only wanted to be successful. Like my sister, I wanted to graduate college and make both of my parents proud. What can I do now though? Maybe it isn't all my fault. Maybe I could have used a male figure in my life who would push me. I didn't have that and I always envied the relationships my cousins and friends had with their fathers. My friend Marty especially who does not talk to me now for reasons that actually are not my fault. It's been a heavy weight to bare. I know it is not my fault but the drugs are so I stopped using. That's all I can do.

Buz had another home in Florida, where he spent a good portion of the winter. I don't know how he usually got there, but I'm guessing he drove. I'm also guessing his adult children and grandchildren were beginning to try to clip his wings a bit, given his recent health scare. I do know that Paul was in touch with one of his daughters, with whom he shared information about the house whenever she asked.

All I know for sure is that in January 2017, Buz asked Paul to drive him to his home in Delray Beach, Florida. Paul would drive

Buz's car—a twenty-plus-year-old little sedan that at one time I think might have been red—and Buz would fly Paul home.

I loved Buz, but I did not like this idea. It wasn't easy to explain why, particularly to Paul.

Me: "You'll miss a week of work and can't afford that."

Paul: "I'll be fine. I have not taken any time off and I'm getting a tax refund."

Me: "Buz irritates you, remember? He's cheap, which drives you crazy."

Paul: "I know. But I love Buz and I want to help him. And you always said I should."

Me: "Yeah, well, I didn't tell you my 2017 New Year's resolution: Every man for himself."

Paul: "Mom, don't be an ass."

Me: "Who is buying your meals along the way? You need these things to be clear."

Paul: "That's true. Can you call Buz for me?"

Me: "No!"

I wasn't nervous about Paul's driving. Frankly, picturing Paul and eighty-five-year-old Buz bombing down the Atlantic coast in that old car made me smile. But what I didn't like was the disturbance to Paul's routine. Paul was in a pretty good place in his life, but with enough heartache and fragility to be at risk, and I didn't want his routine messed with. On January 18, I was unsettled enough to send Don a text:

I'm worried about Paul's pending trip to Florida but don't think he can negotiate his way out of it at this juncture. I wanted you to know this as he could turn to you for advice, although I don't want him to know I contacted you. He just left here and is stressed and knowing this would make it worse. I feel sorry for him and would like to tell you my concerns if you are interested or have the time. Regardless of all this, I hope you are doing well and that your ordeal is as manageable as possible.

Don did reply: "I have confidence that he will do fine and intend on talking to him before he leaves."

I followed up with: "He will come back and be in a bad way."

But there was no reply, so I never had the chance—even cursorily—to express my concerns. I have long believed it takes a village. But I was on my own. Even so, I let my optimism transcend my distress, telling myself there was no reason for it.

Chapter 16

SCREAM IN THE WIND

Surely one day an angel will greet me at destiny's door
and again I'll pack my bags for the divide,
wearing a crown of silver linings and hiking that paradise;
relinquishing my sleepwalk to a realistic pace.

BREEZY VOICEMAIL MESSAGES, providing a running commentary on the drive south, reminded me of a sentiment Paul expressed in the last line of one of his poems, "The euphoria interstates provide."

"Hi, Mom. We're just getting to North Carolina and I wanted to see how you're doing. Okay."

"Hi, Mom. We made it to Georgia. Okay. I love you."

But the Paul I talked with in Delray Beach didn't know breezy; he was agitated. Too many loose ends, and Buz was getting on his nerves. I booked his flight from West Palm Beach to Baltimore. Sean arranged an Uber to get Paul from Buz's place to the airport, with the expenses being subtracted from Paul's rent. I picked up Paul from BWI on January 26, 2017. He was glad to be home, but I could see his anxiety was in high gear.

February was a rocky month. Paul continued to work, two jobs when he could, but business was in a seasonal slump, depleting his income. He asked if I could pay his February rent, saying he would reimburse me when he got his tax refund. I agreed, despite my hope that he would save the tax money. Were it not for going to Florida, he wouldn't have been behind financially, but I didn't say that.

Several weeks passed, and I inquired as to the whereabouts of the tax refund. After stalling for a few days, Paul came clean. He had received it, but it was gone. He had spent it. I was furious with him, telling him that he should be ashamed of himself for lying to me—taking advantage of me. I think I remember telling him not to call me until he could come up with the money. Funny how our emotional selves deliver an ultimatum, even though our intellectual selves know it's fruitless. It's no wonder our children don't entirely trust us.

But more than anything, it scared me. I followed up with a text message:

I am sorry to be so upset and am trying to collect myself, but you misled me, which is just plain wrong. You should have been able to catch up from the trip to Florida. And now the rent for March is almost due. What the hell is happening to your money? I cannot help you anymore until you get back on track.

Paul responded:

I'm stressed out. That is all. I've been depressed. But my job is going well in terms of them being happy with me. Maybe I have nothing to show for the money I've made in the last month but I've made progress over all.

Looking back, I realize this was wishful thinking on Paul's part. He was trying to convince himself as much as me. I also realize I should have seen the "depression" as the tip of the iceberg that it was.

He called the next night and told me he had relapsed—the first time since his one-day escapade in California. He was demoralized, he hated himself, and was sorry he'd hurt me. He said he was going to stop, that he was strong enough to do so. He also said he was going to give me his upcoming paycheck for safekeeping. I didn't know what to say. I could've gotten angry about the money, but I knew better in that conversation. I told him I appreciated knowing the truth and I wanted to help him. "Not with money," I said, "but with exploring options."

He told me he was tired. "I think I'll just go to bed and pray," he said,

Me too, I thought.

After a restless night, I woke up to two text messages:

"I'm dead, Mom. I miss who I was. I need help. I don't want to lose my place."

"I can't lose everything I've gained because of a relapse. That makes no sense."

Shaken, I called him to talk about forging some kind of plan. I asked if he'd told Dr. Kolsky, and he said he had not. I urged him to do so. Paul told me he had confided in his friend, Joseph, who was supportive of him and trying to be helpful. Joseph agreed with Paul that therapy wasn't the answer.

I told Paul that therapy was not the whole answer, but it was an important part of a solution insofar as a professional is a conduit to resources. I said I thought it was too risky for him to do this alone—there plainly was too much at stake.

My voice must have betrayed my attempts to hide emotion. I realized I was pleading with him. "If you have the power to overcome this," I said, "that's good, but most people need support; certainly there is no downside to a safety net."

The next day, he told me that Keely had invited him to dinner for Thursday. He was happy because he didn't have to work Thursday night and was still lamenting the fact that his work schedule had precluded his joining us for the Super Bowl at Keely's. "Please don't tell Keely about my problems," he said. "I'm so depressed and this is something to look forward to. Are you going too?"

"Yes," I said.

"Oh good. I'm excited."

The next morning I was awakened by loud banging on my front door. It was Paul, and he was frantic. By the time I got to the door, he was irrational—yelling at me. But his words made no sense. "Let me in, dammit!" he screamed.

I went out on the porch and talked to him through the screen door. He said he wanted to come in and have a cup of coffee. I told him no, that he was too upset and he could walk to 7-Eleven for coffee. He said he didn't have any money. I handed him a couple of dollars but didn't let him in. Then he started pacing along the side of the house, into the back yard, and returning to the front. Back and forth. Yelling.

"Paul," I said, "you have to calm down. Go get your coffee and call me later. We can talk when you're calm."

Later that day, he came over and said he was sorry about his behavior but told me he was "freaking out" and was going to sell his things and leave Maryland.

"Please don't be rash," I said, pleading again. "It won't solve anything. Please trust me. The only way to move forward is to make good and thoughtful decisions. Running won't help."

I asked when he would see Dr. Kolsky. He said he wasn't sure. He then said he didn't *think* he had an appointment, which meant he didn't have one. I handed Paul the phone and told him to call Dr. Kolsky and leave a message. "Tell him you're in a crisis," I said.

Paul did as I suggested. I heard him.

After he left, I called my dear friend Nancy Leventhal, who has always been a resource for me in general and, in particular, a great help in thinking through situations like this. She agreed that Paul was unlikely to be able to fight this on his own and—expressing grave worry about me—said she felt strongly that I couldn't be his only support person. After we talked, she sent me a list of doctors she thought worth investigating.

Later that day, I received a text message, prompting a texting exchange between us:

If I killed myself would you be sad or would you be relieved? I've never gone completely off the deep end. I've always held back because of the fear I had of you. In some ways it's kept me from hitting bottom. I am scared. And you are mad at me. And I know I've made your life hard but I guarantee that you are happier than I am.

Me:
I'd be devastated. I have so much hope and love for you. But I can't say it's not hard. Maybe I am happier . . . But also I'm more stable, probably because I take better care of myself. I'm not mad at you. I'm just deflated because I am helpless. I'd give anything to be able to talk with you and have you take some of my advice.

Paul:
The funny thing is I care about your happiness more than my own. I always have. I'm just complicated.

Me:
I know you care about me and I know you have a good heart. But you aren't helping yourself to the degree that is needed. And until you do, we will continue to suffer. Both of us. In different ways, but the suffering will be constant. And I have no control. I understand you cannot control your addiction, but you can control getting help. I'm helpless.

Paul:
Well maybe you won't have to deal with me much longer.

Me:
I'd like to think you'd try getting the support you need before giving up. Life is not for the faint hearted. You have to buck-up and seek help. Otherwise it's a miserable journey. You are worth the investment of time and effort but, if you disagree, what can I do?

Paul:
Nothing. Tell Keely I can't make it Thursday. I think I've made a hell of an effort.

Me:
You tell her.

Paul:
No.

Me:
Not my job. Besides, if you don't want her to know your problems, how do you explain being excited one minute and declining the next? And asking your mother to deliver the news? Not stable behavior on either count and there's a game in there too. Exhausting.

*

WE DID GO to Keely and Sean's for dinner, and Paul was in good spirits. He looked good, too, which soothed my frayed nerves. After dinner, Paul and Keely made sandwiches for Paul to take home because he told her he hadn't had time to get groceries. They stood at her kitchen counter, side by side, laughing together as they worked. Since it was such a sweet moment for me, I snapped a photo of them.

None of us knew that they would never see each other again.

The next day, I called Dr. Kolsky's office and left a message. I also called Paul's friend Joseph, who told me he too was worried about Paul and was talking to him daily. I asked if he thought Paul was still using. He wasn't sure, he said, but he was meeting Paul for coffee in a few minutes and was going to find out.

Later that same day, Paul took himself to the Anne Arundel Medical Center Emergency Room, where he reported being suicidal—a strategy for being seen, he told me. He was put in a flight-risk room. I called the hospital and spoke to a nurse, who said he'd been admitted but that she couldn't give me any more information. Paul called me multiple times. In one call, he told me that he was being transferred the next day to a behavioral health hospital in Columbia, Maryland. After we hung up, I called Jimmy John's to tell the manager that Paul had been hospitalized. I said I wasn't sure about the duration, but that I would stay in touch.

On the day of Paul's arrival at the behavioral health hospital, a social worker called to tell me that the hospital program was designed for short-term crisis intervention and that Paul's stay would be limited to two weeks. The next step would be a dual diagnosis inpatient program, she said, and for this they were looking specifically at Warwick Manor in East New Market, Maryland. A bed was available for Paul, but there was a snafu with his insurance. Because she believed he was eligible, she had completed the application on his behalf and hoped it would be processed before Paul's time at the hospital ran out. Usually, she explained, the turnaround time was a month, but they were doing everything they could to expedite the process.

I was relieved to hear from someone working with Paul, and I welcomed the opportunity to provide an overview of his history, his disabilities, and his mental health. But as I spoke, it became obvious that she hadn't called to get information, so I limited my remarks. I figured I would have another opportunity to speak with her. In any case, I was hopeful. Paul had been placed in Warwick Manor twelve years before and had loved it. "I want to stay here for the rest of my life," he'd said.

But in thinking about what the social worker had told me, I realized I was confused and had follow-up questions, both about the insurance and alternatives without it. Seeking clarity, I called the hospital multiple times, leaving messages for the social worker, but did not get a return call. I did speak with Paul each day, and he was hopeful too. But he was as much in the dark about the insurance as I was.

Somehow Paul had managed to take one of his black and white composition books to the hospital. The boy would forget his head before he would his journal. He didn't write much while there, but later I did see this:

I pray for silence everytime I wake up.
My road to recovery began at Warwick Manor.
To this day, I hold value to the serenity there,
By the river, in my dirty underwear
With my mother, walking.

Sara visited Paul during his stay in the behavioral health hospital and had been disappointed to learn that Kayla was too young to accompany her. As the visiting hour was coming to an end, Paul wrote a message for Sara to deliver to Kayla. "I LOVE YOU, KAYLA! XO, DADDY." Written with crayon in Paul's awkward hand, this now framed note hangs on Kayla's bedroom wall.

Prior to Sara's visit, Paul had asked her to bring him a pack of cigarettes, and she had obliged. One of the life skills Paul picked up in Central Booking was how to smoke a cigarette in the bathroom without its being detected. He told me about it once, and I must not have been listening, or maybe I didn't want to know. Either way, I don't remember the details. I already knew more than I wanted to about bail bondsmen and pawn shops.

But I do know that, in spite of how clever this secret smoking maneuver may have been in theory, it didn't get by the powers that be in the behavioral health hospital. Paul was caught breaking the rule and was dismissed from the program, rendering the insurance scenario moot—or so I guessed. He was back home. And, once again, my calls to the hospital, now frantic, were ignored.

I've had to reassure Sara several times that she wasn't to blame for Paul's dismissal because she had supplied the cigarettes—this was on Paul, not Sara. Paul had no better friend in this world than Sara, something she had demonstrated time and again in their twenty-year relationship. The last thing I want is for Sara to reflect on their final minutes together with any regrets.

When the need to cast blame sweeps over me, I blame the hospital. Institutions have rules. I get that. At the same time, I have wondered why a place that exists to promote recovery can't choose its battles and prioritize. After all, Paul wasn't in the lung cancer ward. And couldn't the consequences of breaking a rule have been less dramatic? Take away his journal and his pen for a day, and he'll fall in line. But no, he was dismissed.

Cigarettes are deadly all right.

I spent that whole day with Paul. He went into work to get his schedule. We took his bike to Velo—the local bike shop he swore by and where Jimmy John's cyclists get a discount—and shopped for groceries. I enjoyed his company.

We talked about next steps. Paul told me he was disappointed in the loss of Warwick Manor as a possibility but said he never did understand the insurance and got the feeling the hospital was becoming less optimistic. "But I'm going to look on the bright side," he said, "I can return to work."

I could see that. He had become discouraged when he'd started to slip behind financially, and it had spiraled down from there. Yet I knew that he needed support, and lots of it. One of my overriding concerns was that, long before the relapse, he hadn't been appropriately medicated, making him more susceptible to mood swings and depression. My highest priority had been—somehow—to encourage or facilitate his getting on the right medication.

In that, I failed. I know I did.

*

PAUL WANTED TO find a doctor who would give him Suboxone, saying that, with it, he knew he could fight this on his own. I told him that Nancy had given me a list of local doctors who treat addiction, and my understanding was that some of them prescribed Suboxone or similar medications. I said I was ready to start making phone calls, an offer he jumped at. In fact, he said my help eased his biggest fear—being alone in this.

For a variety of reasons, my phone calls didn't turn up any resources. One office told me the doctor had met his limit in terms of the number of Suboxone patients he was allowed; another said the current doctor didn't have the needed waiver to prescribe Suboxone. In one case, I got a stern lecture on the pitfalls of Suboxone. "Substituting one substance for another only prolongs addiction," I was told. I now know that this statement is one hundred percent false and, moreover, that saying this to me was downright immoral. I'll tell you what medications such as Suboxone prolong: LIFE.

I was distraught, and I desperately wanted an anchor, a safety net—something I had pretty much given up on Dr. Kolsky providing. I did tell myself that Paul had relapsed in California and, after a week in a rehabilitation program, was able to make it from the end of May through the following February. Paul also told me he had learned that people who ultimately beat drug addiction relapse on average nine times beforehand. *Please, dear God, tell me this was the ninth*, I thought, even though I knew better. I did get the sense that Paul was feeling less shame and more self-acceptance, which I saw as a good sign.

On St. Patrick's Day, Keely and Sean decided to Uber to a local pub for dinner. Keely noticed a Jimmy John's car topper on the floor of the back seat, inspiring her to tell the Uber driver her brother worked at the Main Street Jimmy John's. As it turned out, the driver, Steve, knew Paul and loved him. In telling me about it, Keely said, "He raved about Paul."

I paid Paul's rent for March and his electric bill—there was no choice. I told him he now had to work toward April. He signed over his paycheck, which got us halfway there—another good sign—and he started to put cash through the door slot again. One of the silly things I haven't been able to do is move the stack of envelopes from under the rock on my porch.

In early April, my neighborhood book club held its meeting in a home on Conduit Street, where it's just about impossible to park due to the proximity to downtown. Knowing that Buz was in Florida, I asked Paul if I could park in his driveway, just two doors down from the meeting. Paul checked with the second-floor renter and cleared the way. I picked up my friend, Amy Clements, and was appreciative of the premier parking spot. I knew Paul was working, and I was pleased to see that he'd turned off the lights in his third-floor apartment.

At the end of the evening, as I was backing out of the driveway with Amy and another friend, Paul came along on his bike, delivery bound. I lowered my window to say hello and quickly introduced him to my friends. He was sweet, and as we drove away, he called out, "I love you, Mom!" This is a moment that, in the frenzy of the month, I didn't think of again—not one time—until Amy recounted it some-time after Paul's memorial service. I was grateful.

I had a few more uplifting moments with Paul, but the day I figured out that he had sold his phone, my heart sank. Already holding on to shreds of hope, I was frozen. Paul came over, and we talked. He said his tips that night would cover his phone and that I shouldn't worry.

He then asked to borrow my phone to call his father. I suggested he text first to give Don a head's up that Paul was the caller, which he did, and they spoke. Paul asked for some money, explaining that he was still behind after having been in the hospital. Don said he could give him a couple of hundred dollars, for which Paul was appreciative. I would make sure he used it to pay for a needed bicycle repair and some groceries. Paul was fragile and got a little teary as we retrieved the check from Don's mailbox at the end of his driveway. "Why do you think he didn't want us in the house?" he asked me.

"A thousand reasons I can think of, Paul! Don't worry about it."

Just a few days later, Paul told me he needed some of his rent money back—that he had "plans with some friends." My answer was an unequivocal "*No!*" This didn't sit well with Paul—I knew it wouldn't. But, frankly, at that point, I wasn't focused on the rent money or *any* money matter, per se. It was what he might do with it that frightened me.

I had stopped by Cheryl's to wish her a happy birthday, an occasion I hadn't missed in sixty-odd years. While chatting with her, I ignored my ringing phone. Maybe I shouldn't have. Then again, it wouldn't have mattered. As Cheryl walked me to my car, I picked up Paul's call. He was over-the-top, demanding. Again, I said, "No." I don't remember all of what was said, but Cheryl remembers me telling Paul, "I'm scared."

As I drove home, I spotted him on his bike on West Street, making a delivery. He saw me too, which I wasn't too happy about. I pulled over, and he asked one more time. He needed $140. I refused.

Paul looked at me through the passenger side window and said, "You know what, Mom? You are just a bummer."

Those would be the last words he ever spoke to me. We had traveled a long road since I had declared, "Mommie, I had a boy!"

Only it wasn't long enough.

Chapter 17

GOOD NIGHT, MY CHILD

In these times, life seems both true and surreal
And burning passions for verse awaken when my thoughts are even keeled
Like hyper children they are hungry, and my stresses arise
As a need for release festers in my idle mind
Much like a river of rapids, rampaging into a channeled inlet
My mind, body, soul meet poem, and become my beautiful quartet
Once released, the birth of my creations can run rampant and wild
I rock them and treat them to eternity
And say good night to my nourished child

IT WAS A Saturday evening when I last saw Paul. I didn't hear from him Sunday, which was unusual, but I figured he was working, or mad at me, or both. Not that either meant he wouldn't call.

When I hadn't heard from him by midday Monday, I was unsettled. As I've admitted, I didn't like it when he called too much, or too little—and this stretch was out of the ordinary. Then again, he often forgot to charge his phone. Or he misplaced it.

At 2:24 p.m., I received a call from an unrecognized number, which normally I wouldn't have answered. But since Paul frequently borrowed phones for one reason or another, I picked up. I don't get that many calls, and I was pretty sure it was he. "Hello," I said.

Caller: "Is Jessie Dunleavy there?"

Me: "No, she's not. Can I take a message?"

Caller: "Yes. Would you ask her to call the Annapolis City Police at . . ."

Me: "I'm so sorry, this is Jessie Dunleavy—I was in a hurry,
        but if this is important . . ."

I was thinking, *What did he do now?*

The caller's voice was garbled, with the exception of his final
word, which was crystal clear: ". . . deceased."

Me: "WHAT did you say?"

Caller: "Your son is deceased."

I remember the officer asking if I needed help. "No," I said, but I
guess I wasn't convincing because within minutes there were two peo-
ple at my door—a man and a woman from Anne Arundel County's
Crisis Response System. Some part of me realized that I was not alto-
gether grounded because when the call came in, I was upstairs; but
when I heard the knock on the door, I was in the basement and didn't
know why. Anyway, those crisis people held me like they were family.
I needed them more than I knew.

The first person I called was Don. I left messages on his cell and
home phones and sent a text, all of which said, "Call me as soon as
possible." Keely was teaching. I didn't want undue attention to make
this news any harder for her. I thought maybe I should wait until the
school day was over. I didn't know . . . I called Sean and told him. He
said he would take care of telling Keely and would get her from school
to my house in as many minutes as it would take to drive from his
office to her and then to me. I did think to tell Sean I hadn't yet heard
from Don, so Keely couldn't tell people at school.

Next, I called my sisters—leaving a non-specific message for one
and speaking briefly with the other, who was out of town but who
would return to lend a hand in the days to come. Then I called two
old friends, Cheryl and then Maureen; both of them were in my living
room in what seemed like seconds. I do remember Cheryl answering
her phone saying, "What's wrong?" rather than "Hello."

Keely and Sean arrived. Keely—my other baby—grief stricken,
in despair.

I didn't know what happened to Paul, or when, or where. Did he suffer? Was he hurt? Where was he when he died? *Where is he now?* And why would they tell me over the phone?

I kept saying that we couldn't tell anyone else until Don knows. Then Sean was able to reach him. And in a few minutes, he, then Lucy, joined us. We sat there—Keely, Sean, Don, Lucy, Cheryl, Maureen, and the crisis people.

Then a policeman arrived, giving me Paul's watch and wallet. I put the watch on my wrist. We now learned several things, though I don't remember the order, or who told us—the policeman or the crisis people. Paul had been scheduled to work that day, Monday, and when he didn't show up—a first for him—the people at Jimmy John's called the police.

The police found Paul in his bedroom. There was no sign of a struggle or foul play.

The cause of death would be determined by an autopsy, which was the law, given his young age. They gave me a phone number. Paul's body was being taken to the State Medical Examiner's Office in Baltimore. We needed to arrange for where his body would go from there. Thankfully, Sean didn't waste a second before saying he would manage that. I couldn't bear the thought, and I needed to remove myself from it.

The policeman said, "Your son sure was neat." (Meaning his belongings were well organized.) I wanted to scream—"HE WAS SO MANY THINGS! YOU PEOPLE HAVE NO IDEA!"

Don and Lucy left first. Cheryl and Maureen sat a while longer—each would be in and out over the coming days. Then Sean and Keely took me to their house. A note was taped to their front door. It was from Steve, the Uber driver, who didn't know Keely's phone number or even her last name, just her address. He was so sorry.

I had to call Sara. I called her parents first, thinking they could advise me. Was Sara with Kayla? Is there something I should know about their schedule? I didn't want to call if she was driving. But after trying all numbers several times, I couldn't reach either Sara's mother or father. I didn't want to wait any longer. I called Sara's number, and she answered. I asked if Kayla was with her, and she said that Kayla was in Florida with Sara's parents. Okay, all clear. I told Sara. No call I made was as hard. God bless her. A couple of days later, when Sara had collected herself a bit, she shared some feelings on Facebook:

> On Monday I got a call from Paul's mother, the call I never wanted to get. Paul and I knew each other for over half our lives. We may have started out as a couple but we ended as friends with a beautiful daughter. For all the work we both put in to allowing us to have a friendship and maintain it and show Kayla we loved her and cared about each other was a true blessing I thank God for. I see Paul when I look at Kayla. Kayla loved her Daddy so much as did I, and I will help Kayla honor his memory whenever and wherever I can. We love you Paul. XOXO

*

THE NEXT DAY, we started the inevitable logistics. The obituary, a joint effort with Keely, and helped along by Paul's cousin Cassie who was at my door—flowers in hand—first thing. The service. A program. It's a blur. But it's all a brilliant distraction, not one of mundane busy-work. You are drawn in by a passion to honor your person as well as you can. It's what you have left, and you cling to it.

In getting people to speak, Keely and I instinctively turned first to family friends Jack and Maureen, who were like Godparents to Keely and Paulie, never missing a beat—be it a birthday, a graduation, a play, a sporting event, or a parents' weekend—throughout their growing up and beyond. Next, we asked the three children-turned-adults who had grown up next door in commune-like proximity to us—Josh

Falk, Danny Falk, and Lara (Falk) Wilson—and whose lives had intertwined with ours in countless ways.

To round out the speakers, Keely and I agreed that we needed someone from Paul's current life. I thought of the note taped to her door, a gesture that had touched me. "Does that Uber guy speak English?" I asked.

"Yes, of course," said Keely.

That was my only question. I called Steve Wallwork, whom I had never met and whose name I'd just heard. He was quick to say he loved Paul and would be honored to speak about him. Okay—we had our speakers. We didn't give direction to any of them. On to the next thing.

Our friend and popular local musician, Bridgette Michaels, agreed to provide the music. Keely and I made the music selections, one of which was for Kayla. Don chose a poem to read.

With help from loved ones, the details fell into place.

It was a beautiful spring day. The Overlook Pavilion at Port Annapolis Marina turned out to be perfect for Paul: overlooking the water, a stone's throw from Paul's and Sara's sailing camp. I think the event proved a fitting tribute to Paul, as much as those things can, with many heartfelt words portraying his goodness, shared with a couple of hundred people, all paying their respects and providing much love and support. Steve Wallwork's insightful remarks, capturing Paul's final year, were given to me in writing, and included:

Paul was like a living watercolor to me. . . . He was a soft and gentle impression in my mind . . .

I met Paul upon entering the store one night and was greeted by those who knew me . . . I remember Paul had this curious look in his eye, a look of wonder about who I was . . . The manager introduced me to Paul . . . and we engaged in conversation and instantly became friends. He eagerly told me about his family, whom he loved, and how much he enjoyed his job.

We continued to meet most Friday and Saturday nights at Jimmy John's. Paul would greet me with his warm smile and would always want to know if I had any interesting Uber experiences to share. His eyes would light up as I'd tell him about some of the customers I met and share their stories with him. Paul seemed to take a real interest in people's lives . . . He said he could tell that I had a genuineness in how I related to people and that he wished he could be that way. I remember being surprised at that statement and told him that I thought the same way of him, that he was a sincere and genuine man and that he probably had a long list of friends. He seemed surprised that I had that impression of him. He was always questioning my statements with, "Really?"—as if no one told him those things before.

What I loved about Paul was his willingness to share his feelings about anything. He was open about his life and expressed many things to me that allowed me to get an impression of Paul as a complex man. I began to see that Paul's life had been filled with challenges. I could see in his eyes a sense of loss at times, a sense of discouragement about his relationships, his choices, but then, suddenly, his eyes would sparkle with hope as he told me about wanting to do more with his life and experience new things. His watercolor palette was always changing and becoming an image of a man in search of himself, knowing there was so much more he could do.

One time Paul was telling me about his love for adventure.

We were sharing stories about things we'd done and places we'd been . . . So when I told him that I'd lived in Cambodia for five years, he was fascinated and wanted to know how I got to go there. The discussion led to me telling him my wife and I were Mormons and originally went to Cambodia as missionaries. . . . Paul became very curious and wanted to know about my church, my family, being a missionary, the culture of Cambodia, the Khmer people, the food, and said he admired me and my convictions and he hoped one day to spend time helping others.

Paul had a good sense of humor. We laughed a lot as we'd tease each other about various things and try to outwit each other. After I met Keely, I knew I'd play a joke on him about knowing his sister. I couldn't wait!!!

So that night, we were standing around talking and laughing as usual when I said that it was a good thing his sister didn't look like him. He instantly stopped laughing and asked how I knew what his sister looked like . . . He said I was joking and that I couldn't possibly know his sister. I said then how was it I knew she had blond hair and was very pretty? He told me I wasn't funny and got very serious and suspicious of me. You could see the protective brother emerging. Then I said, how was it I knew her name was Keely? His mouth dropped open and his eyes bugged out. Of course, I started to laugh and told him how I had picked up Keely and her husband and dropped them off for dinner. Paul burst out laughing and said he was going to pay me back for that.

Paul's peers from Jimmy John's said Paul was a hard worker and always "stepped up to the plate" whenever he could help anyone. They also said Paul always made himself available to be there whenever anyone needed him. He's remembered as a good friend and a "stand-up" guy.

As sad as I am for the reason we're all here today, I'm happy I got to know Paul as I did. I'm happy for the memories I have of him. Given more time, I know his watercolor would have become an image of a man happy with his life and satisfied with his decisions. He left us as a work in progress and for each of us to complete the painting in our own hearts. I, for one, will miss him. I already do.

Surreal as it was, snapshot-like moments come back to me. People from Paul's past: Carpool mom, Freddy. Beloved babysitter, Molly. Teachers. Neighbors. Little league soccer coach, George. Playmates. Paul's first psychologist, Tony Wolff. Ross Dierdorff. Joan Gillece. Mentor, Ben Ballard—who made his way to Annapolis and introduced himself to me and said, "Paul was such a pure spirit . . ." My cousins, Alice, Bobby, Diane, Erica . . .

Keely—so frail and pained; Kayla—stoic, bewildered, a pre-teen facing life without the father she adored. I love them so. I reckon with my inability to protect them, spare them the pain.

I wished Paul were there. Maybe he was.

It's possible I hold on to these moments, simultaneously fleeting and emotionally gut-wrenching, because there was never an event to honor Paul. No college send-off. No wedding. No promotions. No accomplishments recognized. Yet, he was so incredibly amazing.

As Keely put it that day:

He was my pride and joy when he came home from the hospital. And we played endlessly. I have so much going through my head and can't believe I won't hear his voice or his laugh. He made us all crazy at times, but he was my hero. He always will be. And I hope I made him proud.

The gathering after the service was at home, where good friends—including the owners of Jimmy John's—provided endless food and refreshments and otherwise managed every detail, for which we were grateful.

For two days following the memorial, we cleaned out Paul's apartment. The furniture moving day was organized ahead of time by Lucy, which I appreciated. I was up for the physical exertion but couldn't have orchestrated the process as she did, even on a good day. I went back by myself to clean. I swear I scrubbed off a hundred years of living in that place. His things were gone. He was gone. But he loved that place. I did too. For him. He didn't want to leave it, and I didn't either. I kept finding more things to clean. What sense that makes, I can't say.

Buz called me daily for weeks. He was sorrowful and worried about me. He returned to Annapolis within the month, and I went to see him. He loved Paul. What an unlikely duo they'd been! Buz died nine months later, less than a year after the two of them had driven to Florida. How could they both be gone? I was sad to learn of Buz's death. He was another piece of Paul's life, and I don't like letting go of any of it. I have let go of so much, none by choice.

*

I LEARNED A lot in the weeks just after Paul died, partly because hindsight provides clarity, but also because I sought information from people who knew Paul and from any other source I could think of that would help me understand.

Then, of course, there was the autopsy. The Pathologic Diagnoses from the Medical Examiner: "This 34 year old, white, adult male died of mixed drug intoxication with fentanyl use. The manner of death could not be determined."

I talked with Jeremy, a coworker and friend of Paul's, who had been with him Saturday night. He told me he and Paul watched TV at Paul's place. Jeremy had been drinking but was not aware of any drug use. Jeremy recalled Paul asking him if he wanted to see his poetry. Jeremy left around 1:00 a.m. Paul was awake and in his living room.

I know that Paul called me at 1:15 a.m. that Sunday morning but didn't leave a message. I was unaware of the call until seeing Paul's call log. He sent his last text to his friend, Joseph, within the same hour, saying, "What's up?" I believe Paul died shortly thereafter, in the wee hours of Sunday, April 9, 2017.

Not long after Paul's death, I received a thoughtful message and a photo from Paul's friend in L.A., Shaun, who now is a research project coordinator for a behavioral health and treatment center.

Hey Jessie.
I took this picture of Paul when he was in California. He was sober at the time. I'm sorry for your loss. I loved your son and considered him to be one of my closest friends. I'll miss being able to call him. We talked just last week. I have rarely met someone I connected with so easily. We had a similar sense of humor and taste in music. Let me know if there is anything I can do to help your family during this hard time.
Shaun

Later, I called Shaun, whom I had never met or talked with before. He told me stories about things he and Paul had enjoyed in Montgomery County as well as in L.A., and how frequently they spoke. Shaun said, "Paul was so much fun and so smart. Plus, he was an amazing poet and guitarist." These strengths, Shaun told me, made it hard to figure out why Paul would get down on himself sometimes.

I learned from Shaun that Paul's recent relapse—his first since California—occurred when he was in Delray Beach in late January 2017. I was surprised. Beyond that, I was curious about how one gets drugs in an unfamiliar city. Shaun didn't exactly laugh at me—he's too polite—but he explained how very easy it is. If anything confirms that Paul's choices weren't the result of partying or even socializing, this does. Paul's only companion was Buz.

In processing what I'd learned in recent weeks, my eyes were opened to a shocking reality: It's hard, if not impossible, to get life-saving medications such as Suboxone, but it's easy to get illicit drugs on the street. One saves lives; the other kills. WHY, I continue to ask, can't we do better?

I discovered that Paul had not seen Dr. Kolsky since December 22, 2016. I know this because the bills were re-routed to my address. I could see that Paul had made an appointment after that, for January 4, 2017, but he didn't go—meaning there was no insurance coverage, and Paul was billed for the entire balance. I would bet that when Paul got the bill, totaling $377, he didn't know how to maneuver. He would've been afraid to tell me, so he didn't go back. To some people, this bill or this circumstance may seem insignificant, but for the vulnerable—those who live on the edge—it is life-altering.

Had Kolsky and I had any line of communication whatsoever, things would have gone differently. If Paul's former mental health providers could have found a way to wrap me in, things would have gone differently.

Paul had significant disabilities—long before mental health was an issue—that confounded every special education school he ever attended. These well-documented disabilities ultimately enabled Paul's Social Security support. Yet, he was supposed to be the sole advocate for himself in complex situations, and his was to be the only voice in critical decisions about his treatment. When HIPPA privacy laws trump the agility to individualize care, saving a life gets the back-burner.

As of January, then, Paul was both unmedicated and without a therapist—the very same scenario that led to his self-medicating in the past.

According to the discharge paperwork from the behavioral health hospital, Paul was being released to the care of his psychiatrist, David Kolsky, whom they contacted, leaving a voicemail message. Did Kolsky ignore messages—Paul's, mine, the hospital's—because Paul owed a balance? I really don't know. How would I? In fact, the doctor never once acknowledged me until after Paul's death when—without a hint of condolence—he let me know, via the U.S. mail, that I was expected to pay Paul's bill.

*

I AM PAINFULLY aware of my own confused state over the last weeks of Paul's life. Even though I felt consumed by him and by fear, I was paralyzed in ways I can't explain. I am not helpless by nature. The fact is, I think of myself as a problem solver, tenacious.

I should have been more resourceful in seeking needed treatment, finding the right doctor, and recruiting others to help me, to research, to explore options, to think clearly, and to prioritize. Even a damn shoulder to lean on could have changed the outcome. But I am to blame for that too. I had isolated myself, not wanting to be a burden with relentless and seemingly unsolvable problems. Nancy was right—I was too alone. If you can't have a village, try at least for a tag team.

Another poem I found in one of Paul's journals:

HIDDEN
She's the love of my life
My moral disgrace

When she travels my veins
I take on new traits
Unbound by glory
Or something catastrophic
She hides my skeletons
In my bedroom's closet

It saddens me that Paul viewed his addiction as a moral disgrace, making for yet another way he felt isolated and ashamed.

Paul suffered feelings of abandonment and was riddled with self-doubt, stoked by his years of going from school to school, with a downward spiral in his overall plight. How tragic, then, that his turning to drugs as an escape from his pain brought on incarceration and shackles and hunger and otherwise degrading treatment, serving only to reinforce his shame.

Adding to all of this, Paul had not gotten over the loss of friends he'd known and valued his whole life. It was yet another situation in which he was not allowed a voice and, in truth, was dehumanized.

It occurred to me that maybe Paul gave in to the hopelessness of it all, that maybe he felt the fight was impossible and threw caution to the wind, risking his own life. Because I don't really think so, it would be too great a leap to say that he died *of* a broken heart. But I do know he died *with* a broken heart.

My solace: If there is a place where good souls go, he is there. If there is not, at the very least he is now pain free.

Good night, my child.

EPILOGUE

The rails that carry the city's restless passengers,
May fail or falter.
But the tin cups in the hands of the oppressed,
You can count on them.

STANDING ON THE beach as a toddler, Paul pointed to an airplane pulling a message banner and exclaimed, "Look, Mommie! The plane with the A's!"

I smiled to myself as I thought about all there is to learn: Each one of twenty-six unique characters in our alphabet—formed differently depending on case—has a name and, beyond that, it makes a sound. Several strung together make a word, and the nuances of it all are endless. But Paul, of course, was too young to know any of this and was confident if not proud in his declaration.

What I am getting at is that sometimes in life, we don't know enough to know what we don't know. Needless to say, for a child this is to be expected. And, even as adults, we can't know everything. *But as caretakers—responsible in any way for the welfare of others, and particularly those who are vulnerable—we must strive to be in the know.* It is incumbent on us to seek information, to discern fact from myth, and to resist the temptation to adopt popular belief at the expense of the truth, the scientific truth.

Maybe Paul's and my fight was ill-fated due to factors beyond our control—such as the multitude of barriers to effective health care—but I'm increasingly aware of mistakes I made, or gaps in my understanding, pieces of the puzzle I didn't connect. I could try to avoid this reality by telling myself I always had Paul's best interest at heart, and I never turned my back on him, but that would be only part of the story because there was just too much I didn't know and, in some ways, I thought I knew more than I did. My instincts are good. I'm capable and attentive. And I loved him unconditionally. But was that enough?

*

PAUL FELL VICTIM to senseless regulations and ignorance. And as I analyze the forces at play, I confront the fact that his death was preventable. The realization sickens me but propels me to delve deeper. I study the science, the legislation, and the current state of treatment options. As I contend with all I didn't know, I turn my attention to how I can use what I've learned to help others.

I wish I'd had a better understanding of the importance of addressing the root cause of addiction. I knew Paul's struggles well, and I had no doubt he discovered that drugs eased his emotional pain, providing him an escape from his feelings of inadequacy and social isolation. I was less aware of the implications for healing.

Decades of scientific studies reveal that not all people, or even all users of highly addictive drugs, are equally at risk of developing a substance use disorder. The fact is, most drug use does not lead to addiction; even when it does, most people outgrow it, often on their own. As people mature, they find that a purpose in life is more meaningful than the effects of drugs. This natural process isn't sensational enough to get any press coverage, but it's important to understand.

People whose chronic drug use escalates beyond their control and wreaks havoc with their lives, almost always experienced some sort of childhood trauma—divorce, abuse, the loss of a parent—and often struggled with learning differences, anxiety, or depression. These are the people whose drug use is a means of escaping the pain of the past and the fear of the future. Theirs is a reality riddled with despair and hopelessness. They can't walk away and for the most part are doomed without help. Surely, it isn't hard to see how the tactics of shaming and self-condemnation are counterproductive.

I knew that jail was not the answer. And I fought to save Paul from a fuller extent of its perils, but I bought into some form of punishment, years before his run-in with the law, as I delivered him to a homeless shelter in the name of letting him "suffer the consequences of his decisions." I now know I was wrong and that the following days for Paul were among his most harrowing, without which his trajectory could have been different. I may have been worn down and bewildered by the struggle of it all, but sometimes I wonder if I could have been somewhat predisposed by a culture that imbues the sufferer with blame. I'm not sure.

I do know the cultural bias is powerful. Many families, at a loss to know what to do, turn their backs on a loved one, threatening abandonment or legal consequences—unwittingly contributing to the pain. Some plan "interventions" and other forms of "tough love." But research indicates that these tactics are rarely effective and may even risk being downright destructive. Another pseudo-scientific notion is that a person has to hit "rock bottom" in order to be receptive to recovery, a belief that serves only to further marginalize people—people who need connections and compassion, not detachment.

It's just common sense. Treating the afflicted as criminals and stripping them of dignity not only fails to promote positive outcomes but also feeds the societal stigmatization that has hobbled needed progress on multiple fronts. Those who believe that addiction is a moral failing, and that punishment is the solution, are just plain uninformed.

Paul blamed himself for his hardships—from his learning challenges to his battle with addiction. How was he to overcome these challenges in the face of ongoing humiliation and reinforcement that his condition was shameful?

And how is it that even those who have evolved to understand that addiction isn't a character flaw are okay with treatment programs that scream "morality alert!" by employing redemption as the focus?

I wish I'd had more clarity on the simple fact that addiction is a medical condition. Research confirms that there are two medications—buprenorphine (Suboxone) and methadone—that have proven to reduce overdose fatalities by fifty to seventy percent, with long-term maintenance associated with the best outcome. People on one of these medications report transformative effects, saying they no longer feel compelled to use illegal drugs and instead can focus on recovery and restore their lives.

While medication may not be right for everyone, it should be readily available and presented as an option at the outset of treatment. But treatment programs that operate without medical oversight do not offer medication and often provide family guidance that is counter to scientific evidence, neglecting to speak about the benefits of medication and often instilling unfounded fear of it, promoting gross misunderstandings that include warnings about the perils of long-term use.

I can't blame myself for the fact that addiction treatment in the United States is not regulated and has no federal standards by which families can evaluate programs. Nor do I consider it my fault that this absence of regulations has enabled the proliferation of programs that often do more harm than good.

Research scientists and addiction specialists continue to make the case, stressing the need for low threshold access to medication in all settings, urging lawmakers to lift pointless restrictions, and calling for an end to the unethical but tragically widespread practice of denying services such as housing to patients taking one of these life-saving medications.

Paul benefited from some aspects of the various twelve-step programs he experienced, especially those he sought outside of treatment programs and where he made friends and enjoyed the camaraderie. But as an inpatient, Paul suffered tactics that were counterproductive and was deprived of the medical care he needed, a fact he knew better than I did. It's more apparent to me now why he left the twelve-step program in Florida to return to the treatment facility where he worked with physicians and had medical attention, as well as peer support, and why, a couple of years later and in his final days, he wanted Suboxone. He knew how much it helped him, and he desperately wanted help—he was on the upswing in his life and terrified of losing his footing.

When addiction is widely understood to be a medical condition, other thorny issues become obvious. In addition to having access to evidence-based treatment, patients would get support from primary care or emergency room doctors, none of which was available to Paul.

I wish I had known that a relapse doesn't mean failure. Addiction is defined by the National Institutes of Health as "a chronic, relapsing, brain disorder characterized by compulsive drug-seeking despite harmful consequences." By definition alone, we should understand—beyond the fact that negative consequences don't work—that a relapse is not uncommon. Yet, the abstinence programs I came to know considered a relapse grounds for immediate dismissal and the shaming that went along with it. The patient failed, they reasoned; consequently, treatment was terminated, and the patient was booted out to fend for himself despite being at great risk of incarceration or worse. What sense does this make?

My advice for those who seek treatment is to begin with a comprehensive psychiatric evaluation to clarify any co-occurring conditions that need to be addressed and choose a program accordingly. Whether inpatient or out-patient, make sure the range of needed services, including the option for medication-assisted recovery and the professional staff to deliver them, are in place. They do exist, you just have to know what you're looking for.

I wish I'd been more familiar with the principles of harm reduction. Based on a deep commitment to patient-centered care, public health, and human rights, harm reduction programs are designed to minimize the danger of drug use. The priority is to keep people safe, eliminate needless suffering, and avoid preventable deaths while promoting social justice and resistance to the assault of stigmatization and criminalization.

In essence, harm reduction proponents accept the fact that people use drugs, recognize that social inequality and oppressive public policies exacerbate the harm, and believe that driving vulnerable people into back alleys is counterproductive and inhumane.

Some drug users are not ready to seek treatment or may have tried it and "failed." Some are afraid. No matter what, those who suffer from addiction are human beings who did not forfeit their right to health care or their right to be treated with dignity. When you factor in the severe shortage of evidence-based treatment programs, harm reduction services become even more imperative.

Evidence shows that most people who develop addiction do recover and go on to lead productive lives, but given the perilousness of our current reality—with street drugs easier to access than health care and laced with unknown synthetics and potency—people are dying at a pace we couldn't have fathomed ten years ago. And they are dying before getting the chance to recover, a fact that underscores the urgency of harm reduction initiatives: overdose prevention sites (sometimes called safe consumption spaces), clean needle programs, and access to other life-saving supplies such as the overdose antidote naloxone.

With a track record of reducing the spread of disease and preventing fatalities, overdose prevention sites allow people to inject on-site under the supervision of a nurse or a trained health care worker.

Bringing drug users out of the shadows, minimizing the compounded misery of arrests and incarceration, and often serving as a bridge to job placements and evidence-based treatment, these sites have saved countless lives.

While such programs initially seem counterintuitive, the data speaks for itself. In the 120-plus sites throughout Europe, Australia, and Canada—some in existence for more than twenty years—there have been zero fatalities. Furthermore, such sites have brought about an increase in public awareness of addiction as a medical condition rather than a moral or legal issue.

If we were to understand that a substance use disorder is a medical condition, we wouldn't dream of denying measures to reduce harm—and this is true regardless of whether or not recovery is the immediate goal. The lung cancer patient who continues to smoke or the diabetic whose lifestyle aggravates his condition are cases in point.

While some harm reduction programs are finally gaining a footing in the United States, tragically, none of these services were available to Paul thanks to our legislators' prevailing belief that such practices encourage drug use, a stance maintained despite the absence of substantiating evidence from anywhere in the world.

For Paul, I prayed for appropriate medical care and ultimate healing, but harm reduction services would have saved his life until that opportunity was a reality. Furthermore, there is no doubt that the kindness and the respect embedded in the premise of these health care services would have been reassuring for Paul, promoting a sense of self-worth and a renewed hope for the future.

If you are confused about harm reduction, think about Paul. He couldn't get help in the emergency room, he was denied the inpatient treatment he sought, and he was unable to get the life-saving medication he needed. Without the benefit of a safe haven or any medical oversight, he died. And he died alone. I am not confused.

At this juncture, for me, merely understanding the humanistic principles of harm reduction has inspired my advocacy for the rights of those who use drugs, for their right to health care, and their right to freedom from arbitrary degrading treatment.

I wish I had known that the risk of accidental overdose rises sharply after short-term treatment. I was heartsick and angry that Paul was discharged prematurely from the behavioral health hospital. I also knew that he was vulnerable. I was on edge. But I did not know that following short-term treatment, a person is more susceptible to dying—and dramatically so. It is a fact that the risk of a fatal overdose is three times higher than before entering treatment.

What I now know about the first days and weeks after discharge is: (1) Drug cravings are not under control and coping strategies are weak, increasing the likelihood of a relapse; and (2) A brief period of abstinence significantly diminishes drug tolerance, upping the odds of a relapse being fatal.

It's shocking to me that short term programs or criminal justice systems release people without a medical safety net and without dire warnings. How can this be when life and death hang in the balance?

I wish I had been more focused on seeking community support. I wasn't ashamed of Paul, a condition that I know keeps some from reaching out for needed guidance or connectedness. But having weathered so many bitter disappointments, I had inadvertently adopted a "suck-it-up" kind of stoicism that was foolish. Regardless of what breeds the mindset, I'm here to tell you that the devastation of addiction—its unimaginable suffering and heartache—is compounded by uncertainty and confusion, and confusion is the enemy of grounded decisions.

As the number of families facing this nightmare grows, I have to emphasize the fact that our silence—shame-based or not—does not serve us. Nor does it help turn the tide on the societal ignorance that in many significant ways underpins this deadly epidemic.

Share your story, seek support from others, and draw attention to needed reform. There is hope. And each of us has the power to find it and affect change. Bewilderment weakens your hand. Shame is a waste of time. Acknowledge your fragility—get help!

*

FROM MY PERSPECTIVE, the war on drugs morphed into a war on individuals, marginalized individuals who desperately need help. It's not just the staggering death toll and its faceless numbers at stake, but it's our fellow citizens, our children, and, in so many cases, the most vulnerable among us who need and deserve care. In essence, the war on drugs has failed—and failed miserably.

My fight was challenged by forces I didn't fully understand. But now, rather than dwell in regret, my fight has come full circle. Information is power, as is joining hands with like-minded individuals to stand up against those very forces: unregulated treatment, restrictions on life-saving medications, resistance to harm reduction services, and the criminalization of those who suffer.

Each of these obstacles lies at the feet of our policymakers, most of whom have little incentive to make substantive change; whether they care or not, too many lack the depth of understanding needed to make a difference. As is true with other societal issues, legislators follow the electorate. But deep-seated stigma, fed by criminalization, has tainted public support and, absent systematic coherence within the rehab industry, needed progress moves at a glacial pace.

Studies show the need for policy interventions that target the demand for drugs, without which supply-side efforts will continue to fail. In spite of the research, however, legislation emphasizes the supply side of the equation with tactics that have created the world's largest prison population, without reducing the number of addictions or overdose fatalities.

With prohibition as the mantra, laws target a source—inevitably giving life to a new source that may be easier to smuggle in smaller amounts but with higher potency, leaving more fatalities in its wake. Imposing cruel restrictions on needed prescription medications for pain sufferers is another supply-side strategy, one that has also fed the lucrative underground markets.

Curtailing the pharmaceutical companies' greedy and profit-driven practices is understandable, but cracking down on prescription medication for chronic pain patients—the last people who would share their prescription meds, and some of whom in desperation have turned to suicide or street drugs—has created unnecessary suffering and a whole new set of victims. Furthermore, as the prescribing rate has dropped significantly, overdose fatalities have not.

Layers of governmental restrictions on needed medications—buprenorphine and methadone—preclude access for the vast majority of those who suffer. Deregulation of these medications would save thousands of lives as proven in countries that have done so and reduced the death toll by eighty percent. It is hard to fathom why Congress has yet to take this simple step but easy to see why the United States has the highest number of overdose fatalities in the world, without a close second.

It's time for policymakers to focus on unified public health policies that regulate evidence-based treatment and expand harm reduction services.

Equally important, we must invest in our children. We need prevention initiatives that identify children at risk and provide programs accordingly. Preaching "Just say no" doesn't work, any more than scare tactics do. But helping children forge constructive interests and develop self-respect will serve them as they encounter life's inevitable challenges.

I worry that childhood suffering, so often the harbinger of addiction, is on the rise due to growing poverty and other societal trends that promote despair—increased stress, heightened fear, bullying, dislocated family units, fractured communities, and a propensity to dehumanize or even vilify those who are different. These tendencies, coupled with drug policies that are nothing short of oppressive, sustain the vicious cycle that will require a dedication and coordination, as yet unseen, to overcome.

We have a choice: Do we want to be a society that compounds the misery that breeds addiction, or a compassionate and socially responsible one in which the commitment to public health and human rights trumps the tendency to punish and shame those who suffer? Our lawmakers have the ability to combat this crisis but not the collective will.

Activism and *civil disobedience* represent our best hope. But only if we join forces.

When my child, or anyone else's child, falls victim to the laws of the land, it is nothing short of horrifying.

Paul deserved to live. And I can't rest easy.

Sara and Paul in 2006

Paul and Kayla in 2011

Paul and Casey, ringing in 2012

Keely, Paul, Sean's cousins, and me, Thanksgiving 2014

Keely and Paul crabbing, 2015

Kayla's goodbye to her Daddy, before his departure for Florida

Paul's visit with Shaun in LA

Wedding Day!

Paul with Kayla in his new apartment

Christmas Day 2016

Apron Man

Keely and Paul, a final moment

Poetry

Chapter 1

GOD THE ARTIST

God has a paintbrush and his abstract portraits grow to be.
Their lines, shapes and colors connect
breathing life into the 3 dimensional sculptures
that began with a thought and ended with civilization as we know it.
The universe is the back ground, twinkling with stars in its horizon
and earth is the center piece for our lives to be carried out.
Emotions and spirits are there to greet our every move that he inspired.

Despair was painted black,
blinding our vision to move forward and prosper.
Hope was painted yellow,
lighting a path and guiding us when we thought we were blind.
Compassion was painted blue,
the color of the sky, because once its within us, it goes on forever.
Last but not least is love, which was painted gold,
because there is no value greater than its gifts.

Chapter 2

NATURE'S GIFT

Off in the sunset, resting on the cue of night,

There lies a horizon, sinking in neon light.

While nature below rustles in its chilling gust,

Trees dance to its music, all throughout dusk.

Then as we sleep, by enormous shaded skies,

The western world awakens with day light at its side.

Every day withers, after its destiny is fulfilled,

Then gives another opportunity, to accompany man's will.

And here it is again, out my window, pushing away my sheets,

Beginning where I left off, inspiration takes me from sleep.

Chapter 3

MIRACLES

Miracles are sometimes stretched few and far between hardships.
And though battles may rage in our communities
and though our hearts keen sense of injustice may be felt;
when miracles surface, they will carry us back to refuge.
And what may seem like everlasting gloom now,
will once again appear to be that flawless limelight that will again guide
*   us home.*

Chapter 4

THOUGHTLESS

Thoughtless but provoked to think

Empty but forced full

Lame but expected to carry

Simple but demandingly complex

Creative but left without canvas

Anxious but made to sit

Different but pressured to conform

Chapter 5

CONNECTION

I'm so fed up with trying
My life makes sense to me now
The spirit of youth is gone
And I ask myself what is left?

Reawakened dreams grab a hold
And take footing on the ledge of my ego
A series of books
Written by me

Then there's my heart that craves
Mostly connection
And a good deal of rest
In between conversations
So that I can be recharged
And ready to talk again

My life… It means everything
That I get the chance to connect
I don't know how else to put this into words
I'd give you a hug but my hands,
They're behind my back.

Chapter 6

DREAM CHILD

Though I dreamt of this mansion as a child
my senses still could not orient themselves
to what lay behind its red doors.
Back then, my nighttime slumbers
still comprehended into unbearable nightmares,
which seemed to cripple me in a paralysis,
always leaving me a few thresholds away from my mother's arms.
It was then I clung to my sheets in fear,
while my boundless imagination clipped its own wings,
and subjected my body to terrible hallucinations
and ultimately a fear of dreaming...

Perhaps I had developed a misunderstanding
of what my dreams were trying to get across to me then.
They nearly drove me to insanity
before I was thrust into psychotherapy against my will;
as a pubescent skeleton lain out for examination in cruel light...
or so I imagined.
And the pacing mantras of the next ten years
along with the droning cocktails of psychotropic drugs
would zombify me in a lethargic sleepwalk through time....

But I think I get it now;
my priceless desire to create was forged then,
in the fire of what was a very realistic hell.
And now, unconfined, I can find beauty in such ugliness.
The most horrifying imagery of all is, in fact,
just another painting in need of restoration
or another verse in need of revision.

Chapter 7

PLEADING WITH GRAVITY

Oh gravity why do you blind me with your wicked, ill-fated tempers?

Every time I attempt a climb up and out of your crippling power,

You welcome me with a fall from grace, back to your cold ground.

Am I destined to your chains?

Am I a part of your city sidewalk, in a puddle of beer or cracked glass?

Do you contain my prayers so they'll never reach the maker?

Do you intercept these wishes and hide them?

I want to sing and climb on stars, gravity.

I want to do a handstand on the moon and dip my feet in the pacific.

I want to cover miles to grasp a notion of what infinity means.

I want to cover my dreams in ink and repel you with my pen.

I want to hide in my poem and sleep with my own inspiration.

But I'm stuck here with you gravity,

And I'm bearing your weight for you.

Chapter 8

A SMOOTH AIR

A smooth air beats its chills upon
The shingles of this rooftop sinking
Down into an empty apartment
Building; welded from rusted metal,
Lying bodies; a smelly trash.

Outdated innocence compels
Itself in a crude state
And has lost the right to move
Through the town naked
In the presence of such emptiness
So stranded, we sit.

If only the church steeples
Could rescue us from several flats
Over, the cosmic zombie of the Jewish faith
Could electrify our stunted growth
Set in by what seems like rigormortis
With fervent prayer
And we too could be giants.

But its steeples are much too high
Our feet and hands are restrained by the
Humility of watching the world
Move freely below us in swift movement;
With camouflaged work attire
And batons concealed to briefcases,
Ready for the battle of youth.

We however, came unprepared;
Meeting the dawn with our eyes
But brains still stuck in their wet,
Midnight slumber... searching.

The rude crosstown traffic
Makes pointless music to our ears
And skips my phonograph in
1000 beats until the record is
Scratched and broken. No good

So in what seems like eternity, we
Wait for the stampede to vacate
The sidewalk. Because behind these masks
We cannot breathe

Chapter 9

FOR FRIENDS IN THE JUNGLE

Through my guitar strings the creature speaks to me,
In my darkest hours it juxtaposes its many black and white
Photographs of the past with my current thought process,
Then turns, and molds its face to the sounds I create; inspired by his calling.

Life is lovely when you allow yourself awareness of an alter ego,
An imaginary friend, sometimes a darker half
Who rather than imagined can be frighteningly real.
Tortured in his own right, he's experienced all the turmoil I have.

He's been there all along. I didn't give him much choice
But to tag along with me through my 10,000 hours of hopelessness
And the many bologna sandwiches awaiting us upon consciousness,
Or the bag lunches at the end of filthy lines with three teeth in all.

Through drunken stupors that left us bleeding on cold porcelain,
Waking up to drink rubbing alcohol, and be ok with that,
In our underwear; shaking violently.
Through mad streets, searching all day, to find peace of mind
In between the cold bouts of the city storm,
Only to scream in the wind of a society in which we had no voice,
That choked our cries down to ten cents,
And a cheap bottle of vodka.

Through family homes built on wholesome values
Whose walls in the end began to breathe cocaine
And witness the death of close friends.
Through the vinyl hallways of rehabilitation, 20,000 miles in all,

For momentary revelations of hope,
Only to be released for another march through
The unaccountable blocks of the cement jungle
To cultivate the very same habits;
Leaving our feet and hands blistered.

Through church houses searching for truth,
Then sobbing on alters only to find that Christ was just a statue
Who couldn't speak a word in return; and then reverting to atheism
And self-fulfilling prophecies,

Returning our faith to the narcotic haze that induces nightmares;
A life time in the making. Through beautiful friendships
That lost their meaning as their cause became a distant plea
After the once recreational euphorias overcame morals
And robbed us of our sanity.

Through the park benches of Patterson to recite our nods to passersby
Then falling on our knees for shelter.
Through row home dwellings and office building squats, in all but a few short
    months,
and in what seemed like an instant, bad choices got worse.
Bad choices became mandatory, bad choices defended themselves
In front of correctional officers, judges, and street corner thugs;

After working for counterfeit 20s in a mile block radius of slum,
And finding ourselves staring down a steel barrel at point blank range,
For the few real dollars in our pockets, until left stranded in a foot of snow,
    penniless.
Then succumbing to involuntary ranting's in the piss drunk of night,
Clueless as to how this happened and stumbling towards grocery store isles
Or detoxes, adopting the calmest façade,

And though still mad, with the purest of intentions.

I look back in shame but I can't help but wonder where you all are
I can't help but wonder how much more it will take,
How tragic your life will have to become before you see what I now see
I love you all, and if I could reach any of you from the fire in which you are
    standing,
I would do my best to take you home.

But I can't until you wake up.
The best I can do is serve whoever is ready to listen to what I am saying
Whoever will understand the nightmare of the roads we walked
and the profound toll taken on us all,
our mothers, our children, the community surrounding us.
What a tragedy it is to have them all witness our dying
over and over again
and not even be able to describe to them why.

I know now that you yourselves don't know either.
Because I still don't understand.
Some things can't be put into words but I am telling you that there is a way
    out.
I am not abandoning you.
We are one in the same.
I'll be here if you need me.

Chapter 10

MOUNT WASHINGTON

In her arms I've again found refuge
And above my sorrows, I will recognize
This city's streets have new meaning
As I again take notice of constellations in the skies

To me they resemble all I've found this December
Inspiring emotions I once chalked-up to lost
And here in this room above Mount Washington
Lying on peddles, she's strewn across

Here the magic that is her radiant smile
Transfers heat from her heart to mine
In effortless motion she awakens my senses
With small electric pulses stimulating my mind

Chapter 11

THE CAGE

The machinery of poem churns at my heart stems
Plucking its many strings and
Humming off its irregular vibrations.

Perfectly imperfect; words tell stories of my subconscious
And awaken its many hidden memories of my past
And immortalize them on white tablets; unable to age in time.

Like pedophiles in trench coat stealth;
Artsy cravings study my pubescent youth from dark corners
And capture them down to a science; to a beautiful cage;
Where they can lie naked forever
For another's unprotected pleasure.

Chapter 12

FLOATING BETWEEN

Several bad thoughts away from the fall leave me hanging on summer's cusp.
This in between season seems to symbolize my nonexistence to the world outside,
Which does not pay mind to the grumbles from beyond their storefront windows,
From behind wet denim jackets, and mouths hung wrong,
From the bad postured bums, scraping for a meal in the downtown harbor noon.

I'm in between work, in between relationships, my whole life: in between.
And an epic level of worth has yet again been cut short as I left my last threshold,
Leading away from liberty's arms, only to take off for the next.
But perhaps to a better world where ranting's are valued as gold.

So, my mindless stagger again goes UN noticed.
Neither here nor there, I've at once found solitude within vast crowds;
I've found limbo in state of mind and I've found a cigarette and a warm cup of
*   coffee as a blessing.*
So, upon my fall from grace, I will rise again, grateful for all things taken for
*   granted.*

Chapter 13

EXPERIENCING TO BE LOST

From alligator's jaws to midwest dust

Excitement, overwhelming as yesteryear

Hometown-dreams decay into dirt

Propelling my yearnings to wander languidly

Through America's many rest stops and soup kitchens

To quench my taste, to keep reality closer

Professing my many dreams...of floating

The dreams that pair well with struggle

But also with the euphoria interstates provide.

Chapter 14

COME BACK...

I see you standing there

in what would be your wedding dress.

Your hair is crashing all around itself

like waves on a beach.

I'd like to rest on your shore

and take photos of the sunset

for our children to admire.

My peace of mind is captured so effortlessly.

I wish all moments could be as eternal as love.

Come back to me in echoes

and repeat to me what you said,

the time before you left,

when I said I didn't care.

Chapter 15

REVELATION DREAM

I walked down the hallway of my sub conscience
and Its paintings dating back to my birth came alive.
The portraits of events I thought just circumstance,
were signed by artist angels.
Then in what seemed like an instant,
their visionary hearts fused my wishes with fate,
and new portraiture was born.
Its enlightened colors foretold my future
and its gray areas showed me the way to overcome my faults.

Abstract strokes of my every crisis,
and contemporary lines of my every success,
were explained on a living canvas.
For that instant, destiny was not distorted;
I saw through their eyes… they had shown me how to love.
They turned my dreams of prosperity into realities of triumph.
I no longer had to sit and think of all that could have been,
but could instead be satisfied with what already is,
and understand where those things will take me.

I fell to my knees, not in gratitude
but in prayer that I not forget this dream
and in turn forget the miracles it foretold.
To retract my pen is to converge inwards.
And as this revelation of my heart consumed me in its joy,
my fulfilled spirit swooped forward to be as one with my waking body,
now running toward morning's doorway,
over the threshold, into new a new day.

Chapter 16

SOUND OF AIR TO BREATH

A stone hitting water makes tiny tidal waves for man on his mental beach.
If I could once again find myself in those chatty chambers,
I'd fly like a bird and flutter the mountaintops;
but I am here with you in a basement of the senses drinking coffee.

Surely one day an angel will greet me at destiny's door
and again I'll pack my bags for the divide,
wearing a crown of silver linings and hiking that paradise;
relinquishing my sleepwalk to a realistic pace.

Chapter 17

NOURISHED CHILD

In these times, life seems both true and surreal
And burning passions for verse awaken when my thoughts are even keeled
Like hyper children they are hungry, and my stresses arise
As a need for release festers in my idle mind
Much like a river of rapids, rampaging into a channeled inlet
My mind, body, soul meet poem, and become my beautiful quartet
Once released, the birth of my creations can run rampant and wild
I rock them and treat them to eternity
And say good night to my nourished child

ACKNOWLEDGMENTS

I HAVE MANY people to thank for their support throughout this project. At the outset, I had no concept of the scope of such an undertaking. In truth, I went into it without any depth of understanding about my own role, much less those of others.

I simply have to start by acknowledging Paul, whose life taught me more than words can express, whose gifts inspired this book, and whose challenges galvanized my life's purpose and my passion for making a difference in the lives of others, particularly the vulnerable. Beyond the humility and coping strategies fostered by raising a child with disabilities, I learned countless lessons *from* Paul—a person who knew nothing of life other than a fight—but whose resilience continues to reinforce mine.

A sincere thank-you goes to Stewart Moss for encouraging me in the very beginning, for believing that "Paul possessed the soul, if not the outright talent, of a poet," and for all the cups of coffee over which this book took shape. I am grateful for my literary agent, Laura Strachan, whose experience is as remarkable as my inexperience, and who believed in my story enough to take me on anyway, and whose patience in answering my endless, wordy, questions did not go unnoticed. I am indebted to Cynthia Sanders at Baker Donelson for her legal guidance, her expertise, and her genuine kindness.

My editor James Morgan—a master of his craft and an invaluable resource to me in multiple ways—has my lasting gratitude. While our long-distance work was launched with me feeling intimidated by his distinguished literary credentials, it evolved to include an easy rapport, a discovery of shared values, and a friendship—with an open invitation extended to Jim and his wife to join us for "one of those Maryland crab feasts."

I am extremely fortunate to have my friends of forty-five years, Maureen Sullivan and Jack Siggins, who read multiple drafts, offering important feedback and critique, and who otherwise allowed me to routinely exploit their anomalous capacity—born of intellectual depth and love for Paul.

I give huge thanks to my lifelong friend Cheryl Morgan for her thoughtful support, both practical and emotional, and for being a constant source of comfort. Heartfelt thanks are due as well to my old friends: Nancy Leventhal for being a dutiful proofreader on a moment's notice and for just being there all along; and Emily Legum for teaching and caring for both Paul and me and for being an inspiration.

My appreciation goes to others who provided vital support—giving me advice, proofreading, providing technical help, serving as a sounding board, or lifting my spirits—including Colleen Connors, Sean Fitzpatrick, Matt Franko, Lisa Hillman, Mac Kearney, Sarah Khan, Joe Manck, and Robin Weiss. I extend special thanks to Ruth Weinstein who, in addition to providing feedback and guidance, helped me discover unrealized aspects of myself and inspired my continued quest.

The entire team at Apprentice House, especially Kevin Atticks, Shelby Ehret, Kelly Lyons, and Grace Marino, deserves much praise for their hard work, skill, and enthusiasm in the multiple aspects of what felt to me like magic—turning a manuscript into an actual book. I thank Taliah Lempert—whose bicycle sketches and paintings stole my heart—for permission to use one of her prints for the book's promotion as well as its cover.

I want to acknowledge my website followers, who hung in there with me over the many months when this book was little more than a pipe dream, responding to my emails and showing an interest in my cause. Your support has meant more to me than you realize. I would like to express my gratitude for the attention and generosity of nationally recognized thought leaders, renowned journalists. and authors who read my manuscript and offered early praise including Will Godfrey, Ryan Hampton, Ben Levenson, Roger Parloff, Helen Redmond, and Ben Westhoff.

I am incredibly thankful for my dear granddaughter, Kayla, for her permission to use her father's poetry and, most important, for being a blessing in my life. Also, I thank Kayla's mother, Sara Wallace, for her unwavering love and support for me and for her exemplary devotion to Kayla, manifesting itself in countless ways not the least of which was her ongoing friendship with Paul and her intuitive grasp of its lasting importance for their daughter.

My abiding love and deepest gratitude go to my whole family—from those who came before me and gave me everything through to the generations after me who nourish my spirit and give me hope for the future.

Through it all—every step of the way—there was Keely, who read each page, as I cranked it out, giving me feedback and cheering me on. And most significant, it is Keely, and only Keely, who walked this path with me, cried with me, laughed with me, and mourned with me the loss of Paul, and celebrated with me in the honoring of his goodness and the ongoing discovery of his gifts. A mere "thank-you" doesn't begin to measure up. So I honor you, dear Keely, for your incredible strengths and for the joy you bring to my life. You have my deepest respect and my unwavering admiration, and, of course, my wholehearted love.

ABOUT THE AUTHOR

INSPIRED BY ALL she learned through her son's tragic death, Jessie Dunleavy finds herself increasingly in the role of activist. In opposition to the devastation inflicted by the war on drugs—particularly for vulnerable populations—she is an advocate for drug policies based on human rights and scientific research and is committed to combating stigma and other impediments to humane and effective strategies to reduce the harms of drug use.

In addition to lending her voice through opinion editorials, speaking engagements, broadcast interviews, and social media, she has joined forces with like-minded groups at the national, state, and local levels, including the Maryland Harm Reduction Action Network. She is certified by the Maryland State Department of Health as a Master Presenter on the Stages of Change and advocates for her cause within the Maryland General Assembly.

Her thirty years as a school administrator in a pre-kindergarten through grade twelve college preparatory school entailed community outreach, public relations, marketing, and written communications that ranged from newsletters and website content to a blog in which she offered general parenting advice. She holds a master's degree in library and information science and served as an academic librarian for nearly a decade at the outset of her career.

She can be contacted via her website: jessiedunleavy.com

Apprentice House is the country's only campus-based, student-staffed book publishing company. Directed by professors and industry professionals, it is a nonprofit activity of the Communication Department at Loyola University Maryland.

Using state-of-the-art technology and an experiential learning model of education, Apprentice House publishes books in untraditional ways. This dual responsibility as publishers and educators creates an unprecedented collaborative environment among faculty and students, while teaching tomorrow's editors, designers, and marketers.

Outside of class, progress on book projects is carried forth by the AH Book Publishing Club, a co-curricular campus organization supported by Loyola University Maryland's Office of Student Activities.

Eclectic and provocative, Apprentice House titles intend to entertain as well as spark dialogue on a variety of topics. Financial contributions to sustain the press's work are welcomed. Contributions are tax deductible to the fullest extent allowed by the IRS.

To learn more about Apprentice House books or to obtain submission guidelines, please visit www.apprenticehouse.com.

Apprentice House
Communication Department
Loyola University Maryland
4501 N. Charles Street
Baltimore, MD 21210
Ph: 410-617-5265
info@apprenticehouse.com • www.apprenticehouse.com